Be Smart Home Buying With 500 Years Experience

by RICHARD C. SMITH, Appraiser/Inspector

35 Horror Stories + 72 Nasty Problems = 107 Hassles to Avoid

(107 Secrets They Don't Want You to Know)

Worth at least $285,850-plus

COVER: 15 Horror Stories / Nasty Problems
Can you find them? (Answers at rear)

Bloomington, IN

Milton Keynes, UK

AuthorHouse™
1663 Liberty Drive, Suite 200
Bloomington, IN 47403
www.authorhouse.com
Phone: 1-800-839-8640

AuthorHouse™ UK Ltd.
500 Avebury Boulevard
Central Milton Keynes, MK9 2BE
www.authorhouse.co.uk
Phone: 08001974150

First published by AuthorHouse 1/31/2006

ISBN: 1-4208-8633-9

Library of Congress Control Number: 2005909230

Printed in the United States of America
Bloomington, Indiana

This book is printed on acid-free paper.

MY PROMISE:
To Help You Become a Smart Homebuyer Today

WHO: Richard C. Smith, A.I.C. (Residential Appraiser, Inspector, Associate in Claims). Licensed Real Estate Salesperson since 1974. Assembles, relates, and reveals over 500 years of home buying experiences from appraisers, assessors, architects, bankers, brokers, builders, inspectors, salespersons, surveyors, and homebuyer victims.

PURPOSE: This is a crash course to enable future homebuyers to become **smart** homebuyers.

GOAL: To enable you to:

1. Act in your own best interests.
2. Be knowledgeable.
3. Act in a wise manner in "an arm's length relationship"
   (without being pressured by outside influences).
4. Act in a reasonable length of time in a competitive market.

All of these elements can be achieved through learning the experience and wisdom in this manual.

DISCLAIMER: This material does not intend to provide complete information of any area of law, and should not be used as a replacement for legal advice. Seek legal and professional advice where necessary.

Estimates of repairs are general projections -- check local rules, ordinances, and customs.

P.S. - **BLUNDER**: A stupid and serious mistake usually caused by ignorance, stupidity, or confusion. (Per *The American Heritage Dictionary.)*

"NO! I'm not a 500 year old Appraiser!"

FOREWORD

Congratulations. Buying this book puts you on the road to becoming Smart Homebuyers.

Forgive me. My writing style is not like Hemingway's, Steinbeck's, President Clinton's ($30 how-to book?) or that of other famous authors. It's just the real world accounts of a working real estate appraiser.

One could promise you instant Magical Wisdom. I won't.

First read the checklist at the rear. Two or three readings will give you more and more understanding.

SECTION I deals with home-buying secrets to save your wallet and your sanity.

SECTION II includes bonus chapters to give you a leg-up on other buyers.

There is no chapter on mortgages. Why? That field has hundreds of constantly changing products/services. Most bankers are hard pressed to keep up with what their bank offers, let alone what other banks and mortgage companies offer. Shop around, get a trustworthy banker or broker to serve your personal needs.

Don't let someone else mismanage your home buying details ... manage them yourself, or supervise them with your newfound knowledge.

Let's have fun as we learn to become smart homebuyers, avoiding the **nests of rattlesnakes** and **skunks** on your home-buying adventure.

TABLE OF CONTENTS

SECTION I

APPETIZER: THREE SMART HOME-BUYING-WITH-500-YEARS-EXPERIENCE TIPS!

Salty Wells, Private Mortgage Insurance (PMI), Flood Insurance. Could this be worth:

1. - $1,500?
2. - $3,000?
3. - $9,000?

Check it out!

Appetizer #1: Educate Yourself.

Be Warned of Costly ($1,500) Salt Water Damage.

In a rural setting in an $80,000 value range, I appraised a home several years ago. After completing my inspection I chatted with the homeowners, who had purchased the home a few years earlier. The small neighborhood was notorious for its salty ground water content. The homeowners told me they bought the home after the public water line had been installed, and I listened as they related that the *previous owner had real problems* **before** *the public water line was installed. NOT ONLY IN LIVING IN THE HOUSE, BUT IN* **SELLING** *IT!*

The previous owners had no idea about the high salt content in the wells when they bought the house. Their family went through two water heaters, a dishwasher, and an automatic washer in a few years time, due to rusting out.

If the previous homeowners had water tests performed, or tasted the water, or talked with neighbors, they would have avoided replacing TWO WATER HEATERS, A DISHWASHER, AND AN AUTOMATIC WASHER (This cost at least $1,500 out of their pockets) -- PLUS OWNING A HARD-TO-MARKET HOME!

Certainly, water tests could be required if a bank or mortgage company is involved, but probably no one requires it in a cash deal or land contract sale between two private parties. A BAD EXPERIENCE CAN BE A VERY EXPENSIVE TEACHER!

Appetizer #2: Is PMI Insurance Necessary?

If you plan to pay less than 20 percent down, understand Private Mortgage Insurance (PMI).

Typically, down payments are 20 percent when home buying. If the down payment is less than 20 percent, banks and mortgage companies require the homebuyers to buy insurance to protect the banks and mortgage companies from losses if homeowners default on their mortgage. The theory is that with larger down payments, homebuyers having more equity in the home are less likely to default on their mortgages. Conversely, homebuyers with smaller down payments, thus less equity in the home, are more likely to default on their mortgages. Banks and mortgage companies want protection from this possibility.

Obviously, buyers with 5, 10, or 15 percent down have been able to buy homes because they can buy PMI insurance.

Using rates on a government-monitored chart based on 1997 fees, let's run through an example. The example is of a $100,000 sales price.

With a 5 percent down payment, or $5,000, the monthly PMI insurance is $61. The yearly premium is $732.

With a 15 percent down payment, or $15,000, there is a monthly premium of $26. The yearly premium is $312.

AS YOU GAIN MORE AND MORE EQUITY IN THE HOME, AND AS THE PROPERTY APPRECIATES, YOU MAY NOT EVEN NEED THIS INSURANCE! But homebuyers may not be notified if their equity exceeds 20 percent, and they often keep paying for this unnecessary insurance.

DON'T PAY AN EXTRA $312 or $732 PER YEAR FOR NOTHING. Multiply this for 10 or 20 years. COULDN'T YOU USE THE $3,000 to $14,600 BETTER THAN SOMEONE ELSE?

Recently I appraised a home for homeowners whose total motivation was to demonstrate to their bank how much their home had appreciated. They could show how much equity they had in the house, obviously. The $250 appraisal fee saved the homeowners thousands in unnecessary PMI insurance.

There has been some correction to this problem. Effective July 29, 1999 the Homeowner Protection Act of 1998 has provided some relief. If you got a mortgage after July 1999, the PMI insurance is to be automatically cancelled when the equity in the home reaches 22 percent.

BUT ... GUESS WHO IS ASKED TO MONITOR THIS? That's right -- the banks that require it! Don't you think you should be aware of this and watching for this also?

I want you to become a smart homebuyer, not only in this first home-buying experience, but so that you are the authority through multiple home-buying experiences over your lifetime.

"Didn't I tell you to check out flood insurance and flood plains before we bought this cheap **!?! house!."

Appetizer #3: Flood Plains and Flood Insurance. "Enter at Your Own Risk!"

Some residential areas are in flood plains. These areas can be along rivers or streams that are prone to overflow and flood. Obviously this is a natural phenomenon, but it can also involve man-made areas. Along the Mississippi River in New Orleans there are levees built with huge pumps to remove the water from these low areas where homes have been built. Failure of those pumps has caused some disastrous flooding. Flood insurance did help people recuperate some of their financial loses. Not only does my training/experience include being a licensed real estate appraiser, but I was also a licensed and trained insurance adjuster for many years. I have flood insurance training.

Flood maps are drawn up by the U. S. Department of Housing and Urban Development/ Federal Insurance Administration through the National Flood Insurance Program. These maps show enlarged areas, whether it be a city, town, or township. It shows the drainages, the streams, rivers, lakes, or even coastal water areas that are prone to flood. There are a total of 10 zones, and they rate the various severity and frequency of flooding. In the mid-western area of the country we basically deal with three zones. Zone A, which is areas of 100 year floods; Zone B, which is areas with 100 to 500 year floods; and Zone C, where no flooding is indicated per the flood maps.

If a residential property is located in a zone on a flood map, this is checked out in an appraisal by an appraiser. Also a bank can have a certification company determine if it is in a flood zone. This costs anywhere from $15 to $20. A survey, which is much more expensive, will indicate the boundaries of flood zones.

BANKS/MORTGAGE COMPANIES WILL **NOT** APPROVE A MORTGAGE IF FLOOD INSURANCE IS NEEDED. Homeowners' insurance coverage does not cover floods as defined in the flood insurance program.

Many communities and townships choose not to participate in this program. Determine if your home/future home is in a participating township or city, to avoid charges for a survey (costing $300 - $500 or more) or having a certification done, which serves no purpose because the township does not participate. Sometimes a phone call can be made to government offices to see if they participate in the flood insurance program.

Flood insurance is a very basic type of insurance and does not give the comprehensive type coverages as provided in homeowners' insurance coverages. The insured party(s) will get the bare-bones type settlement. If in fact they qualify as being in a designated flood plain, and if a real "flood" is involved, as defined by the federal government. The cost of flood insurance depends upon the value of the house and the zone that it is in. THIS MIGHT RUN APPROXIMATELY $300 TO $400 PER YEAR. MULTIPLY THAT AMOUNT TIMES THE LIFE OF THE MORTGAGE (UP TO 30 YEARS), AND THIS COULD MEAN AN ADDITIONAL $9,000 IN INSURANCE COSTS TO YOU. Beware of this additional cost which could be sneaking up on you.

Study the specific layouts and adjacent areas of where you are shopping. Look at county maps, township maps, and city maps for the possibility of flood hazards. A comprehensive real estate appraisal completed by an ethical, experienced, and forthright appraiser will address many of these issues. Having a second opinion (consultation/written report) could save hundreds if not thousands of dollars.

Bonus $1,000 Horror Story

Recently I appraised a 5-year-old upscale home on a newly developed golf course for mortgage refinance purposes. Mr. and Mrs. Homeowner had the home built and never needed flood insurance.

Review of the poorly drawn flood maps indicated the property was not in the flood zone. My appraisal noted that. Small cattail-filled swamps were 100 yards to the west.

The mortgage company ordered a routine flood certification report by a specialized company. Its report indicated the property **was** *in a flood zone. Flood insurance was needed, costing* $1,000/year. *Their report was final and could not be challenged.*

The loan officer called in a panic. "I've processed thousands of mortgages and never had this happen."

A survey to dispute the report could cost $500-plus and there would be a 2-3 month waiting list.

Solutions (free) were: letters from the local township building department, and from the developer, detailing that the specific flood zone boundaries were away from the subject property.

If you are home shopping in flood zone areas (or questionable flood zone areas), smart homebuyers ask for and get documents **up front**. *Get copies of surveys (detailing the house location on the lot and flood zone boundaries), certification reports, letters from local government offices verifying and challenging unclear flood maps.*

Smart homebuyers know how to challenge the bureaucracy and possibly save **$1,000/year** *in unnecessary flood insurance.*

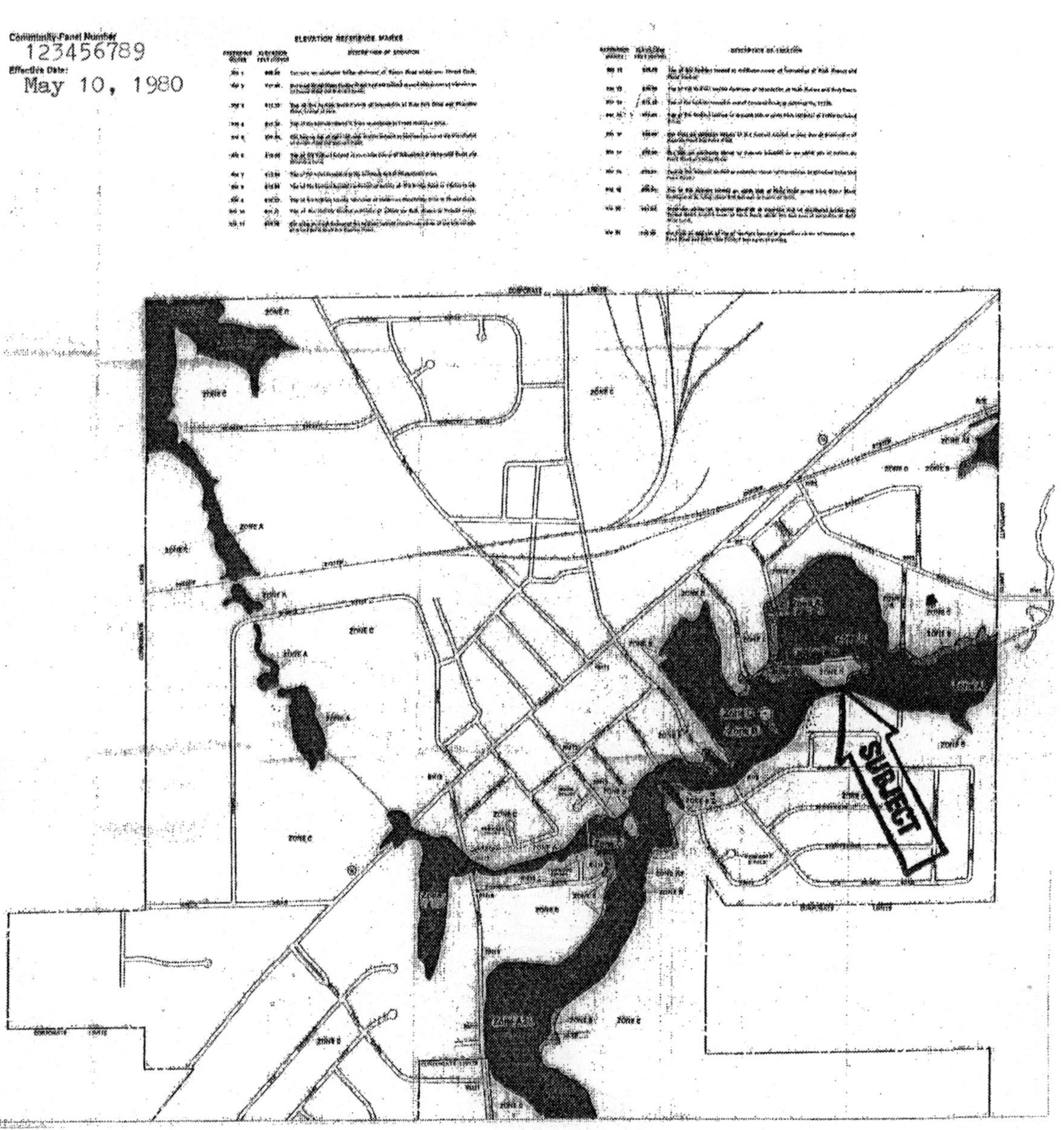

FLOOD MAP SHOWS GENERAL AREA OF FLOOD PRONE AREAS

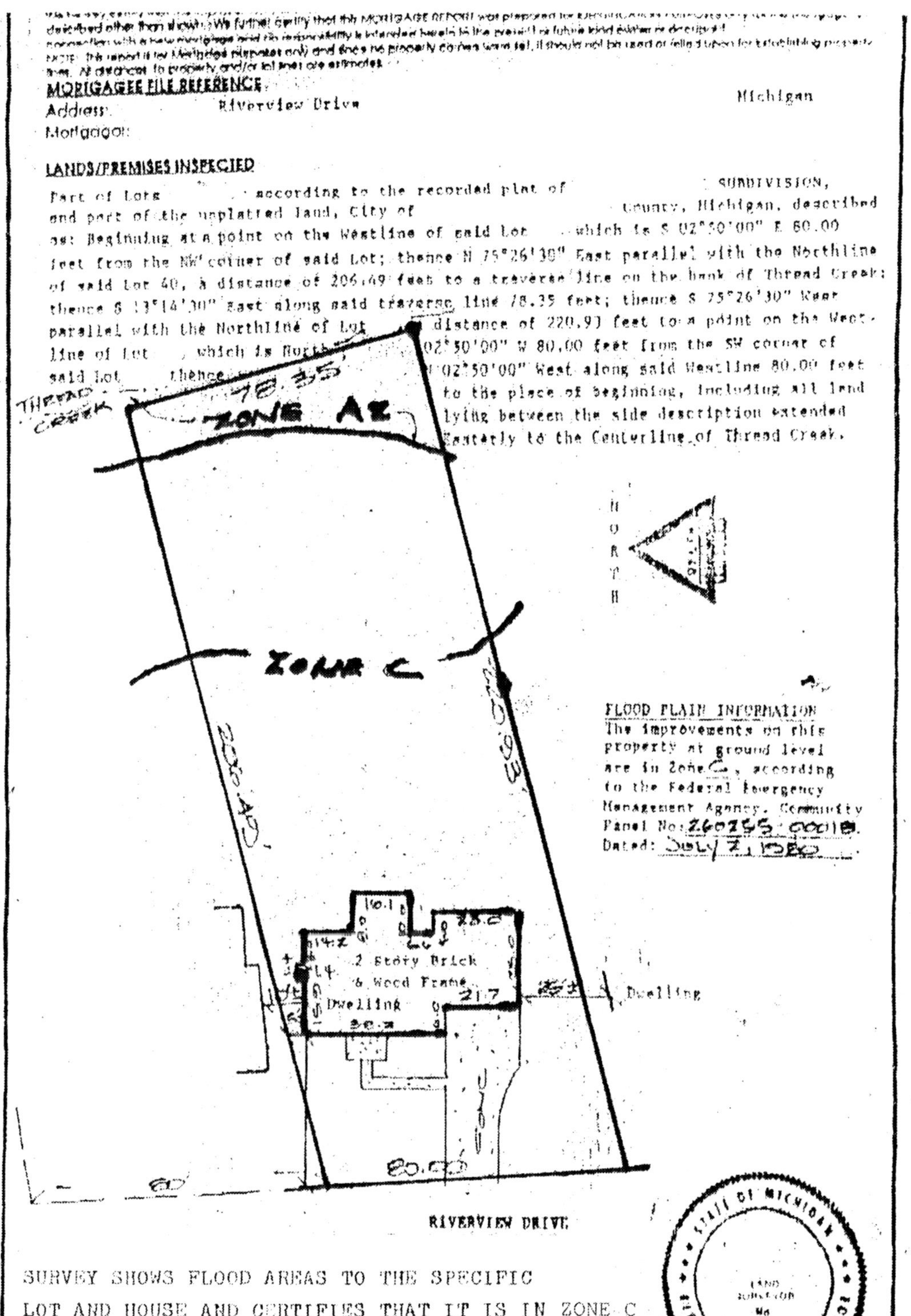

...described other than shown. We further certify that this MORTGAGE REPORT was prepared for ... identification purposes ... no responsibility is intended herein to the present or future land owner or occupant ... connection with a new mortgage ...

NOTE: This report is for Mortgagee purposes only and does no property corners were set, it should not be used or relied upon for establishing property lines. All distances to property and/or lot lines are estimates.

MORTGAGEE FILE REFERENCE

Address: Riverview Drive Michigan

Mortgagor:

LANDS/PREMISES INSPECTED

Part of Lots according to the recorded plat of SUBDIVISION, and part of the unplatted land, City of County, Michigan, described as: Beginning at a point on the Westline of said Lot which is S 02°50'00" E 60.00 feet from the NW corner of said Lot; thence N 75°26'30" East parallel with the Northline of said Lot 40, a distance of 206.49 feet to a traverse line on the bank of Thread Creek; thence S 13°14'30" East along said traverse line 78.35 feet; thence S 75°26'30" West parallel with the Northline of Lot distance of 220.93 feet to a point on the Westline of Lot which is North 02°50'00" W 80.00 feet from the SW corner of said Lot thence 02°50'00" West along said Westline 80.00 feet to the place of beginning, including all land lying between the side description extended Easterly to the Centerline of Thread Creek.

FLOOD PLAIN INFORMATION
The improvements on this property at ground level are in Zone C, according to the Federal Emergency Management Agency, Community Panel No: 260255 0001 B
Dated: July 7, 1980

SURVEY SHOWS FLOOD AREAS TO THE SPECIFIC LOT AND HOUSE AND CERTIFIES THAT IT IS IN ZONE C

Appetizer Review

H.S. = Horror Story

N.P. = Nasty Problem

H.S. #1 - $1,500 of costly appliance replacement due to salty ground water wells (talk with neighbors). Get water tests. Ask local well drillers for saltwater maps showing salty water areas.

N.P. #1 - Hard to sell property.

H.S. #2 - Paying too much for unneeded PMI insurance ($3,000 to $14,600). Check on appreciation rates and equity level in the homes and areas.

N.P. #2 - Don't rely on other people (banks, mortgage companies) to monitor this.

H.S. #3 - Additional flood insurance cost of $9,000.

N.P. #3 - Constant worries/hassles about flooding and almost flooding conditions.

Be Smart Homebuying With 500 Years Experience

I Want You to be a Smart Homebuyer

LESSON #1:
AVOID THE $500 MISTAKE AND THE $50,000 BLUNDER

Case #1

You are actively searching for a residential lot to build a dream home. Needed are: paved streets, good school district, a suburban-like setting in a rural area, easy commuting within 1/2 hour to an hour to major employment centers (city), nearby shopping and essential services, and reasonable access to the interstate highways. The budget also places limits on what you can afford.

Then the perfect lot is found. It's less than a football field length from a rural intersection, has paved roads, shopping and essential services are within two miles north, good schools are nearby, access to the interstate is 2½ miles north. There is a 20-minute commute to the major employment center. The lot size per the local unit of government will accommodate the size of house that you plan to build.

However, it has no public water or sewer. The seller's representative advises that the percolation test is suitable for a septic tank, so there should be no problem. Perfect, right? Well, let's look at the big picture.

Down the street at the corner there is concrete curbing and paved drive-through driveways on the southeast corner. Metal light posts, and an abandoned, dilapidated, small building sit less than a football field length away. An abandoned gas station. Big deal?

It is a big deal! Those thousands of abandoned, boarded-up, torn-down gas stations around this country are in that condition usually for a reason. Leaking underground gas storage tanks! The prohibitive environmental clean-up costs have bankrupted many station owner/operators. Contamination to nearby wells is a possibility. How does the idea of carrying plastic gallon milk jugs of drinking water into your new dream home, and the never-ending trips to the laundromat, sound? If you apply for a mortgage, the bank could insist upon a Phase I environmental study that could cost in excess of $2,500.

Then there's the future resale of the property. Does this sound like a fantasy? Well, it's based upon an actual appraisal that I started. The buyer backed out of buying the lot apparently after re-evaluating the situation, forfeiting the $500 purchase agreement deposit.

Potential dangers cannot always be proven, but because of the emotional factors in home buying, perceived problems in future buyers' minds can kill a deal.

You will not own that home forever! It can be a difficult asset to sell. Don't let them paint yourself into a corner based only on emotional decisions. Think of future resale: a job transfer, a promotion, a change in health, family, or marital situation, all could dictate the need to be flexible.

"How about this for a neighbor?"
With a leaking underground storage tank near your well!

Case #2

A potential $50,000-$75,000 location Blunder!

People with money and limited common sense can be a dangerous combination, even in the face of the obvious.

Some time ago, a bank assigned me to appraise a proposed new-built home in a rural setting in the $150,000-plus value range. The homeowner jump-started the project, building a detached garage and pouring the concrete basement walls. He couldn't wait for completion of the appraisal, and the bank's mortgage approval process.

My inspection of the lot found it to be approximately 200 feet directly across the street from an 8-foot high cyclone/chain link fence surrounding a 200-acre **regional landfill**. *Signs prohibiting trespass on landfill property were spaced on the fence, in easily visible intervals. Within a quarter mile down the road were boarded-up houses fenced in because the landfill company had bought out the adjacent residences during a recent expansion! There had also been widespread publicity about the landfill!*

When the bank heard this, the sh_t hit the fan! The bank officials personally drove by the site. Ultimately, the bank declined the mortgage. The bank did not want a possible repossessed home with marketability problems if the homeowner defaulted on the mortgage. Be cautioned that all appraisers or all bankers may not discover such problems, or reveal these problems.

Two years later, the house had been built. The landfill now has a methane gas-electricity conversion station half a mile away. Driving by that area on the local interstate on a hot, humid, sultry August night, I was almost gagged by the smell.

It appears the second appraiser did not do an accurate analysis of the external factor in his appraisal for the second mortgage company. Make sure not to get involved in a money pit situation such as this. Be aware that external situations can and will affect the value and marketability of the property. Drive around the area and the neighborhood. Talk with neighbors working in their yards. Be current; read the local newspaper. Do your homework to become smart homebuyers.

"Man.. you won't believe the deal I got on this place."

Lesson #1 Review

H.S. = Horror Story

N.P. = Nasty Problem

H.S. #4 - Lose $500 deposit (check out adjacent problem properties).

H.S. #5 - Pay for $2,500 Phase I environmental study.

N.P. #4 - Carry in water for drinking, extra laundromat trips.

H.S. #6 - $50,000 external depreciation/hard to market home (don't build across the street from a landfill!).

N.P. #5 - Fumes, wind-blown papers from landfill.

LESSON #2: AVOID HIGH TRAFFIC AREAS

High traffic volumes on the home street can make living there a nightmare. It can also be a real bummer for future resale.

Recently I appraised a home in a small city. The home was situated on a tree-lined, 2-lane paved street in a city with a small population of 8,000 people.

The land use was 95 percent single family residential, with homes 20-50 years of age, in the $50,000-$100,000 value range. At first glance it appeared to be a quiet residential neighborhood. I parked my car on an adjacent side street to keep my car out of the front photo of the house. As I walked across the street to the subject home, I noted heavy traffic and had to wait and wait to cross the street. After I did my appraisal inspection, the homeowner attempted to back out of the driveway. I watched as she waited, waited, waited, and waited in her driveway, attempting to back out onto the street. The time was not unusual, like with a shift change at a factory. Apparently this was the usual ebb and flow of traffic on this street. The street was one of six arteries to the downtown area.

The next stop was verifying the city assessor's record at City Hall. The assessor had deducted 5 percent from the assessed property tax value, due to high traffic. Believe me, they don't reduce this value without good reason!

This could result in a 5 percent locational depreciation penalty in this particular appraisal.

Compared to a house with a $100,000 value on a side street that did not have this heavy traffic flow, our subject property on the busy street could easily be penalized $5,000.

An appraisal near the city limits of a large city of 200,000 people presented a similar, but less obvious situation. It was located near the entrance to a 30-year-old regional hospital less than a block away. The entrance to the hospital was out of sight behind a wooded area. When I mentioned this to the homeowner, he reluctantly admitted that at certain times of the day the traffic was very heavy, making it next to impossible to back out of the driveway. If you had visited the home during low traffic times, or were not familiar with the proximity of the regional hospital, a far different impression would have been formed.

Also the proximity to high traffic volumes can be very detrimental to privacy and one's peace of mind.

Another appraisal involved a suburban subdivision of 25-year-old homes in the $90,000-$150,000 value range. The subject home was on a **corner lot** *at the entrance to the subdivision. The lot's frontage was on the subdivision street, and the east lot line abutted a major paved 2-lane county road. The back yard was exposed to traffic, and at night the shining headlights of cars turning into the subdivision. Add to this the sound of cars braking and accelerating at the stop sign. The owners had lived there less than two years. Both the husband and wife worked long hours away from the home. They mentioned the "great price" they paid for the home. (I wonder why?)*

An extremely long, 6-foot-high, solid wood stockade-style privacy fence ran along the east lot line. I asked about the fence and the owners related that the previous owners had built it. (Probably the high traffic, and the shining of the headlights into the house and back yard, were driving them nuts!)

Not only would $5,000 or more of external depreciation affect it, but it could take forever to market the property due to noise and loss of privacy.

"Don't grow old waiting to get out of the driveway."

Tip-offs to traffic influences include high, solid privacy fences, back around/turnaround areas added to the driveways, berms, and extra shrubs/landscaping. Be aware of these red flags and consider them in your negotiations, and the quality of the housing needed, and what is tolerable. Walk across the street, stand in the middle, and stare both ways, as if taking a mental photo. Observe and note what is seen at different times of the day (like shift changes), and on different days, (weekdays are different than weekends).

Make yourselves smart homebuyers by learning to notice those property features that are different from other properties.

A lot of home buying is done on Saturdays and Sundays, when the traffic patterns may not be as obvious. Drive around the neighborhood on weekdays, during peak traffic and commuting hours, in doing the smart home buying homework.

Lesson #2 Review

H.S. = Horror Story

N.P. = Nasty Problem

H.S. #7 - $5,000 external depreciation due to high traffic volume (research traffic volume -- check the assessor card).

N.P. #6 - Spending 5-10 minutes every time backing out of driveway.

H.S. #8 - Corner lot at subdivision entrance decreases market value by $5,000 or more (and possibly lengthens marketing time for resale).

N.P. #7 - Need to build privacy fence to enjoy rear yard; must keep windows closed in summer due to traffic noise stopping and accelerating at stop sign.

Doesn't really fit with the neighborhood does it?

LESSON #3: GO WITH THE FLOW AND FIT IN WITH THE NEIGHBORHOOD

Your dream home should fit into the neighborhood. A white elephant misfit can lose 20-30 percent or more of its value.

Don't be encouraged to get a "great deal" in a sinking neighborhood.

To become smart homebuyers, understand what a neighborhood is. It can be a compatible mixture of styles and values of homes. Across the street can be a different neighborhood based upon the same factors of value range and styles. A neighborhood can be a rural subdivision of 100 to 600 homes, which is a community in itself. It can be a whole township, or part of a county in a rural area. Boundaries can be natural or manmade, such as an interstate highway, river, commercial park, or change in the school district boundary.

It is far better to be in the lower value range and to be pulled upward than to be overbuilt for the neighborhood.

Pay attention to the age range and value range of the houses in the neighborhood.

I once appraised a mansion in a rural township with a suburban-like setting. A dead-end residential street came in half a mile from the east portion of the section. Short streets branched off from it. The development of the subdivision began six years earlier and it was about 90 percent built up. The homes *averaged $200,000, with an average gross living area of 2,000 to 2,500 square feet. The lot sizes averaged about 100 front feet, and were about 3/4 of an acre in size.*

From the west section line, a dead end residential street ran .4 of a mile east. This subdivision was 100 percent built up. The average age of homes was 25 years, with gross living areas of 1,500 to 1,800 sq. ft. The average value of homes was $125,000. The lot sizes were 125 front feet, and were about 3/4 of an acre in size.

A mansion was built between the two subdivisions, within golf driving range distance of each subdivision. It had a man-made pond about a half-acre in size. **It took me over half an hour to measure the mansion's outside dimensions!** *The gross living area exceeded 4,000 square feet. The stained glass windows, marble floors, and chandelier in the foyer were imported from Europe, and cost more than many homes. The foyer resembled the entrance to a museum or church. The finished basement with recreation room, den, office, and bath, cost more than many homes. The basic construction materials exceeded those of the best homes in the county. The cost to build it was easily 3 to 3½ times of the nearby subdivision's $200,000 homes!*

My analysis of the market value for the bank placed a heavy penalty (known as external depreciation/obsolescence) as it was overbuilt for the township and most of the county. An external depreciation penalty of $150,000 was considered.

The homeowner was dissatisfied with my appraisal. I explained that the best comparable homes were in suburban neighborhoods **50 miles away** *and it was overbuilt for this area. The marketing time could take 1½-2 years to find a qualified and interested buyer, while the typical marketing time for homes in this area was less than 90 days. Even then, the homeowner most likely would not collect all his investment back.*

Neighborhoods do change. They have life cycles like everything else. Usually these cycles are: growth, stability, decline, and revitalization. This is defined per *The Dictionary of Real Estate Appraisal/American Institute of Real Estate Appraisers.*

A retired couple bought a retirement home in an urban area of 200,000 people. It was a well-built, 70-year-old home in good condition. The buyers could not believe the great deal they got. What they did not consider was the change in the neighborhood, from owner-occupied homes to absentee-landlord rental homes. The care, maintenance, housekeeping, and pride reflected and exercised in owner-occupied homes is easily recognized. Unfortunately, renter-occupied homes can often be very evident by the lack of or disregard for the earlier mentioned qualities. **Ages of the homes and economic backgrounds are not always the basis of this change.** *I know of an eight-square-block suburban subdivision with no natural or manmade barriers, where the rental houses can be readily distinguished from the owner-occupied homes. The homes are 25 to 30 years of age, in average to good construction quality, and many houses have the same builder.*

The owner-occupied homes are in the $30,000-$45,000 value range. A block away, the value range for rental homes runs $15,000-$25,000.

Some 80- to 90-year-old homes that are owner-occupied are in high demand because they are in revitalized neighborhoods. They can be in the $100,000 value range. Others that have been converted into single- or two-family rental units are in the $15,000-$30,000 value range in declining neighborhoods. The sizes and quality of construction are comparable, but they are in different neighborhood life cycles.

Drive through the neighborhoods, being alert to changes in use. Outside stairways to the second floor signal a conversion to an apartment. Often driveways are full with cars, forcing parking on the lawn due to too many tenants. Disrepair and neglected housekeeping and maintenance can be apparent.

Many times the assessor cards in a city or town record several years of the property's tax assessment value. They can reflect evidence that declining values every year over the last five, 10 or 20 years, and should **signal a red flag** for the smart homebuyer.

Smart homebuyers check out homes that are compatible with the neighborhood value range. Avoid declining neighborhoods, where "good deals" can trap buyers many times with a slim chance of recouping the original sales price.

Lesson #3 Review

H.S. = Horror Story

N.P. = Nasty Problem

H.S. #9 - Mansion amongst regular homes can cost $150,000 in overimprovement/external depreciation (build/buy compatible homes).

N.P. #8 - Marketing of this property could take 1-2 years with extensive publicity to qualified buyers 50 miles or more away.

N.P. #9 - Buying in declining neighborhoods makes the chances slim or none of recovering your original purchase price (learn to recognize the stage of the neighborhood's life by driving around/reviewing the assessor card).

LESSON #4:
LOTS AND BUILDING SITES

Homebuyers are buying a lot either as a vacant building site or as an improved lot with a house, site improvements, and other structures.

The height or elevation of a home site compared to the other portion of the lot is critically important. Visualize the 100-150-year-old farmhouses in the rural areas. Not only did they get first choice in the neighborhood for building sites, they are usually built upon the highest portion of the lot or farm. This allows for excellent drainage out and away from the house for surface water, house drains, and underground water movement and pressures.

Recently I appraised a 50-year-old home in the $70,000 value range on a paved county road with concrete curbs in a suburban area. The view from the asphalt street showed a sloping driveway and lawn. The slope ran down from the roadway, toward the home. Not only was the home below the road level, but the rear yard leveled out. Surface water would be funneled toward the house and basement from the higher street. Houses can be equipped with a drain water collection pit and sump pump, to pump the water out from excessive rains and drainage. It should not be too much of a surprise, but this house had two sump pumps with two collection pits. Do you think there was a real possibility of an ongoing flooded basement, or water damage or pressure affecting the footings? **You can bet on it.**

Sometimes the situation isn't that obvious. *One homeowner owned a modest home with a basement in a suburban area with a 4-lane paved street and a concrete curb in front of the house. The lot is fairly level. To the south about 300 yards, in a very slight sloping grade, is a major river. But that's not the problem. To the north is a residential area at a higher level. This created a stair-step or terrace-like effect. The homeowners were on the middle step of the three levels: the river, the house, and the higher neighborhood. You can guess whose basement gets flooded in a severe rainstorm, and the water from surface water runoff and from subsurface water that flows towards the river.*

Over 20 years ago, I spent considerable time with a prominent local architect examining alleged damage to homes, foundations, and basements. A nearby construction site allegedly caused cracks when dynamiting excavations for a sewer line. We checked out dozens and dozens of homes in modest to upscale value ranges. What we actually found were walls built against sloping hillsides without consideration to hydraulic/hydrostatic pressure of aboveground and underground water. Building site selection many times contributed to or aggravated problems, such as cracked walls, wet basements, sinking and/or settling footings, foundations, and slabs.

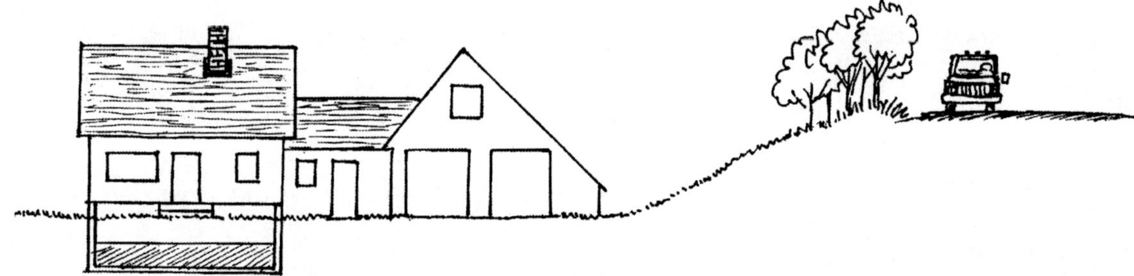

(Basement fills with rain-water from surface runoff)

Better placement of the homes on the lots, or special drainage considerations, would have saved a lot of maintenance problems, grief, and expensive loss of property.

One homeowner suggests shopping for homes after rains or rainy days. She and her husband learned this lesson in their first house, which was built on a slab. The neighborhood rainfall runoff collected to 4-inch depths on their lawn, until trenches were dug for drainage. They obviously did not shop for and buy this house during a rainy season.

Obviously the type of soil can accelerate or eliminate this problem. Sandy soils don't have these problems, but clay type soils or rocky soils do.

A tip-off to a problem can be a freshly painted basement floor, or walls covering recent repairs. New paneling and carpet can cover walls and floor to cover water stains and repairs. Some states require a seller to complete a written seller disclosure statement regarding this problem, or recent problems, or any history of problems. Educate yourself to ask questions, when and why, especially when recent repairs can be seen.

Let's make you into smart home buyers, avoiding buying a swamp property by inspecting the home's location on the lot, observing the lay of the land of adjacent properties, and inspecting the basements, crawl spaces, or slabs, for problems of cracking, heaving, bulging, dampness, mildew, and mold.

Lesson #4 Review

H.S. = Horror Story

N.P. = Nasty Problem

N.P. #10 - Lots below the road level sloping to act as catch basins which lead to chronic flooding from surface water, wet basements, extra expenses (wearing out of sump pumps, wash out/settling of asphalt or concrete driveways or concrete service walks), and loss of use of flooded yards for days or weeks.

N.P. #11 - Higher adjacent properties, with a home on a terrace above the natural flow of water to a lower river means constant flooded wet basements and driveways, with a lot composed of heavy soils.

Don't buy a house on an unmaintained, impossible private road where you need a tank to get home!

LESSON #5: AVOID ROADS OF NO RETURN, PARKING WITH THE NEIGHBOR, BAD PARTNERSHIPS WITH FLAKY NEIGHBORS, CHEAP LOTS, SALTY WELLS

Be cautioned to avoid some commonly overlooked problems of private roads, gravel roads, joint driveways, joint wells, small driveways, cheap lots, and poor water quality.

Some rural and suburban residences are only accessible by private roads. Many times the local Road Commission posts a traffic sign indicating that the road is not maintained by them. Often the road is so poorly maintained that potholes and washouts restrict travel to 10 miles-per-hour or less. You should know if there is a written, formal road maintenance agreement among the neighbors. It can require money donations to hire contractors for snow removal and road maintenance. Sometimes the neighbors own trucks or tractors, and voluntarily do the maintenance. Do not get stuck doing all of the maintenance while the deadbeat neighbors are too busy to honor their obligations. I have seen some private roadways that were better maintained than public roads. But I have seen some that took my four-wheel-drive truck to navigate them.

Years ago, the spring thaw made rural gravel roads so impassable that it was very common for people to park their cars half a mile or more away from their homes on the main roads. Two weeks of walking in to their houses, lugging groceries and small children, tired a lot of people of rural living. It can happen on public roads also. But private roads often have maintenance problems. Be warned that this can be very detrimental to future resale.

In some cities, especially in older neighborhoods with narrow lots, joint driveways between two houses are common. They can lead to parking areas or garages behind the houses. You will not want to be the only one constantly repairing and paying for driveway materials if your neighbor is a deadbeat. Often, selfish neighbors park in the drive, blocking access.

In some urban areas, common fences on property lines and a common garage wall can create similar problems. Get an agreement in writing as to use and maintenance.

A local rural subdivision of 30-year-old homes in the $50,000-$70,000 value range has some unique circumstances that many may not be aware of. In the first phase of the subdivision, many homes share common wells. These are often situated on the property line between the two homes. In such cases, it is wise to insist upon a written agreement as to who pays for what, and when, regarding repairs and usage.

Things don't automatically work out between neighbors. How about the neighbor watering his lawn and garden all summer and you don't have the water pressure to have a functioning home? Don't go into a blind partnership with a neighbor. Believe me, you don't need these problems a year or two years after the sale.

Consider other overlooked problems.

The size of a driveway isn't always checked.

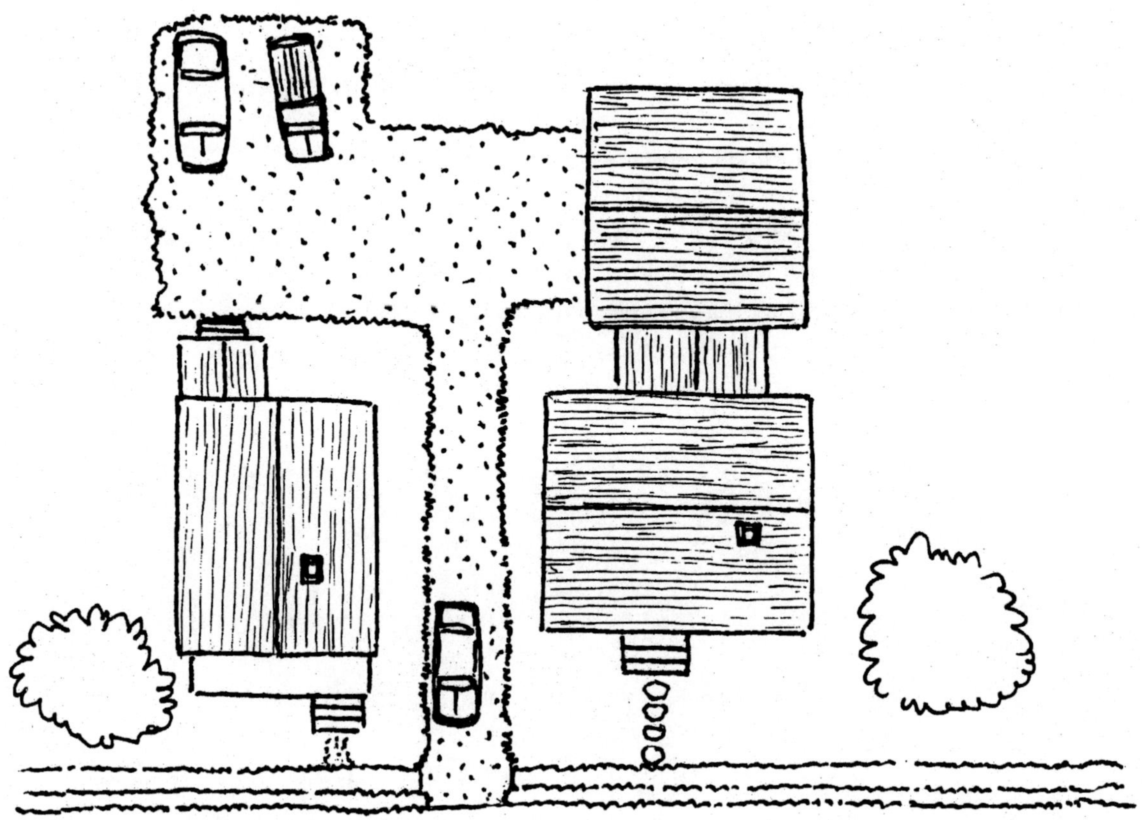

Don't go into partnership with your flaky neighbor.

One homeowner in a small city started to feel like a parking lot valet. The typical lot sizes in this subdivision were 60 X 150 feet, with concrete driveways often leading to a one-car or two-car garage. The driveway widths would only accommodate one car. Parking was not allowed on city streets. When the homeowner's two children got their drivers licenses and their own cars, the shuffling began. The husband, wife, and two children were constantly jockeying their four cars. One needs to consider if the number of drivers in the family will increase beyond the driveway's capacity in the near future.

Don't be tempted to buy a cheaper lot that needs fill dirt; do some serious thinking. Consider the cost of filling the lot to make it into an acceptable building site. Many times a standard lot is cheaper in the long run. A bargain is not always a bargain. A $5,000 lot needing $7,000 worth of fill and excavating is not cheaper than a similar $10,000 lot, which is ready to build a house on.

Water quality in private wells can be a tricky business.

Before buying a lot, a couple talked with a farmer across the street about the water quality. His water was fine. The couple bought the lot and discovered salty water after drilling five or six **deep** *wells. The water even burned their skin after showering. What wasn't pointed out was that the farmer had a* **shallow** *well. Shallow wells might not be legal now, but were acceptable at the time of the old farmhouse. If the couple had checked out several local well drillers they would have found out about researching saltwater area maps and well depths. Many well drillers have maps indicating local salt-water areas. It would have made a smarter decision before buying their lot. The builder indicated to me that they had to pay about $6,500 for a water treatment system to make the water tolerable.*

"Oh well, at least the flowers get watered."

Lesson #5 Review

H.S. = Horror Story

N.P. = Nasty Problem

N.P. #12 - Being the only one to maintain (grade or snowplow) the private road, or being the only one with $$$ to pay for it.

N.P. #13 - Enduring damaged shocks, mufflers, tailpipes on your car getting in/out to your home (I heard of one case where the homeowners wore out/bounced-out their cars and bought new ones every 2 years as a result).

N.P. #14 - Joint driveways with flaky neighbors and their guests parking in the common driveway, and they're not home, forcing you to park down the street or constantly hound them to move their *!!** car.

N.P. #15 - Walking in .5 mile to your house on impassable muddy roads. Never keeping your new car clean due to caking on of mud. Tracking of mud into the house and on your clothes every time you get in and out of that filthy car!

N.P. #16 - Nobody fixes the dilapidated common fence, as it isn't their problem.

H.S. #10 - Installing a new well, due to the neighbor hogging the common well (cost, $2,500). Lack of water pressure, can't water lawn or garden if the water drops below supporting two homes and two families.

N.P. #17 - Driveway is too small to handle all the cars in the family, with nowhere else to park. (Does provide experience when applying for valet job!)

H. S. #11 - Spending $2,000 more to fill in a bargain lot than the market value of a lot ready to build upon.

H.S. #12 - $6,500 for a water treatment system due to not consulting local well drillers with their salt-water-area maps. (P.S. - Suggest that you get a well test of the volume of water pumped. An extra-large holding tank may be a clue that something is wrong with the well. Its flow and capacity may be limited, or very slow.

"And they don't pay no rent, neither."

LESSON #6: BUYING AN EMPTY HOUSE (REPO OR ESTATE) CAN BE A BLESSING OR A CURSE. DON'T LET ROVER SOAK YOU OVER.

You should know how long the house has been empty. Do not believe everything the seller or the seller's representative says. Be a detective and call the local utility company to determine when the power and gas were disconnected. The city water department could confirm when service was terminated.

If a home has been vacant for some time, determine if the heating and air conditioning systems functioned during that time. Was the plumbing drained? Has it been recharged, and for how long? Sometimes slow leaks take a while to appear. Plaster and drywall may be adversely affected without heat. Heating and cooling systems may be slow to function if they sit idle for some time.

Varmints and insects love empty houses. Where termites, ants, and a variety of insects are common, an inspection should be performed.

In many areas of this country, the varmint removal business has become a rapidly growing industry. With decreased hunting and trapping activity due to the lack of interest or the outlawing of these sports, the populations of raccoons, opossums, skunks, woodchucks, and squirrels has grown out of control. These animals are not the cute little creatures as seen on TV or in the movies.

They can dig holes under a porch or under a foundation; they can chew holes in the roof and in siding. Nests are built in chimneys and fireplaces. The attic can be turned into their private litter box. This not only causes hundreds of dollars in repairs and removal costs, it can make a house unlivable.

Be alert to holes, scratch marks, claw marks, and roof access from a close-by tree or telephone pole. Raccoon manure on the roof or in gutters demands further investigation. Specify that the home inspection company look for these signs of problems.

Don't underestimate these varmints. They can scratch and chew through aluminum siding, shingles, and roof boards. *One homeowner spent more than $500 in re-siding the second story gable area, after a raccoon moved in when he was out of town!*

It can be wise to pull the damper lever in a natural fireplace, not only to be sure that it is functional but to be sure that there are no nests of creatures living there.

Make sure that you inspect or specify to the home inspector that the chimney is capped with wire mesh to prevent creatures from nesting inside.

Constant air traffic of flying bees in, out, and around the eaves, overhangs or chimney could signal a hidden nest inside somewhere.

Buzzing bees, fighting skunks under the porch, and chattering and squealing raccoons or squirrels in the attic are not good house guests.

Undetected water damage from roof leaks or burst and frozen pipes can leave a real mess. A home inspection by a conscientious and honest home inspector should determine this. However, you should insist and ask these questions.

Determine if the neighbors have taken over the use of part of the property by extending a driveway, building a fence or shed, or storing items onto the property when it was empty.

Dampness, mildew, mold, and humidity can build up without proper ventilation. Did a handyman or management firm check on the property when it was left vacant? Renters and evicted homeowners don't always leave pleasantly. Sometimes angry tenants turn on the faucets and plug the drains, allowing the floors to be saturated and flooding the basement.

Floors may be spongy or soft, or there may be mildew in the area. Sometimes only part of the damage is covered by insurance, and the remainder may have received partial or temporary repairs. These are good questions for you to raise, such as recent insurance claims and what repairs have been made.

Be on guard to uncover the mysteries before getting surprised. One appraiser of repossessed houses carries a can of flea spray. If he smells dog odors when he enters an empty house, he retreats to his car to spray his pant legs and shoes. Often a person doesn't realize he has fleas until he gets in his car or back to his office. Fumigating the house could cost hundreds of dollars.

"Rover's Revenge."

I have heard of a case where the odor from cat and dog urine surpassed the usual cleaning and sanitizing. After the replacement of the carpet and cleaning of the floor, the only solution was to tear out and replace part of the wooden floor. In winter, without heat in the house or with a broken window, the odors may not be so pronounced. This happened in an actual appraisal case. The appraiser estimated the cleanup repairs would cost $300. The bottom line repair cost was close to $3,000!

Never assume anything is as it appears! Do not assume by the existence of a house feature/machinery that it actually works.

I know of a case where an empty house had a central air conditioning condenser, but on the seller disclosure statement, which had been faxed to different parties at various times, it was barely legible that "Air Conditioner broke -- hasn't run in several years." Whether this was an oversight or accident is anyone's guess, or perhaps it was an intentional misrepresentation. It certainly would be wise to get it in writing.

You should be on guard as to poor maintenance, incomplete repairs, varmints, encroachments by neighbors, and Rover's Revenge when inspecting vacant/unoccupied homes.

Lesson #6 Review

H.S. = Horror Story

N.P. = Nasty Problem

N.P. #18 - Drywall and plaster may need repairs in unheated, vacant houses – FIND OUT how long it was vacant. Check local utility company records.

N.P. #19 - Unused heating and air conditioning system may require extra servicing to become operational.

N.P. #20 - Insects, fleas, raccoons, bats, bees, ants, termites, squirrels, mice and rats may have moved into a vacant house. (Removal could cost hundreds or even thousands of dollars.) Skunks and woodchucks love to dig dens under wood decks.

H.S. #13 - Look out for and don't buy into $500 of raccoon repairs.

N.P. #21 - Have the neighbors taken over part of the lot making a new parking area, driveway, storage or building onto the property while it was vacant? (As they say, "SH_T HAPPENS.")

N.P. #22 - Intentional flooding by disgruntled tenants often warps or softens floors.

H. S. #14 - Don't let Rover soak you over for $3,000. **Appearances can be deceiving! Never assume anything!**

LESSON #7: INTERIOR INSPECTION -- PART A: SYSTEMATICALLY CHECKING OUT THE FUTURE DREAM HOME/KEEPING FAT UNCLE LOUIE OUT OF THE BASEMENT

A person may rely solely on the home inspector, or perhaps he or she is a do-it-yourselfer. Or you may wish to know an inspection process to double check on the home inspection. Here are some guidelines.

I carry a small carpenter's pouch on a belt. In it is a small flashlight with a wide beam, 30-foot tape measure, 100-foot tape measure, and two screwdrivers. Carried also is a clipboard with a pad of paper, and a camera with a built-in flash. In my car I have rubber boots and a change of clothes. Some inspectors carry a marble and a short level.

Most appraisers and inspectors have a systematic inspection routine, to insure that no important areas are overlooked. The logical way to inspect a house is to start in the same order that it was built.

If there is a basement, I start there. The basement can reveal a tremendous amount of information about the quality of materials and workmanship of the house. Often I start in the furnace room, as many times the remainder of the basement is covered with ceiling tiles or paneling and this may be the only area that is open for inspection.

Old Midwestern farmhouses may have stone foundations with concrete or mortar. When built correctly, their extra thickness can make the house sturdy as a fortress. Poured concrete, concrete blocks, and wood foundations in modern homes are just as adequate.

Severe settling, bulging, cracking, and collapse are signs of potential serious structural problems. Walk around all four walls inside and outside for visual inspection. Minor hairline cracks could accelerate dampness, but may not be a serious structural problem. If you can see daylight through a crack, I recommend consulting a builder or engineer. Large floor cracks and heaving need expert evaluation. A look down the walls can reveal bulging. Sometimes fresh paint or paneling covers recent repairs. In some areas, a forced silicone injection can close and seal cracks in the walls adequately.

A white powder residue, green mold or mildew, or chipping paint can be evidences of water and dampness problems.

The type of structural members used in the flooring can indicate the builder's choice and budget in building the home. Floor joists of 2" x 4"s spaced at 20 inches apart in older substandard homes would not carry the floor loads of 2" x 6"s, 2" x 8"s, 2" x 10"s or 2" x 12"s. The larger materials, the more expensive it is to build the home. Usually the better quality homes don't skimp on materials. Measuring the floor joists and the spacing between can be a guide to the quality of construction. The local and national building codes will provide minimum standards. In this area of the country, 2" x 8"s are standard, but 2" x 10"s and 2" x 12"s are found in the higher quality homes. Quality framing has double floor joists under wall partitions and bathtubs. Floor trusses are often used now. Engineered I-beams and H-beams are also becoming quite common. These are helpful in freeing up the basement area for future finish, so that support posts or pillars may not be needed to support the floor structure members.

Sub-flooring of diagonal boards or plywood is more expensive than compressed board.

All copper water supply lines are superior, and more costly than galvanized or plastic type lines. A mixture of copper to galvanized pipelines can cause future problems, due to the different chemistry of each material and the chemical action that can happen between these two types of pipes.

Most modern electrical services have circuit breakers rather than fuses as a matter of convenience. If a circuit is switched off it can quickly be reset, rather than finding a replacement fuse.

Electrical boxes can be found in the basement or garage, and sometimes even inside of a cupboard or behind a picture on the wall. A look outside near where the electrical lines come into the house is a good starting point for finding an electrical service box on the inside.

Do not touch the electrical service if there is dampness on the floor, or there is any possibility of a shock or electrocution. Many inspectors touch a box with the back of their hand before opening it to make sure that there is no short, as a safety measure. The inside printed page of the box cover door often indicates the capacity as 100, 125, 150, or 200 ampere electrical service. Many times the main circuit switch has the number on the front or on its side of 100, 150, or 200 ampere. The larger capacity allows for future expansions, such as for a second garage or pole barn, or central air conditioning. Newly built homes with low amperage service may need an additional box to accommodate future upgrades. Checking with a local electrician can determine the minimum size needed for the square footage of the house. Then give consideration for future upgrades and additions. **It could cost hundreds of dollars more if an additional box is needed. Note this for your negotiations, should the house need a larger box to accommodate future central air conditioning or a second garage or a hot tub.** A local electrician should be able to tell you the size of the service that would be needed when you get into the specifics of the square footage of the house and various appliances and load that will be needed.

Fat Uncle Louie Finds A Short-Cut To The Basement!

High efficiency forced warm air furnaces are common in newly built homes and as replacement furnaces. The 90 percent high efficiency rated units are more expensive than the 70 percent and the 80 percent, but more savings are realized on the heating bills. The 90 percent rated systems have PVC/plastic exhaust pipes vented to a wall. The others have metal exhaust pipes, which can be attached to a chimney.

Some people like the steady heat of hot water heating systems with baseboards or radiators. However, if central air conditioning is to be added, it could cost twice as much as a forced warm air system. **This is because the air ductwork will need to be added. This could cost an extra $1,000-$1,500 or more. The forced warm air system already has ductwork to use for the air conditioning. Keep this in mind for your negotiations.**

If homes have sump pumps and/or well pumps, the general condition of the pumps should be examined. Age should be determined as well as recent repairs, and any applicable warranties if they are newer.

Many times, finished basements are completed by the homeowner. Inspect corners, moldings, and see if the paneling is loose from the wall. Check for evidence of flooding; the bottom edge of the paneling may crumble or warp after absorbing the flooded water.

Basement bedrooms usually are required to have escape-sized windows for emergencies. Sometimes in owner-finished areas, they do not have building permits and lack those safety-sized windows to comply. This can be a very expensive procedure to correct, costing hundreds or even thousands of dollars. You should be aware of this for future negotiations.

Don't rush this part of your inspection. Shine that flashlight up underneath the bathroom floor. Look for water stains, rotting, loosening of plywood layers in the area under the toilet where it connects to the sanitary line. A leaking wax toilet seal is easy to repair, but floor replacement or repair can be an expensive project costing hundreds of dollars. Smart homebuyers think about this before fat Uncle Louie sits on the throne and ends up in the basement

Furnaces set up on concrete blocks certainly point to ongoing or past basement flooding. Beware. This is a big red flag.

If the lower sheet-metal portion of the furnace housing is rusting or has peeling paint, this can be the result of basement flooding.

You should learn how to look for problems, listen for dripping or running water, and smell for musty odors or sewer gas.

Lesson #7 Review

Develop a systematic routine of inspection, often inspecting in the way the house was built. Inspection of the foundation's integrity is critical.

H.S. = Horror Story

N.P. = Nasty Problem

N.P. #23 - Recent painting and paneling in a basement could be covering a recent repair for leaks or other problems.

N.P. #24 - White powder residue, green mold or mildew could indicate water or dampness. Quality structural framing members, i.e. 2" x 8" or 2" x 10" can be an indication of the quality of construction.

N.P. #25 - Mixture of copper and galvanized steel pipes can lead to future repair/replacement.

N.P. #26 - Low amperage electrical systems (check with local electrician) may cost hundreds to add sub-boxes if you wish to add a garage or central air. Learn to identify the various types of high efficiency furnaces and their abilities to heat. (Don't be fooled in being told it's a "high efficiency furnace" without an explanation of its rating).

H.S. #15 - To add central air with hot water heat could cost an extra $1,000-$1,500 or more, due to the need to run extra ductwork. Check the age of well pumps and sump-pumps.

H.S. #15 - Adding escape-proof windows for basement bedrooms could cost $500-$1,500 or more per window.

N.P. #27 - Deteriorating sub-floor areas under the commode or drains could cost hundreds in future repairs.

N.P. #28 - Rusty sheet metal furnace covers or furnaces set up on concrete blocks could indicate flooding or basement leaks.

LESSON #8: INTERIOR INSPECTION -- PART B

Develop a game plan for an organized inspection, and understand the important features to examine. In the event that a home does not have a basement, begin with the mechanical systems or utility room on a crawl space or slab. Some houses may have some systems in one room, and some in the laundry room and in the kitchen.

Start at the lowest level, the ground floor, and work from one end of the house to the other end, sweeping back and forth to make certain not to miss any rooms or unusual features. Ask the homeowner for permission to look in every door and in the cabinets, and ask if you can try the appliances. Open every door, look inside each door, as it is very easy to miss a room or a closet. Sometimes a closet can suffer water damage or a collapsed ceiling or walls or floor that has not been repaired. Make yourself a smart homebuyer.

Diplomatically ask about incomplete repair projects, as we all have them, inside or outside. Determine if they are incomplete because of a lack of time or money, or because the cause of the problem hasn't been solved. An open trench or excavation could signal a sump-pump, septic, well, sewer or drain problem. Unfinished or unpainted drywall could be over broken or frozen plumbing. Ask why. We want to save your wallet and your sanity.

The two most expensive areas in the home are the bathrooms and the kitchen. It is wise to spend most of your inspection time in those areas.

Consider the squareness of a house, and the interior dimensions. It is common, in measuring older homes, to find the outside dimensions of the opposite sides vary in length. I have appraised several older homes where opposite sides of a rectangular shaped home varied 6 to 8 inches. Future remodeling jobs may reveal odd shaped rooms, making it very difficult to fit paneling, ceiling tiles, and drywall sheets. You should consider this possibility if buying a handyman special. Assessor cards and appraisers may round up their dimensions when reviewing their sketches. Actual measurements will give you the true shapes and figures.

Some inspectors put a marble on a smooth floor to determine if the floor is level or slants. If it rolls, the floor is un-level. These are common in older homes.

Check ceilings for water marks, stains, and repairs to plaster, drywall, or ceiling tiles. These could indicate a leaking roof.

Open and close the doors to determine that they latch properly. Sliding patio doors, as they age, stick on their tracks and sometimes don't open fully. Is there a screen for the patio door? If so, where is it? Pocket doors, often in bathrooms, are despised by many carpenters because they present so many maintenance problems. Do they operate properly? Are they warped? Do they close properly?

Check for the quality of materials and the craftsmanship of cabinets. Do all of them have their handles? Does the hardware function properly, or does it stick and not open completely?

Bathroom floors are often problems. Inspection of the bathroom floor around the base of the toilet could show loose, cracked, or curled linoleum from a leaky toilet. Stained or water marked carpet around the toilet could be a clue. Not only can the toilet leak, but many times there can be overflow from lavatories, bathtubs, and toilets.

I once walked across a bathroom floor so water soaked and damaged that I could feel the bounce in the floor. It was in a 40-year-old house, and the bank required complete repairs before they would consider mortgaging the property. Cost of repair: $500-$700.

You need to know the good features along with the bad features. Flush the toilets, turn on the faucets.

Use a flashlight to check dark corners and inside of cabinets, especially in the bathroom. Shine up from the basement on the floors under the toilet, kitchen sink, shower, tub, and dishwasher areas. Look for the drainpipes coming down from these areas. Look for leaks, rotted cabinet bottoms, and rotted floors. Many times water leaks leave a white powder-like residue on wood. The water soaked floor may be softer than the firmer wood around it when pressed on with a finger. If the wood deteriorates or chunks fall off the floor repairs may be necessary, and they may be very expensive.

Sit on the toilet with the lid down. Does it give a little, or wobble? The floor may have water damage and be rotted underneath.

Turn on the faucets in the opposite ends of the house. How is the water pressure if two people are using the water at opposite ends at the same time?

How long does it take for the hot water to arrive hot at the faucet?

Does the plumbing shudder or vibrate wildly when you turn it on and off? This is called "water hammer." You may wish to consult with a plumber. (This not only involves plumbing repairs, but could damage drywall and plaster, costing thousands of dollars.)

Do faucets leak where the handles are attached to the basin? Are there rust stains in the sink from a dripping faucet?

Fill the sink with water to determine the speed of drainage.

After taking possession, one new homeowner discovered that the bathtub lever, which diverts water to the tub or to the showerhead, did not work. The handle for the internal bathtub plug didn't work either. After hundreds of dollars in plumber's repairs, it was revealed that the previous homeowner, a single man, took showers but did not take baths. The repairs cost $500-$700.

Test the showerhead, the tub selector lever, and the bathtub plug closing mechanism. Frozen or broken plumbing can cause hairline cracks in the toilet, especially in seasonal dwellings where the plumbing was not properly drained and freeze-proofed. Cost to replace: $200-$400.

Strip-wood flooring can cup and warp after water damage.

Have there been any insurance claims and repairs from tornado, flood, hail, wind, vehicle damage, fire, frozen pipes, water damage, overflow from toilets or tubs that necessitated major repairs? If so, when, how much, and who repaired it? Major fire repairs are often noted on the "remarks" section on many assessor cards, including the date of the fire, the estimate of the fire, the estimate of the fire repairs, and the date that the building department approved the repairs and allowed for the home to be occupied again.

When inspecting the toilets, lavatories, and kitchen sink, check for shut-off valves in the water supply lines underneath them. With shut-off valves, water can be turned off in one room while repairs are ongoing rather than turning off water for the whole house.

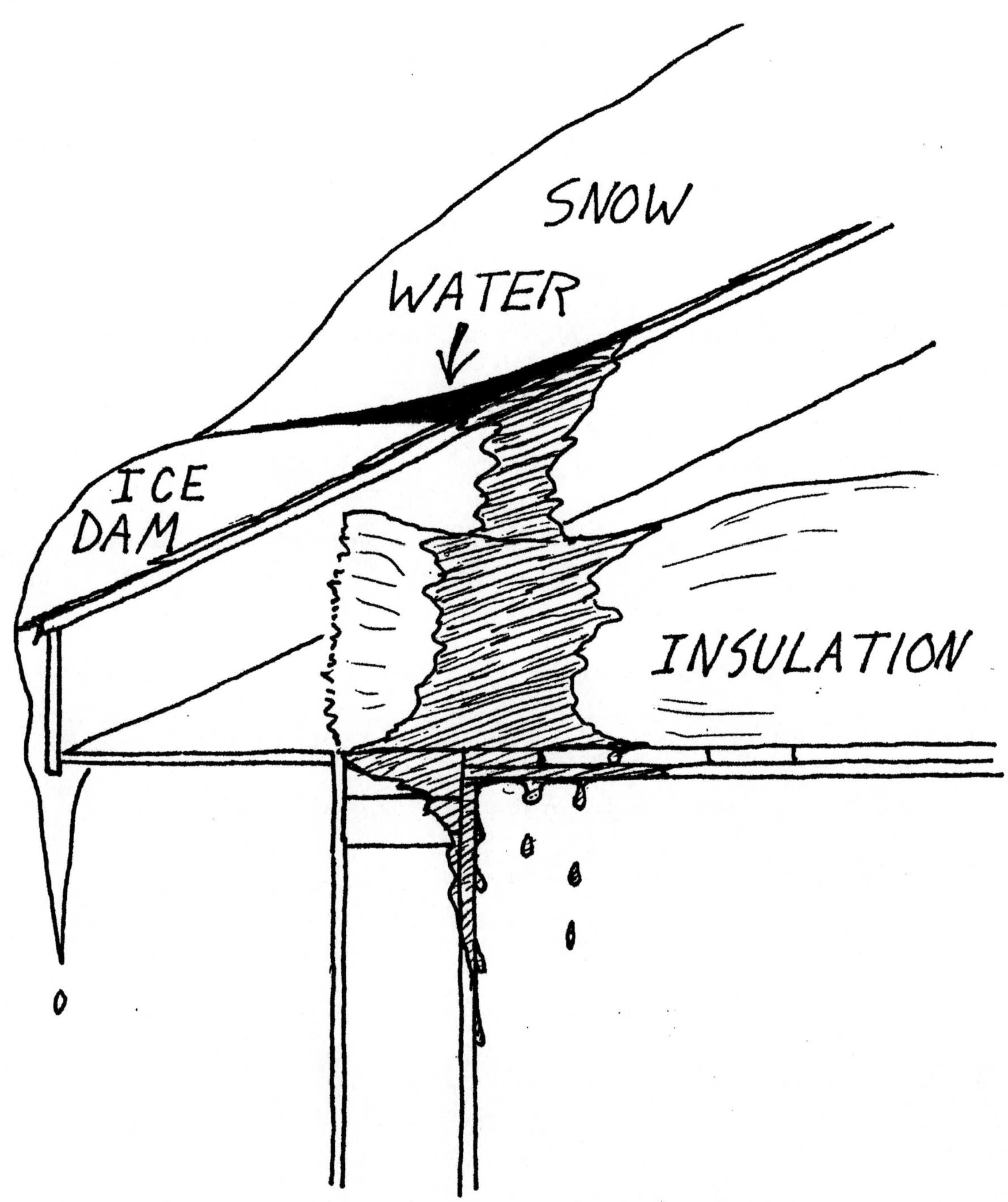

Damn Those Ice Dams!

Lesson #8 Review

Develop an organized routine of inspection: bottom to top, end to end. Ask permission to look in every door.

Check inside cabinets, especially the bases and bottoms -- they may be covered with dishes or canned goods now, but could be rotted out when emptied and the shelf paper is removed.

H.S. = Horror Story

N.P. = Nasty Problem

N.P. #29 - Ask about unfinished home repairs. Is it because of lack of time or money, or because they can't figure what causes the problem?

Spend most of your inspection time in the kitchen and baths (the two most expensive areas in your home).

N.P. #30 - Old homes are usually not square. Measure all four sides of the room you plan to remodel. Be forewarned -- fitting paneling, ceiling tiles, flooring could be a pain.

N.P. #31 - Old houses often have un-level floors.

N.P. #32 - Check for ceiling water stains, usually from roof leaks -- rain or ice and ice/snow damming-build up.

N.P. #33 - Does bathroom pocket door work?

N.P. #34 - Where is the screen for the sliding patio door? (Cost $40-$50)

How old is the toilet? Any repairs? Inspect the bathroom floor for curling, loose linoleum, tiles, carpet at/near the toilet. Has the lavatory, bathtub overflowed, damaging the floor? Any repairs? How extensive?

H.S. #16 - Water soaked bathroom floor with $500-$700 in repairs.

Flush the toilet and turn on the faucets, for water pressure. Sit on the toilet -- does it give or wobble?

H.S. #17 - Water hammer -- repairs could be thousands.

N.P. #35 - Leaky faucets -- replacement $150-$500.

N.P. #36 - Slow draining sink/lavatory/bathtub -- repairs $50-$150.

H.S. #18 - Check out the tub/showerhead diverter lever and tub plug mechanism to see if it functions properly -- repairs $500-$700.

H.S. #19 - Check for hairline cracks in the commode, especially in seasonal dwellings (cabins and cottages) from inadequate draining and poor anti-freeze-proof materials. Cost to replace - $200-$400.

N.P. #37 - Are there shut-off valves at or near sinks, lavatories, commodes, outside faucet? Or do you have to turn off water for the entire house for repairs?

LESSON #9:
INTERIOR INSPECTION -- PART C

Open and close the windows. Do they seal or fit properly?

Many times homeowners install modern windows or replacement windows only in the high visibility areas, or the front of the house. When inspecting the bedrooms, pull back the drapes or shades. Often, original windows in poor condition are still in the spare bedroom or the unused portion of the house. (Replacing half of the windows could cost $2,000-$5,000.)

Test the windows. Do the double-hung windows easily slide up and down? Do the casements crank out, or are the gears stripped, or handles missing or loose? Do the sliders slide, or do the awning types swing out? Do they fit tight? Do they latch and lock properly without forcing them? Are they water-stained around the edges? Do they have screens? If so, where are they?

If there are newer style windows, whether in a new house or as replacement units in an existing house, determine if there is a warranty that goes with them. Who was the installer? Does the warranty stay with the home, or does it go with the homeowner? This could save a lot of grief and hundreds of dollars in repairs.

The rating and size of a garage is based upon the number of cars which can independently enter and exit from it, not the owner's claim that it's 10 feet wide and 32 feet deep, making it a 2-car garage. In that case, one car must be backed out before the other car can exit.

How is the access to the garage? Can a person get to the attached garage from the house, or must they go outside to enter into the garage through the overhead door or a service door? I've seen houses where you did not have a direct doorway to the house. Then a person is forced to park their car and walk outside the garage to get into the house. If a side service door is not put in with the garage, a person is forced from the outside to go into the house for garage access when the overhead door is closed or locked. Not a big deal, but it's a hassle that you should be on guard for, for your convenience.

Determine that the automatic door opener does work. When was the last maintenance? Where are the portable operators? They cost $40 to $50 each to replace.

Measure the inside parking length and width.

One homebuyer had a classic car, which was too long to park in the garage. He decided to park it in the driveway with a portable tarp over it. The Homeowners Association's rules and restrictive deed covenants would not allow it. He had to rent a space at a storage company. (Cost $200 - $300 a year.)

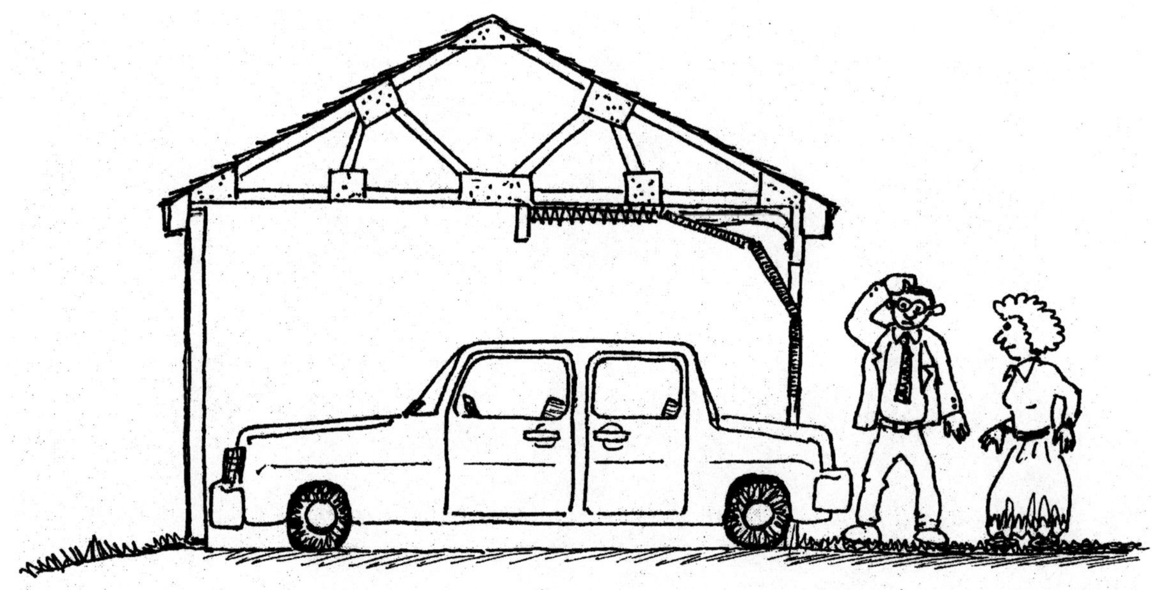

Does your garage fit?

If the garage has an attic, does it have a safe, working fold-down ladder?

Be certain hinged or sliding doors work. Sometimes they are stuck in place because they are not used regularly.

Get permission and turn on the garbage disposal and the hood fan to determine if they work. Test the dishwasher. Do these machines make strange sounds? Is there evidence that the dishwasher has leaked onto the floor, causing serious problems where repairs are needed? If there is a jet-tub in the house, fill it and turn it on to determine that it works.

Test the ceiling fans.

Count the phone jacks and cable TV jacks. Are there enough to suit your family's life-style?

Does the house have an attic? Is it floored? Is it finished? Is it insulated? Is it accessible?

Note the general quality of the craftsmanship of the moldings, and how they fit together with the joints around windows and doors. Trim work, door casings, window casings, baseboards, chair rails, cove moldings in the corners, should all be cut to fit nicc and tight. Gaps around them could be indications of poor workmanship, or cheap or improperly cured materials or green wood, which pulls apart after it's installed.

Keep in mind that no one is perfect in doing inspections.

While doing an appraisal I found half a basement floor covered with personal items. I reported this to the bank, and they insisted that the people move the items. They moved them all over to the side of the basement I had previously inspected, so I could go back and re-inspect the basement. Sound impractical and silly? Read on.

An appraiser inspected an older modest home and reported to the bank that it was in good condition. The occupant had stacked cardboard boxes of personal items on the floor of an enclosed porch before they made their move. This happens quite frequently, and some lending institutions will require that the people moving out move all their boxes and personal contents away so that a thorough inspection can be done. In this case, this was not done.

The boxes that were in this house covered a rotted out floor. The sale closed. The new owner found the rotted out floor after the boxes and the previous owner had moved. They reneged on the sale, and the appraiser was forced to buy the home. Fortunately, it was a modest valued home in the $15,000-$25,000 range.

Lesson #9 Review

Windows: open and close them, crank them, raise and lower them. Older, broken windows are often behind draperies and blinds –- look behind them.

H.S. = Horror Story

N.P. = Nasty Problem

H.S. #19 - Expensive, modern windows in the visible, high traffic areas of the home -- old fashioned, poor conditioned windows, needing replacement in the less used areas of the home (cost to replace half of the windows could cost $2,000-$5,000). Where are the screens or storm windows? Are there warranties with replacement windows?

N.P. #37 - Garage access door to house, outside service door, or do you have to go outside and around to get into the garage (no door to house)? Or do you walk through the house when the overhead door is locked (no service door)? Does the overhead door operator/opener work?

N.P. #38 - Where are the portable openers/controls? They cost $40-$50 to replace.

H.S. #20 - Does your car fit in the garage? Does the Homeowner's Association or deed restrict outside parking? Storage company fees -- $200-$300/year. Is there a safe, functioning fold-down ladder to the attic?

N.P. #39 - Do the garage doors function properly?

N.P. #40 - Machines/appliances -- test them.

1. – Dishwasher. It may serve occasional use of a family of two, but how about hard use by a family of six?
2. - Water heater. Check temperature and volume (size).
3. - Garbage disposal.
4. - Jet-tub.
5. - Ceiling fans.

N.P. #41 - Where are the phone jacks and cable TV jacks? How many do you need? (Installation of extras could run $20-$50 each.)

Easy access to the attic--where is it? A lot of people don't know!

How's the quality of the finish carpentry? Gaps could indicate poor installation or green lumber. (If this shows, **what about the materials that are covered over?**)

H.S. #21 - Boxes stacked over rotted out floor, where the floor couldn't be inspected below! (Horror story for appraiser costing $15,000-$25,000.)

"How come those boxes are always stacked on the floor there?"
"Theyre awful handy if we need something out of those boxes"

LESSON #10: SMART HOMEBUYERS MAKE SURE THEY HAVE A ROOF OVER THEIR HEADS -- A GOOD ONE! AVOID A $3,500-$5,000 ROOF JOB!

Quite often I see homebuyers replacing a roof soon after buying their dream home. Maybe it was negotiated in the purchase of the home -- maybe it wasn't.

Stay on the ground when inspecting the roof, for safety reasons. You can use binoculars from across the street, walking around the different sides of the house. Look for dark spots, cracking, curling, and wrinkling of the shingles. Inspect all sides of a roof. Sometimes one side or a portion of a roof is replaced due to hail or windstorm damage. Thus, one side is older and one side is newer. The colors do not match.

Orange and brown stains and streaks from rusting TV antennas on roofs can give an idea of the roof's age, especially if an old antenna is still on the roof.

Proper ventilation is very important. Vents under overhangs, on roofs, on gable ends are necessary, so heat, air, moisture can flow through and out. This can prevent heat buildup and the curling or cupping of shingles, which insures a longer roof life.

Valleys are the areas where two roofs come together. If tar patches are evident, they could be signs of a worn out valley, and this could be a very expensive area to repair. The valleys carry the most water volume towards the eave troughs.

Shingles which appear to be four thicknesses along the edge where the roof meets the siding at the bottom means the roof probably has two roof layers. If a new roof is needed, most local building departments require the old roof be stripped down to the roof boards before a new roof can be applied. This is a much more expensive process, and could add another $1,500-$2,500 to a roof replacement.

Check for interior leaks from snow and rain where the addition joins the main house.

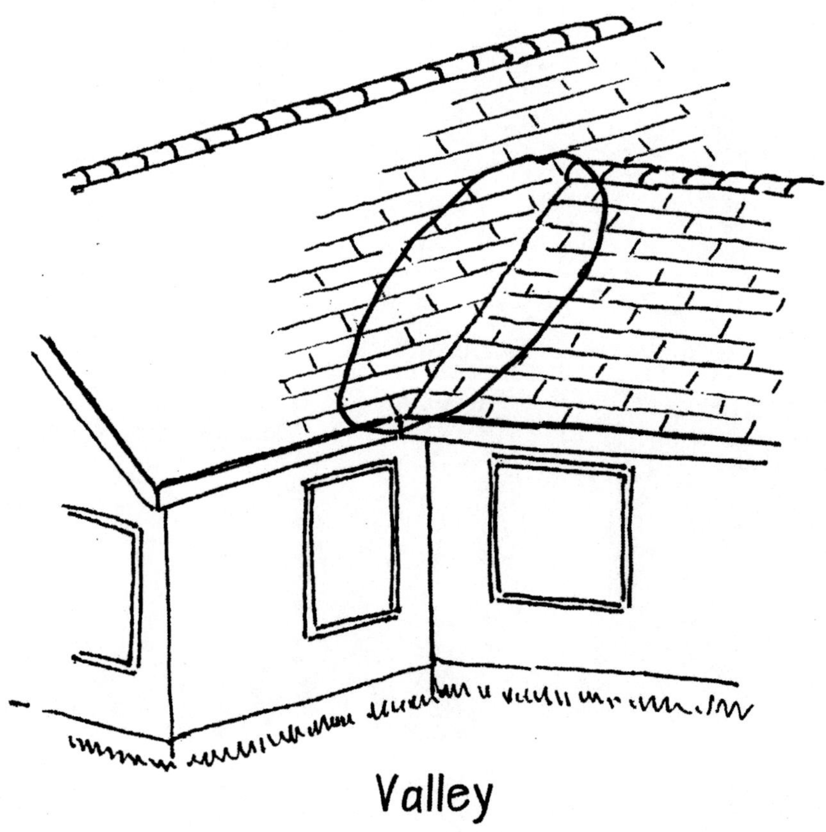

Valley

Sometimes a fireplace chimney or regular chimney is located downstream from where the rainwater runoff flows. The rain or snow flows down the roof against that part of the chimney. This acts as a damming effect, and the water is absorbed into the fireplace and can seep down undetected inside the house, rotting out the roof boards underneath the shingles. Sometimes a white residue can be found on the fireplace. A solution can be a roof structure much like a small tent, built to divert this flow of water. It is like an island in a river diverting the river flow into two channels. Make sure your roof has crickets/saddles around chimneys in the roof area, to divert water.

Frequently an addition or garage is built a few years later. Often the new roof ridge is lower than that of the original house, and an overlap area of the original roof extends out and over the addition's roof. If this is built downwind, rain and snow can accumulate in that area. If it is not properly flashed, roofed, and sided, this area can be a source of water penetration. Inspect the inside of the house at this junction of the two roofs for possible water damage. It could cost hundreds of dollars to repair.

Be certain that you are alert to poor design features that could be an ongoing maintenance problem.

The steeper the roof pitch, the better the drainage. It is more expensive to build a steep roof, but it is superior. Slight roof pitches allow for the accumulation of snow and water. If the water can't easily and quickly run off, it will seep down into the roof.

Gutters and eave troughs should be the correct size for the roof slope area. Sometimes a 5-inch commercial size gutter is needed rather than the 3-inch residential size. Common sense and a roofer's opinion can answer that. You should not assume they are the proper sizes, as sometimes builders take shortcuts by putting on undersized gutters.

Recently I needed to upgrade to 5-inch gutters on the north slope of my roof to handle the water runoff. It cost over $300 wholesale.

Gutters should drain, and not be level. If level they act as a lake with water sitting in them, to freeze or serve as a mosquito-breeding pond.

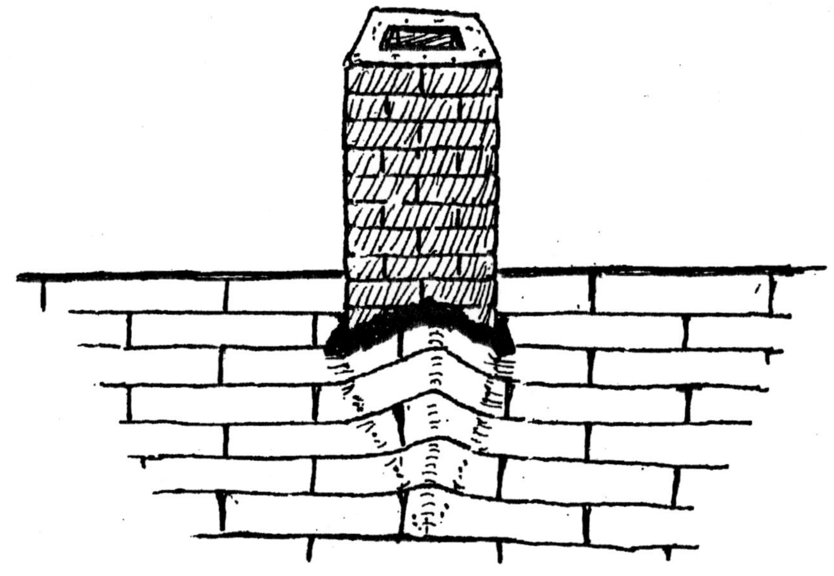

Cricket/Saddle (Top View)

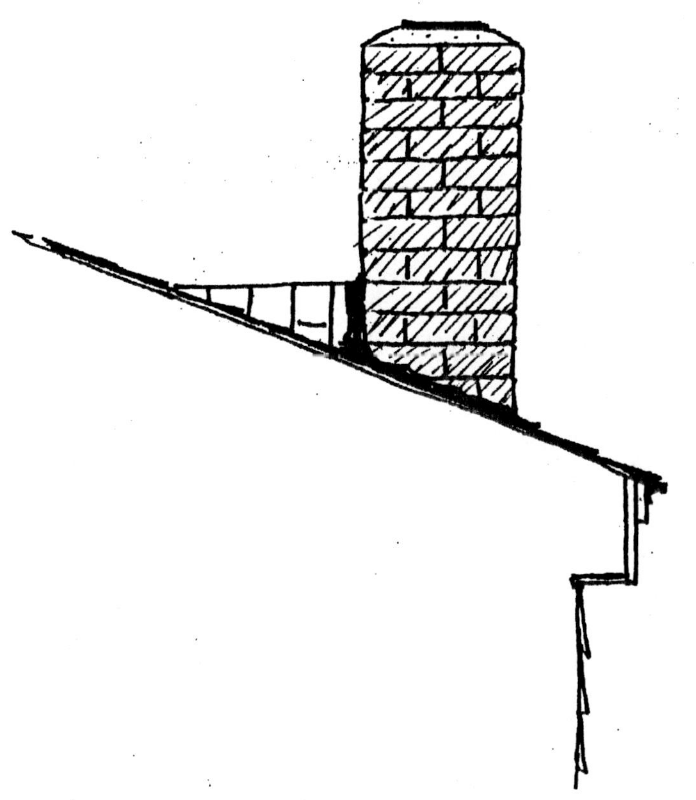

Cricket/Saddle (Side View)

Cracked fiberglass shingles.

Damaged shingles may be from a tree limb or fallen TV antennae.

Take note that the gutters are not pulled away from the drip edge, or that they are not sagging, which could cause an ice buildup area. Numerous trees shedding their leaves and pine needles could plug up the downspout, causing back up water to flood and saturate the edge of the roof. Be aware of trees too close to the house, shedding their leaves and needles.

Missing downspouts, or the lack of the lower outlet pipe (called a diverter) that empties the water 2 to 4 feet onto the lawn, could funnel the rainwater downward into the ground. Water could seep into the footings, or into the basement. I have quite frequently seen where downspouts just empty onto the ground and holes could be 6-18 inches deep by the downpour of water and no place for it to go. The water runs along the footings, and if there is a basement, there is a high possibility of a damp and flooding basement. Excavating and foundation repairs for something as trivial as improper or lacking pieces of gutters could cost $500-$1,500 or more.

There are many types of roofs: metal, tile, slate, rubber, wood shingle, built-up. However, the most common types are asphalt or fiberglass shingle roofs. Many types of expensive shingles have warranties on them for 30 years, or the life of the roof. This is also true with some rubber roof warranties, for shorter lifespans. In many localities, rubber roofs have to be installed by a licensed contractor rather than a home do-it-yourselfer.

Don't walk into a $3,500-$5,000 roof repair job.

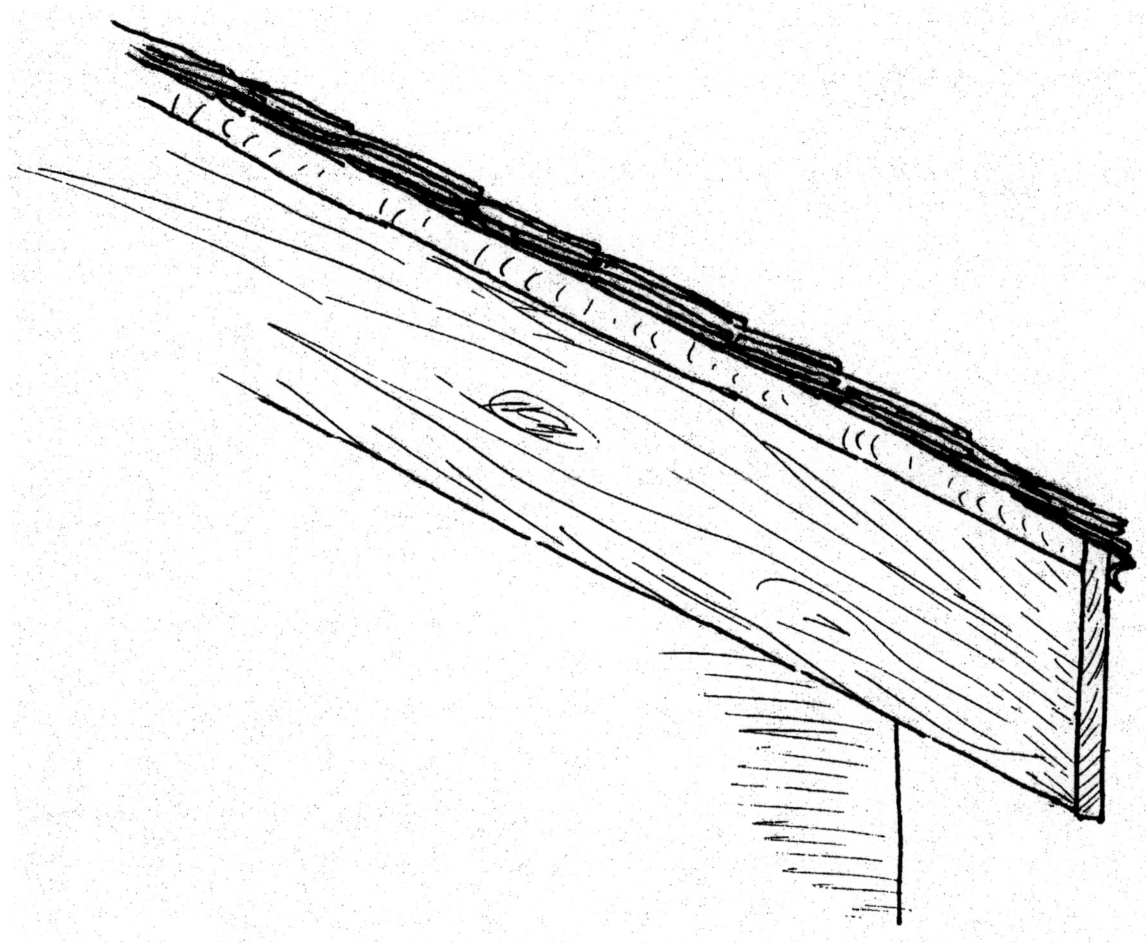

Two layers of shingles will likely require stripping to the roof boards (more expensive) when the next roof is needed!

Lesson #10 Review

Roofs: Inspect them from the ground with binoculars for both/all sides. Sometimes only one side has been replaced due to hail or wind storm repairs.

H.S. = Horror Story

N.P. = Nasty Problem

N.P. #42 - One side of the roof may be older, needing replacement before the other. Matching colors may not be available.

N.P. #43 - Lack of roof vents, gable vents, soffit vents can shorten a roof's life.

N.P. #44 - Double thick roof shingles could require stripping to the roof boards if a new roof is needed (figure another $1,500 added to a typical roof job.)

N.P. #45 - Worn out -- holes in valleys.

N.P. #46 - Added repairs for a cricket/saddle with possible interior repairs (cost to build a cricket/saddle -- $300+).

N.P. #47 - Cost of flashing at junction of addition for rain/snow penetration plus interior repairs to insulation, drywall, redecorating, etc.

N.P. #48 - Roofs with slight pitch wear out quicker and leak more often.

N.P. #49 - Gutters/eaves/troughs too small for the roof area. (My upgrade cost $300/wholesale -- subcontractor's price.)

N.P. #50 - Gutters level, acting as a pond, ideal place to raise mosquitoes.

N.P. #51 - Missing downspouts or bottom diverters (cost $40-$50 each installed).

N.P. #52 - Undermining of foundations from improper rainwater drainage from downspouts. (Costs: excavating and concrete repairs -- $500-$1,500+.)

H.S. #23 - Buying a home and paying to re-roof, $3,500-$5,000 or more, a short time later. This is without knowing the need and negotiating this circumstance with the seller.

More Useful Roof Information

If you are utilizing a home inspector, suggest that they take photos or a video of the roof in its entirety. Also pay him the extra time to have him measure and diagram it. Roof repairs are done by areas; by the square (10 x 10-foot area), by height and by difficulty (number of valleys, saddles, etc.), plus a percentage of waste for cutting the roof materials. Ask him to calculate the area in squares, or do it yourself and divide by 100 square feet.

If you want a house needing a new roof, you will obviously need replacement bids from roofers. After getting the detailed written bids, check or ask how many squares, ask what percent of waste is included, ask how much extra is charged for difficult jobs. Ask the weight of the shingles: i.e. 235 lb., 240 lb., etc.; or the life span of the type of shingles: 20 year, 25 year, 30 year, etc. The heavier the grade, the more expensive and better quality, longer life. Ask for comparison to the brand and weight that is on the house. Don't let him con you with "el cheapos" to make his bid cheaper, or the "super-deluxe" because he gets a mark-up off them. Are there warranties?

If the roofer is honest with you on the size of the roof area, or is willing to compare his calculations to yours, he may be trustworthy on the other areas. Don't let him work you over with his pencil for an extra $200-$500.

The bottom line is: A roof is an obvious thing to check out, but don't overlook them. It could cost big dollars.

Hip Roof

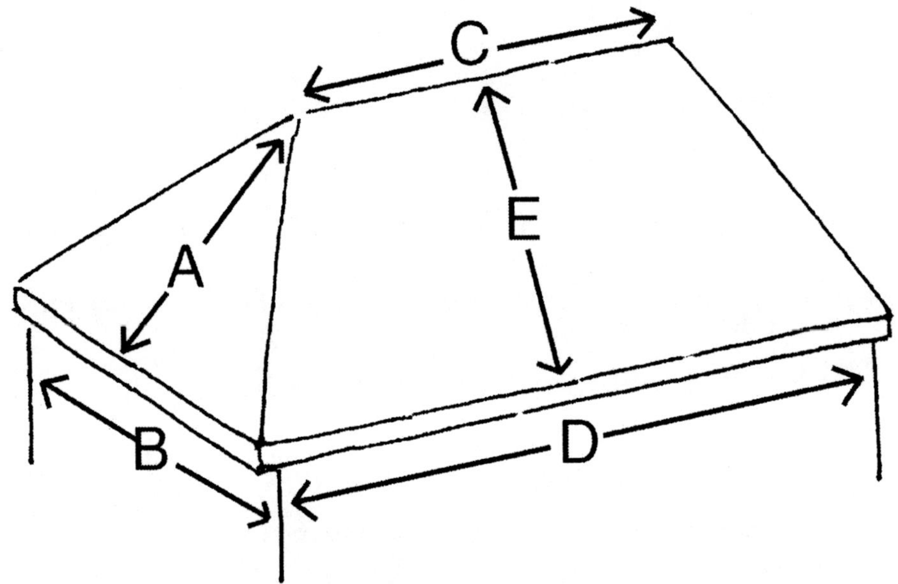

Area = 2 Sides X(AX B/2)= Area of 2 Ends

+

$$2 \text{ Sides } X\left(\frac{C' + D'}{2'}\right) XE = \text{Area of 2 Sides}$$

Total Roof Area

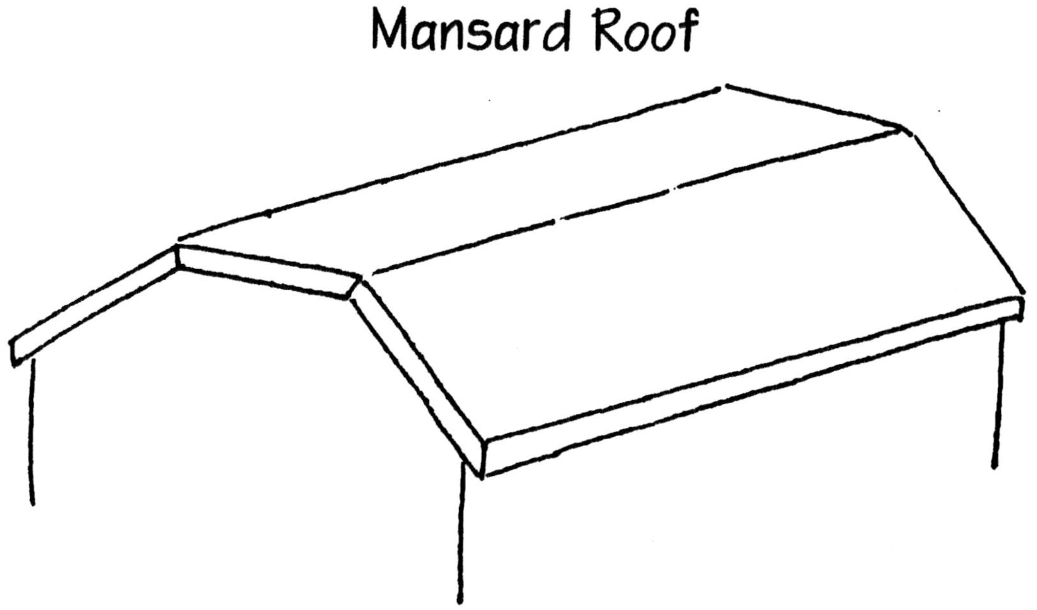
Mansard Roof

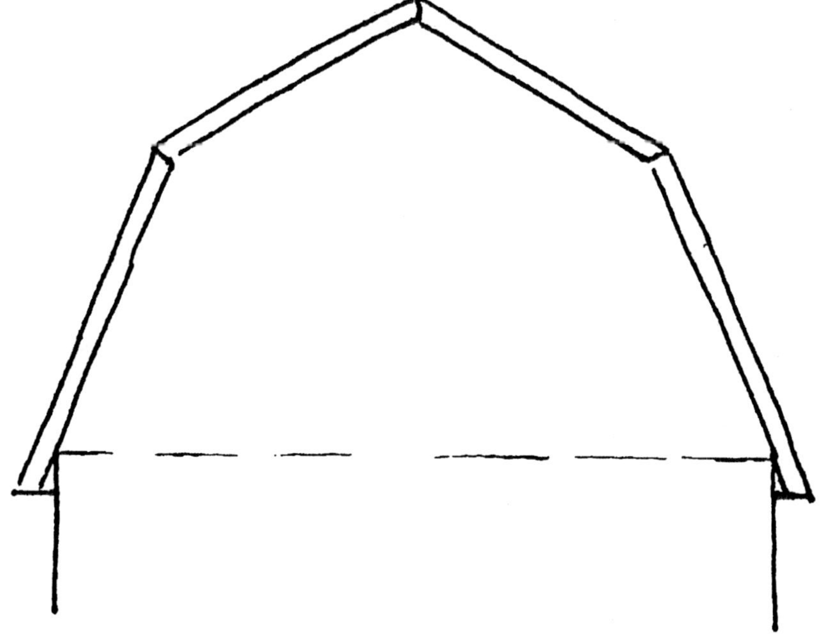
Gambrel Roof Style

Gable Roof

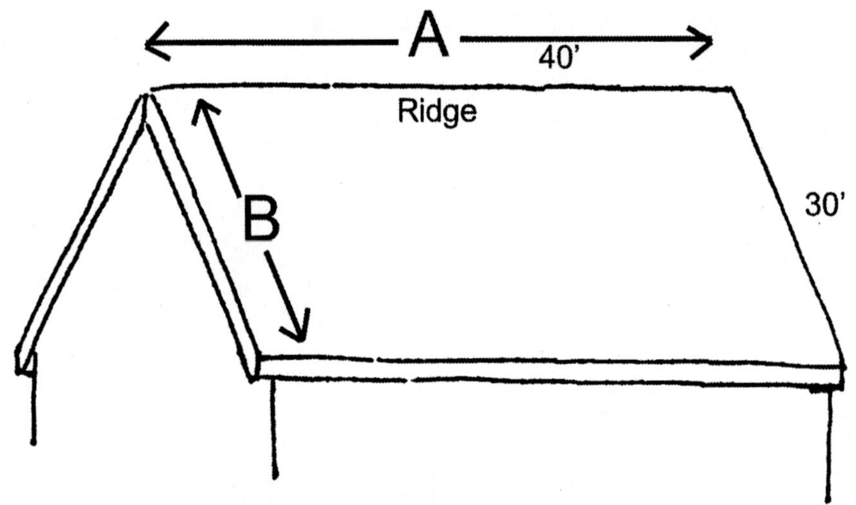

Area = A x B x 2 Sides

40' x 30' x 2 = 2,400 square feet

divided by 100 square feet/square =

24 squares of roof area

Roofing Replacement

Strip 3 tab shingles

Replace 24 squares with L.K.Q. (like kind and quality)
Plus 5% waste = 25.2 squares (rounded=25 squares)

25 squares @ $80	=	$2000.00
Tear-off 24 squares @$15	=	$360.00
Debris Trucking/Landfill Fees/Dumpster Rental	=	$800.00
Permits	=	$50.00
		$3,210.00
Contractors Overhead, Mark-up, Profit	=	$642.00
Estimate Roof Replacement Cost	=	$3,852.00

Also consider scaffolding, steep roofs, extra valley and edge materials, extra ice-dam materials along bottom edge, replacement of rotten/water soaked roof boards.

Curled tabs maybe caused by heat build-up inside the roof by lack of or insufficient number of roof/eave/ridge vents for proper inside air movement in the attic.

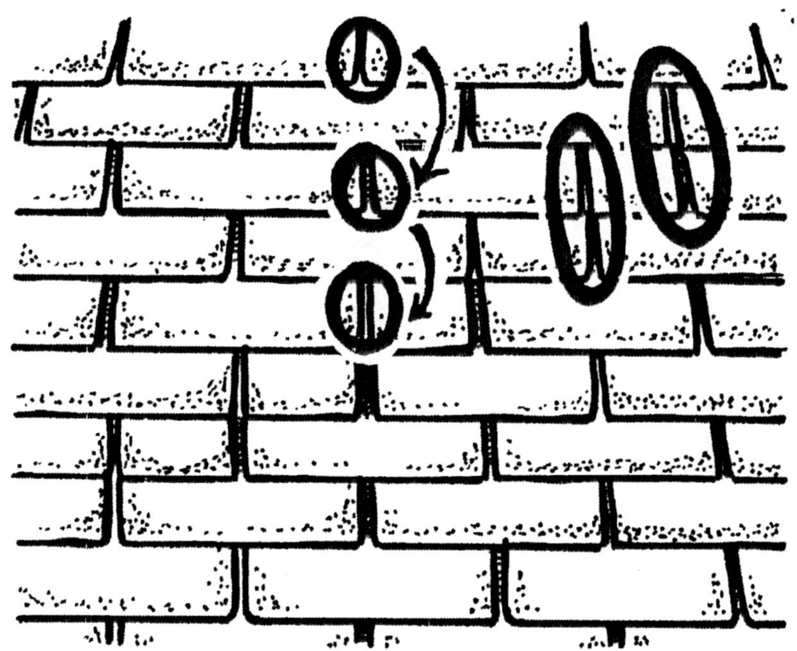

Improper installation- slots should be staggered to prevent premature roof wear

Moss covered roof- which grows under the shade of nearby trees.

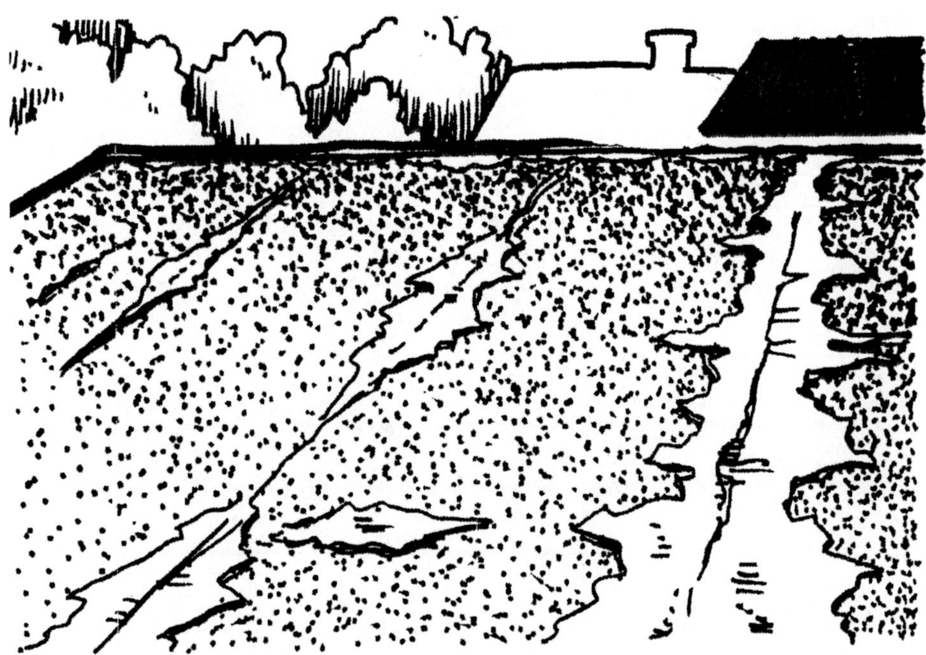

Patched up repairs or built-up/ gravel coated repairs.

Alligatoring: wear problems on flat built-up roof.

Wearing out wood shingles.
Note curling/warping and
deterioration of shingle tab ends.

LESSON #11: EXTERIOR INSPECTIONS

Completely inspect all four sides of the building, the driveway and sidewalks. Note obvious problem areas such as large cracks, sinking or splitting, rotting or deterioration of the siding or around the window areas, or discoloring from rain or mildew.

Houses with crawl spaces are sometimes difficult to inspect. They should have vents through the foundation walls to allow for airflow under the house. Take a photo through a vent, or have your home inspector take photos to check for rotting of the structural members, such as floor joists, or the floor itself, or other maintenance problems.

If the house is on a slab, determine that it is not undermined by water or sinking. Note the overhangs of the edge of the roof. Check to see if there is peeling paint, rotting, deterioration. Check for vents underneath the overhangs that are closed in so the air can circulate underneath the roof for proper ventilation so it is not stagnant and rotting out. Be sure eave troughs, gutters, and downspouts and diverters are in place.

In many 30-year-old houses, it is common to have basement window wells dug around and below ground level. Window wells, if not properly drained or covered with a plastic shell to divert away excess amounts of rainwater, act as a collection basin and funnel water into the basement with resulting moisture problems. If the water gets deep enough, it can rise up to the window and actually come in the basement window.

Asset or Liability?

Be aware of any landscaping that looks freshly installed, planted, or disturbed, which may cover up any defects or recent repairs around the base of the house. It is possible this has been used to cover up some major structural problems to the footing, foundation, slab, or basement.

Go a distance into the back yard. Take photos and review them. You may be amazed of the things that will show up in the photo review, which were missed in the initial inspection.

Note if the lawn is soft or moist. Observe if drainage flows towards the house rather than away from it. Water that flows away is called positive drainage. Negative drainage is where surface water flows toward the house. The soil surrounding the home should allow for rainwater to flow away from the home, not funnel toward it. Poor drainage can be corrected with the placement of heavy soils, such as clay type soils, in a gradual slope to accelerate the flow out and away from the home.

Note any areas where black sludge may be seeping out onto the lawn. This may signal a serious septic problem. Note any sewer gas or unpleasant odors. Perhaps this is only an indication of a septic cleaning process, which could cost a couple hundred dollars. But it could also be a needed major repair of the septic field, costing several hundreds or thousands of dollars.

Look on the inside of outbuildings, sheds, or children's playhouses for electrical services, and the type of floor. Check for holes through the roof, or water stains. Observe any indication that animals have been digging around or underneath the floors/footings of these outbuildings. Look at the chimney. If the chimney is not on the actual ridge of the roof, the top should be 2 to 3 feet above the roofline. If it is on the roof ridge, it should be 2 feet above the roofline. On a flat roof, the chimney should be 3 feet above the roofline. This prevents back drafts of exhaust/smoke coming down inside. (Note: Look for deterioration or leaning.)

Also note the height of the vent pipe from your bathrooms. Are they on top of the roof where they should be? Be wary of vent pipes that are cut off and left at a window level. This allows for sewer gas to come back into the house.

Inspect the house from the front or from the street. Does it actually have curb appeal for you and your family, or is it something that is pleasing only to you and may not be easy to sell in the future?

Positive Drainage with water flowing away from the house.

Lesson #11 Review

Closely encircle/inspect the house exterior -- for siding, brickwork, foundation, window problems.

H.S. = Horror Story

N.P. = Nasty Problem

N.P. #54 - Driveway, service walk cracking and sinking (cracks could be minor and are common; sinking/tilting could cost $500-$1,000 or more).

N.P. #55 - Does the crawl space have vents for ventilation? Better check with your builder or inspector how many are needed for the size of the area.

H.S. #24 - Take photos with a flash (or have your home inspector do so) to see the floor joists and floor through the crawl space vents for rotting, moisture. **Watch out for varmints that slither, fly, smell, or bite that may be living there!** (I've seen rotted out floor areas that would cost $2,000-$5,000 to repair, especially in vacant and repossessed homes. P.S. Was a permit drawn with city inspections when an addition was built? Sub-standard plumbing, wiring, carpentry, foundations could show up in the crawl space.)

N.P. #56 – If the house is on a slab, is the slab undermined by water? (Repair cost, $200 or more.)

N.P. #57 - Do the overhangs/soffit areas need major replacement, or repairs, or painting? (Costs $200-$1,000 or more.)

N.P. #58 - Do window wells drain properly, or have transparent covers/caps?

H.S. #25 - Is there freshly brought in dirt/landscaping? Could it be covering a problem and was installed just when the house went on the market? I heard of a case where freshly planted shrubs covered a major exterior foundation defect costing thousands to repair. Inspect photos of the front, rear, and sides of the home from a distance. How does it look? Anything peculiar? Is the lawn abnormally soft or spongy compared to other yards? (If so, maybe it collects surface water.)

N.P. #59 - Positive drainage -- does the rain water/surface water flow out and away from the home? (Cost to build up and add heavy clay-type soils around the perimeter of the house -- $500-$1000.)

H.S. #26 - Does a hole or swale need to be dug for surface water runoff to collect in (cost, $500-$1,000)?

H.S. #27 - With a septic system -- black sludge seeping to the surface (clean-out cost, $50-$150; reconstructed septic field, $1,000 or more; replace entire septic system, $2,500 to $5,000 or more, depending upon local building codes, soil conditions, percolation rates.

N.P. #60 - Small sheds, outbuildings that are more liability than beneficial (cost to demolish and take debris to landfill, etc., $200-$800 -- some local ordinances forbid burning).

N.P. #61 - Chimneys and vent pipes too short, causing back drafting -- sewer gas (cost to repair, $500 or more). Note: Modern higher rate high efficiency furnaces are vented through the walls. How is the curb appeal?

Don't buy an *oddball* style house unless . . . . .
you're a space cadet waiting the arrival of UFO's.

LESSON #12: DESIGN, APPEAL, AND MARKETABILITY/DON'T BUY AN ODDBALL HOUSE (GOD HELP NUMBER 8 IN THE BATHROOM LINE!)

Once I reviewed a multiple listing book with a picture of a house that looked like a flying saucer! It had over 4,000 square feet, was on acreage, and had a private lake. Cool ... if you're an eccentric millionaire. But who wants it next?

Design and room layout can make or break the appeal of a home. Younger people often buy split-level homes; quad-levels, tri-levels, and bi-levels. Over the years the constant stair climbing, going four steps up or four steps down to here or there, becomes tedious. Their next home is a one-story or ranch style with a first-floor laundry. Keep this in mind as the general population and baby boomers age: The stairs get steeper and longer and harder to handle.

The better-designed 2-story and 1½-story homes have one bedroom and a bath on the main level. The kids are sent to the second floor bedrooms. Keep this in mind for your family, as 2-story homes are very popular in newly developed subdivisions with limited lot sizes. You will be able to build upward, but don't sacrifice the convenience of the main floor for the main occupants.

Many areas of the country have no basements or crawl spaces under the homes. So be it! But many areas have all three options.

Often, starter homes are built on slabs. As circumstances change, the now smarter home-buyers move to homes on crawl spaces or with basements. Fatigue, leg problems, and back problems are common complaints as a result of living, walking, and standing on concrete slabs. Also complaints of coldness and dampness are common. Of the three styles of foundations available, homes on slabs are the least desirable.

What is the ratio of bedrooms to baths?

An old farmhouse I once appraised had eight bedrooms and one bath. The owner bragged about the suitability for a large family. Wow, I hope I'm not No. 8 in line for the bathroom!

Where is the bath located? Older 2-story homes of the 1910-1930 vintage in this area of the country usually had upstairs baths and bedrooms. That may be suitable for younger people, but for physically challenged and older people, it is not that appealing. It could cost thousands of dollars to add a bathroom downstairs.

Experimental and exotic heating systems may suit you, but what about the next buyer? Electric baseboard heating has been a quick and easy solution for rural homes, cottages, and cabins. But the heating cost compared to forced warm air systems and hot water systems have made them a real boondoggle. Marketing problems have been considerable also. More recently, geothermal heating and cooling systems have been promoted to solve all of mankind's problems. They heat and cool by extracting heat and cold from the ground water. It is claimed to operate cheaper than conventional furnaces -- but installation costs are considerably more.

Heat pumps are common and suitable in some areas of the country, but there is not widespread local acceptance of these systems, and there is a lack of service companies.

Earth-berm homes with only the roof exposed are very interesting and unique. But so is the fun house at the amusement park. Do you want to live there? How about marketing to the general home buying public?

Old farmhouses are hot items for remodeling and nostalgia. But often the heating and cooling capabilities for the second floor are not on a par with the first floor. Additional mechanisms can solve these problems, but they are more expensive to add on. Make sure you are aware of this.

Solar panels were really in demand 15-20 years ago when the energy crisis hit. People got tax credits to install them. Appraisers are bombarded with the wonders of solar panels.

In Michigan, which has the second cloudiest weather after the New England states, few if any new units are being installed. They did not solve the heating problems on a large scale, as promised.

Energy saver features can include insulated windows, insulated exterior doors, thicker walls, and added insulation to the walls and ceilings. Often the brand and model are printed on the lower right corner of the windows. Measure the walls near the windows to check the wall thickness. Have energy audits or rating of the home been done by local utility companies? Many builders receive recognition for these features. Ask to review the utility bills over a year's time.

Buyers are very conscious of energy saver features, and lose interest in model homes without them. In the 1980s, energy features added about 2½ percent to the sales price in this area of the country. Buyers were willing to pay $2,500 for energy saver features in a $100,000 valued home. (Per the research in my 1987 thesis.)

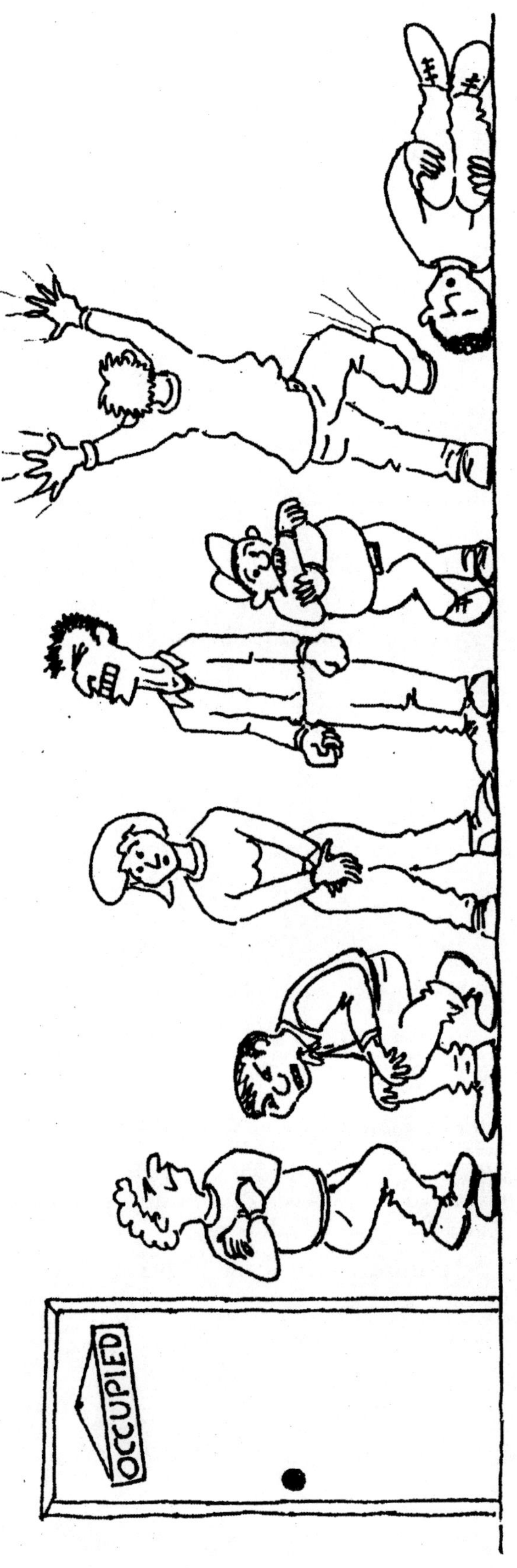

God help #8 in line!

Lesson #12 Review

Don't buy flying saucer design homes, unless you plan to live there ... forever ... or unless you hope to attract extraterrestrial friends!

H.S. = Horror Story

N.P. = Nasty Problem

N.P. #62 - Split-level homes with constant stair climbing are for young, able-bodied people. Better quality 2-story homes have a first floor master suite and bath.

N.P. #63 - Occupants of homes on slabs suffer more fatigue, leg problems, back problems than occupants of homes on crawl spaces or with basements.

H.S. #28 - Inadequate ratio of bedrooms to baths (cost to add/remodel for bath: $2,000-$10,000).

N.P. #63 - Poor location of bath on second floor.

N.P. #64 - Experimental/exotic heating systems--difficult to find servicemen and parts.

N.P. #65 - Electric heat -- very expensive utility bills; hard to market homes.

N.P. #66 - Earth-berm homes are unique, but so is the funhouse; hard to market.

N.P. #67 - Old farmhouses--heating/cooling systems often are not on a par with the main floor. (Check with heating/cooling man -- do they claim extra booster-type mechanisms can solve this?)

N.P. #68 - Solar panels in cloudy-weather states -- you won't recoup your investment on resale. Energy saver features can be positive for your living enjoyment and resale. Ask about energy audits, review of energy bills. Have the owners added insulation? How much? Did the builder win any recognition/awards from local utility companies?

LESSON #13: TIMING/SUPPLY AND DEMAND: GET A FEEL FOR THE MARKET BEFORE FINALIZING HOME CHOICES.

Understanding the forces of supply and demand can help you avoid future disappointment and poor investment choices.

One common mistake made over and over again is the assumption by homebuyers that the housing market always appreciates, and at a tremendous rate.

Job transferees coming to the conservative Midwest market from the east or west are overwhelmed at the size and quality of homes available for the dollars they received from their previous home sale. They take it for granted that values will appreciate at the same rate. After 5- or 10-year periods, they often are rudely awakened to 3-5 % or less on yearly appreciation rates. They assume 10 % per year or more, like in their other home areas.

Research with a library or local salespersons are good sources. Also construction guides such as *Marshall Swift* give national cost rates for building of homes by state and by city, and suggest multipliers. These multipliers reflect the cost to build locally versus national averages. These multipliers can be a rough guide to local economies. They also provide quarterly time multipliers as building costs increase.

Cost of living indexes is another reference area.

You should ask the following questions:

1. The number of days those houses typically are on the market; a normal wait can be 60-100 days. In some hot, high demand neighborhoods, the average could be 6-20 days, with competitive bidding. *I appraised a house in the $70,000 range, 25 years of age, moderate size and average construction, which was in an extremely hot neighborhood. The market for these move-up homes after starter homes was very hot. Young couples with elementary school aged children were close to highly desired schools and in a small town, with urban amenities. The owners got three offers over the listing price! Be aware of this so you do not have your hearts broken.*
2. What is the ratio of sales price to listing price? It can be common in strong markets with 95-97 % ratios. Keep that in mind in your negotiation strategy.
3. What are the customary financing methods? A large percentage of conventional mortgage financed sales occur in the more stable and affluent neighborhoods. State-subsidized or federal-subsidized financing is common in more modest neighborhoods. A large percentage of land contract sales are prevalent in modest neighborhoods.
4. Real estate salespersons or "For Sale by Owners" may be the main method of selling. Some neighborhoods are in such demand that the homes almost sell themselves. I've appraised several homes where very few sales went through the multiple listing service. Sales were researched through sales studies at the local city or township assessor offices.
5. Special assessments can be made by the local government. *A doctor friend of mine tried to help his son buy a home in a suburban subdivision. They did all their homework knowing of a future $4,000 sewer assessment. They offered the listing price less the $4,000 assessment. Someone else offered the full price, and was accepted. That other party ended*

up paying the full price plus the future $4,000 sewer assessment. The doctor and his son moved on to another house that was not over-priced.

Timing that was important 10 years ago may not apply now. In this area of the country 10 years ago, winter off-season downturns occurred in the new home construction market. Construction slowed or stopped. Laborers and tradesmen worked for 25 percent discounts just to keep busy. That is not the situation in hot markets. Be aware of what is going on in your area.

Good sources to ask are builders, lumberyards, building supply companies if you are planning to build or subcontract homes. Ask to get specifics of rates, turn-around times, waiting lists, timing, and premium rates charged by the better tradesmen.

Lesson #13 Review

Understanding the Market/Timing/Supply and Demand. Different areas of the country appreciate, stabilize or depreciate in value at various rates. If moving to a new area, research the local cost of living.

Ask the following questions:

1. What is the typical number of days of marketing time for a region, town, neighborhood?
2. Are there seasonal cycles?
3. What is the ratio of typical sales price to listing price? Is 5 % less than the listing price typical? This could educate you when negotiating.
4. What are the customary finance methods used?
5. Are sales by real estate companies, or by private owners? It could indicate a hot or cold market!
6. Are there special assessments, ongoing or future? Check the local unit of government.

Old cycles of timing may not work now. Check on turn-around time of sub-contractors if you are planning to build.

LESSON #14:
A HOME SHOULD BE A REFUGE, NOT A GIANT TRAP.

Safety Checklist:

1. Are there smoke detectors for every level and every bedroom of the house? Many cities require them. Is radon gas a problem in your area? Has the house been tested? A good question for your home inspection company.
2. How about the presence of lead paint? Another good question for your home inspector.
3. Do the electrical outlets near water and plumbing systems have ground fault interrupters to prevent electrocution in the baths, kitchen, laundry, outside, or other areas? If you do not know what they are, I suggest visiting an electrical supply store, call an electrician, or research a good home construction book. They are easily identified.
4. Are there adequate handrails for every stairway?
5. Does the water heater have a discharge pipe for escaping water and pressure that goes down to 6 inches above the floor?
6. Does the finished basement bedroom have an approved window that satisfies the local building code if an escape is necessary due to a fire or other calamity, or to allow for rescue personnel to enter the house with their rescue equipment?

7. Look for the presence of Urea Formaldehyde Foam Insulation, known as UFFI. There have been health concerns about this type of insulation.
8. Asbestos covering and wrapping of heating pipes and portions of heating systems are fairly common in older houses. It could be perfectly safe if it is not disturbed. Every home should be examined on a case-by-case basis to reach that conclusion. As indicated, this is something that can be found in older homes, often used to wrap around the ductwork and heating system.
9. Structural framing and fastening defects could be covered by drywall or siding. A private inspector could check on nailing patterns, proper framing, and proper construction "practices."

Several years ago I subcontracted the building of a pole barn. After the end of the workday, when the workers were gone, my walk around the framed walls revealed that the carpenter who framed and nailed the east wall, properly nailed bracing and framing. The carpenter who worked on the west wall pounded 25-40 percent fewer nails in critical bracing. He was a talker and goof-off. I nailed the missing nail areas myself. The carpenter's employer shrugged his shoulders when I discussed this with him. But it was I who would suffer future structural problems due to sagging, bulging, or even collapse.

In my 17-year career as an insurance adjuster, I had two cases in which entire drywall ceilings suddenly and violently collapsed. The first one occurred when no one was home. The second one could have killed someone. It was in an upscale suburban neighborhood. Fortunately, the family was in another room. But the collapse was like the fall of a house made of playing cards. It occurred totally or partially in 50 percent of the ceilings. The weight of sheets of drywall could break a person's neck, or inflict serious head injuries.

This was due to nails being too short. Longer nails were the proper fastening technique, but due to someone's negligence in using the wrong size nails, people were almost killed.

The homes were 45 and 10 years of age respectively. The builders were gone, and no one could be held responsible.

A wood stove can be the main heat source with its own chimney, or attached as an auxiliary source to a conventional furnace, or inserted into a conventional fireplace. They have many appealing features.

If possible, it is good to note the type of wood being burned. Green/uncured wood and softwood such as poplar, also known as aspen, and pine, contain a lot of pitch. This pitch can build up an accumulation inside a chimney, and can be set on fire. This is a chimney fire. The fire can crack the flue liners in the chimney, and the cold water from a fire department can crack the hot portions that were not on fire. It could cost $1,000-$2,500 or more to properly repair the chimney.

The burning of seasoned woods, especially hardwoods, and periodic chimney cleaning can prevent this.

Lesson #14 Review

Lack of smoke detectors? Radon gas testing needed?

H.S. = Horror Story

N.P. = Nasty Problem

N.P. #69 - Lead base paint testing needed? Clean up and redecorating could cost thousands of dollars.

N.P. #70 - Lacks ground-fault interrupter electrical outlets (cost $300-$600). Adequate handrails? (Costs $200 or more.) Lack of proper water heater discharge pipe (cost $50). Escape size window for basement bedroom? Inspection for U.F.F.I. insulation? Very controversial; check local health department and local building department as to risks, repair, cleanup. In the past, some homes containing this insulation have become extremely difficult to sell.

Asbestos-wrapped pipes, wrapped heating systems suggest specialized contractor. Inspect and advise; could be insignificant, or could be a disaster!

H.S. #30 - Construction nailing patterns/practices -- inspect or hire a private inspector to check on this as you build your home. There are no guarantees; even the city building inspectors can't monitor this.

H.S. #31 - How safe is the wood stove? Chimney fires and repairs could cost $1,000 to $2,500 if contained in only the chimney. Check out the type of wood burned. When was the last chimney cleaning?

LESSON #15:
THE PRINCIPLE OF SUBSTITUTION/FUNCTIONAL OBSOLESCENCE -- DEPRECIATION AND ZONING

Don't make life's biggest investment decision on an emotional basis. "We fell in love with the house!" I hear this over and over again.

Sales people push the approach that this is the only house in the world, and hurry, hurry, hurry their clients into making an offer.

The principle of substitution indicates that the market value of a house is restricted to the cost of replacing a home with a comparable priced lot, a similar house with its features and similar amenities. So if your Chevrolet is totaled out in an accident, the market value, per the principle of substitution, is restricted to the sales price of replacing a similar Chevrolet -- not the price of a Cadillac or a Yugo.

Bigger is not always better. Bigger may be a liability towards the property's appeal and market value.

Many times homebuyers go beyond reason when building wood decks. I have seen wood decks larger than many homes, and extremely customized. If the typical contribution to the market value of a property with a wood deck in a subdivision and value range is $1,500, would it be wise to build a $5,000 wood deck? The extra $3,500 wood deck cost is **overkill**, known as "functional obsolescence." This is also very common with excessive landscaping, pole barns or second garages, in-ground swimming pools, and customized interior decorating and extravagant finish, such as $5,000 doors.

In areas of the country with short summer seasons, in-ground swimming pools can be gross overkills.

Once I appraised a newly built home with an outside $40,000 in-ground pool in mid-Michigan. The builder and owner were very unhappy with my analysis of the functional obsolescence of the pool. That summer was one of the coolest ever. Some of my friends with pools never used them once. What was the real contribution to market value? Somewhere between nothing and $40,000, tempered with reality.

Some local assessors give 15-20 year life spans to in-ground pools, and depreciate them out to zero. This explains why some homeowners fill in their pools, due to high maintenance costs and the lengthy amount of time to maintain them. There is also the fear of liability and lawsuits.

You should realize that if you plan to make a quick sale with a complete return on the investment, it won't happen.

Many buyers migrate to the suburbs and rural subdivisions to experience open space, fields, forests, and mountains surrounding them. Do some detective work on the present and future zoning of adjacent land. Check with the local unit of government. Do they have a master plan for future zoning land use? Are petitions in process to change the zoning, perhaps from single family to high density, multi-family? This could allow trailer parks, high-density condos, or apartments?

A local builder had a high demand, small, rural subdivision of 40 homes in the $125,000 to $200,000 value range. The first phase was almost completely filled over the last 7-10 years. There was room to expand the subdivision into other phases.

Four years ago a large parcel of 100 to 200 acres, was purchased nearby by the local County Fair Commission. Having the fair nearby for one week in the summer wouldn't have been the end of the world. But the Fair Commission planned to turn the fairgrounds into a high profile exhibition area. There could have been everything from late night outdoor concerts to noisy monster truck shows. The noise and traffic would have been unreal.

No one bought lots or built houses in the three years of debate and appeals that occurred between upset local residents, the local government, and the Fair Commission before the zoning was denied.

Functional obsolescence!

Lesson #15 Review

Substitution -- the cost of rebuilding a similar home (age, size, features) on a similar lot with similar features should be the upper limit to value without consideration of unusual factors of supply and demand or emotional influences.

H.S. = Horror Story

N.P. = Nasty Problem

H.S. #33 - Functional Obsolescence -- overbuilding beyond a market value: i.e. $5,000 wood deck in a situation where wood decks typically contribute $1,500 to the market value. Therefore, $3,500 in functional obsolescence.

H.S. #34 - Outside, in-ground pools in regions with short, unpredictable summer seasons can be money pits.

H.S. #35 - An anticipated major change in zoning in nearby or adjacent properties can stagnate the marketability of homes.

LESSON #16: HELPFUL BITS OF WISDOM TO MAKE YOU A SMARTER HOMEBUYER

In wintertime, snow cover can make inspection of the driveway, roof, sidewalks, landscaping, wood deck and even the street impossible. Most people are proud of their homes. Ask the homeowner to show you summertime photos or videos to fully understand all of the property's features.

Waterfront lot inspection: *When one couple wanted to sell their waterfront cottage, a prospective buyer brought chest-high fishing waders. He waded out into the lake to check on the depth and the lake bottom for boat usage, swimming and docking.*

Fuel oil furnaces: Underground storage tanks can be a liability, as discontinued or abandoned tanks can present clean-up problems. Evidence can be a filler pipe sticking up above the ground about 5-12 inches. Usually the cap is labeled for fuel oil. Many times the tank is left in a basement. This can take up space and be unsightly, but it is not the problem as with an underground tank. Sometimes an outdoor fuel oil tank leaks and can contaminate the ground area, and this could present a very expensive clean-up problem and/or threaten a nearby well.

Beware of stains on the ground from filling the tank.

Twenty-year-old and 25-year-old houses: At this stage of their life span, many expensive systems need renovation or replacement: roof, furnace, well, air conditioner. After 1-3 years, septic tanks need cleaning; after 10 years, dishwasher and water heater replacement will probably need attention.

Kinda hard to inspect the roof, driveway, and lawn with this much snow cover, heh?

Often garage conversions to living areas are done by homeowners, without permits or inspections and without consideration to the increased need for heating and cooling systems. The quality of construction is not equal to the rest of the home. You should be aware of the potential problems in houses where a garage has been converted to a living area because of these oversights.

Home inspection company: Have your home inspector photograph the attic, roof, crawl spaces, and potential problem areas, not only to give you an understanding, but to insure that they actually did inspect those areas.

Home inspectors: Check out their qualifications. Get independent references. Sometimes the inspectors are too chummy-chummy with the salespeople who refer them. Sometimes the thorough and critical home inspectors are not referred because they do **too** good a job.

Find out and get copies if possible of the certificate of insurance for malpractice (known as Errors and Omissions Insurance) for home inspectors. This will show the insurance company's name, address, policy number, and policy dates. If you are extremely conscientious, you might want to call and verify if the policy is in force. Policies do lapse and are cancelled. The home inspector could miss something very expensive, then be non-collectable, uninsured, or possibly skip town and go out of business. This does happen.

Lots and building sites: You will obviously pay more for views of the ocean, lakes and mountains.

Determine location of:

1. the sewer tap-in
2. the septic tank and its clean-out access, with a map
3. the drain clean-outs

4. the well or public water line location (This will be necessary in a future FHA sale with a well and septic.)

Find the instruction manuals for garbage disposal, dishwasher, well pump, and building appliances such as stove, oven and microwaves. You would be surprised at how many people keep a very good filing system, but if you don't ask for them, you won't get them.

You should get warranty information on the furnace, roof, air conditioner, well or sump-pump motors, and replacement windows.

Request and do a final inspection or walk-through before your closing, to ensure that movers or the home seller have not damaged or removed items from the home.

Assessor cards: Most thorough and professional sales persons obtain copies to complete their listing information for multiple listing purposes. Ask for a copy. It can track value trends of the property and the neighborhood, previous sale prices and history, remodeling and permits taken out, age, dimensions, lot sizes, and other valuable information. If the homeowner or the person acting as the representative do not have them, obtain a copy from the local unit of government. It can be a very excellent reference material for you.

(Please see Bonus Assessor Card chapter.)

Be A Smart Homebuyer, Don't Be A Dunce

Lesson #16 Review

Snow cover prevents inspection of the roof, driveway, landscaping -- be wary.

Wade the lakefront property to check on depth, dockage, swimming potential.

H.S. = Horror Story

N.S. = Nasty Problem

N.P. #71 - Leaking underground fuel oil storage tanks can need expensive environmental clean up (costing thousands). Maintenance/replacement items for 20-25-year-old house: roof, furnace, well, air conditioner. Ten-year-old homes may need: septic tank cleaning (every 1-3 years -- when was it last done?), dishwasher or water heater replacement.

N.P. #72 - Garage conversion to living area: Often heating and cooling systems are not adequate. Home Inspectors: Have them photograph or video the attic, roof, crawl spaces and problem areas. Could be good negotiating demonstration to show need for repairs.

Home Inspectors: Get independent references and call them; get a certificate of their malpractice insurance with insurer's name, address, policy number, and policy dates. Call/write/fax to verify the policy is in force. (People buy insurance, don't pay, and are cancelled.)

After all, it's the biggest investment of your life. Who are you going to collect from if the inspector skips town?

Get a list from the owner of the location of:

1. sewer tap-in,
2. or septic tank and its clean-out access
3. drain clean-outs
4. well or public water line

Get instruction manuals for:

1. garbage disposal
2. dishwasher
3. well pump
4. built-in stove/oven/range
5. microwave
6. jet tubs

Get warranty information for:

1. furnace
2. air conditioner
3. roof
4. well
5. sump-pump
6. replacement windows

Get names, addresses, telephone numbers of:

1. furnace and air conditioning company
2. the electrician
3. the plumber
4. the roofer
5. the well driller or well pump installer

Do a final walk-through before closing.

Assessor Cards: Review value trends, check previous sale prices and history, remodeling and permits, age, dimensions, lot sizes.

Apply this knowledge to help you become smart homebuyers! Good luck, and smart home buying!

SECTION II:
BONUS CHAPTERS

ASSESSOR'S CARDS

THE MEDICAL RECORDS
OF YOUR HOME©

LESSON #17: ASSESSOR'S CARDS -- THE MEDICAL RECORDS OF YOUR HOME

One of the methods of taxation in this country is through the assessment of values and property taxes upon real estate, and in particular homes. Methods of taxation differ in various states. Very important to the homebuyer is that government records are kept and updated continuously. They are like the medical records about you in your doctor's office.

They are an extremely valuable source of pure information that can be obtained from the local (city, village, township, county) assessor's office. The most professional real estate people usually have a copy of the Assessor Card as part of their packet, which they use to insert information for the Multiple Listing Service, if one is available. The original cards are best. The modernized versions delete information.

This is valuable not only when inspecting the property, but also after inspection, while doing some serious thinking about purchasing it. If you live out of town or cannot physically inspect the property, it can be a valuable source of information that is basically hard and cold facts.

There are various assessor card forms. Let's review some samples.

Understanding Assessor Cards by Reviewing Samples

Sample #1

In the upper left corner, a Tax ID Number or Tax Identification Number is found. This identifies the home and lot by its county, township or city, and section, and gets specific with neighborhood types in large metropolitan areas. Secondly, note the owner's name and address, which could be different from the actual property address because this could be a rental property, or the owner lives in a different state or a different portion of the city or county.

The next item is the actual property address, with the house number, street, city, state, and zip code.

The next item is the actual legal description for the property in reference to the city, the subdivision, and the lot that it is on.

Land Sketch: Sometimes the land sketch with the dimensions of the lot is on the front of the page, as it is in this example in the lower left-hand corner.

Some cities and townships will provide a separate sheet showing the lot size and its dimensions. These are good indicators, but do not replace the detailed information of a survey.

Topography: This gives the characteristics and features of the lot. It can indicate whether it is level, high, rolling, swampy, wooded, rocky, or landscaped.

Land Improvements: This section covers such things as if the property has public water, sanitary sewer, electric, gas, storm sewer, if the street is paved, if there are sidewalks, and will also indicate whether the property has a well or a septic system. This is very valuable information when differences of opinion arise as to whether the property actually has these types of utilities.

Basically, it provides information regarding whether the lot is improved, such as having a driveway or sidewalks. This will also say if there is a house or building on it, or if it is vacant, "raw" land.

Remarks: In this first sample there are no Remarks.

Sales Record or Sale History: This gives information with regard to previous sales, the year that they happened, the sale price, value, type of sale, what amount of down payment, and the name of the broker listed as the source of information.

Land Value Computations: If this is a recent version of the Assessor Card, it can give an accurate idea of what the actual cost of land is, separate from the building. So a vacant lot that has just been sold for $38,000 as of June 1, 1998, and note is made on the Land Value Computations. If you are shopping around in that same subdivision, you can get an idea on the size and features, and also the rate used on the card and what perhaps the going rate is. Ask the assessor to check sales studies of lots that have sold in that neighborhood. Four or five lots may have sold that may not be publicized or well known. Sometimes you will find discounts to builders on lot sales in developing subdivisions.

Often these builders will buy two, three, or more lots at a time and get a discount for doing so. Their discounted prices are not true market value.

Summary of Appraisal: This is the calculation by the assessor of the land value and the building values together for a total value of what they would consider to be a cash value.

Record of Assessment: This gives a history by year and total assessment of the valuation the assessor has placed on the property through various studies. The assessor collects various sales in that city, neighborhood, or block, to determine if the sales reflect that property values are going up by a certain percentage, if they are stable, or if they are actually decreasing. In this sample, we see for the years 1989-1998 they have been increasing; in fact, they have been increasing every year. You will see in this sample that BOR (which means Board of Review) in 1991 shows that the property value was appealed and the value did remain the same for 1991 and 1992. As an additional comment, sometimes the Board of Review can stabilize the assessed value for reasons other than the neighborhood. Keep in mind that the Board of Review may have reviewed a "hardship case" where the owner had illness in the family and their medical expenses could have exceeded their income or they had been laid off from work and had no income. They then appealed for a stabilizing or reduction from the Board of Review because of the economic circumstances of the homeowner.

Sample #1

2-04-579-015

01/01/76

CLASS 401 RI
TAXUNIT 5201
SCH
DDA
TIFA

KINSON, MARY
1412 W FLINT ST
VISON ,MI

PROP ADR.. 1412 W FLINT ST
, MI

LOT 76 ASSESSORS PLAT CITY OF

MAP NUMBER ___ ___ | ___ PROPERTY NUMBER ___ ___ ___ | ___ ___ ___

CLASS OF PROPERTY ___ CARD NUMBER ___ OF ___

TOPOGRAPHY

✓	Level
	High
	Low
	Rolling
	Rocky
	Swampy
	Wooded
	Landscaped
	Building Site

LAND IMPROVEMENTS

✓	Water
✓	Sanitary Sewer
	Storm Sewer
✓	Electric
✓	Gas
✓	Curb & Gutter
✓	Paved
	Dirt Street
✓	Sidewalk
	Well
	Septic System

CLASSIFICATION

✓	Improved
	Vacant

REMARKS:

PROPERTY ADDRESS 1412 W Flint

SALES RECORD

YEAR OF SALE	SALE PRICE	TYPE OF SALE	DOWN PAYMENT	NAME OF BROKER
	$		$	

LAND VALUE COMPUTATIONS

FRONTAGE OR LAND CLASS	DEPTH FACTOR OR # ACRES	EQUIV. FRONTAGE	RATE	BASE VALUE
66x170				

WELL $ SEPTIC $ $

SUMMARY OF APPRAISAL

TOTAL LAND	
TOTAL BUILDINGS	
TOTAL APPRAISAL	

RECORD OF ASSESSMENT

YEAR	TOTAL ASSESSMENT	YEAR	TOTAL ASSESSMENT
89	$16200	93	$18600
90	17700	94	18600
91	18400	95	23400
BOR 91	18400	96	23400
92	18400	97	24700
		98	27000

LAND SKETCH

N ↑

Lot 76

66 / 170.5 / 170.5 / 66

Flint St

Sample #1a

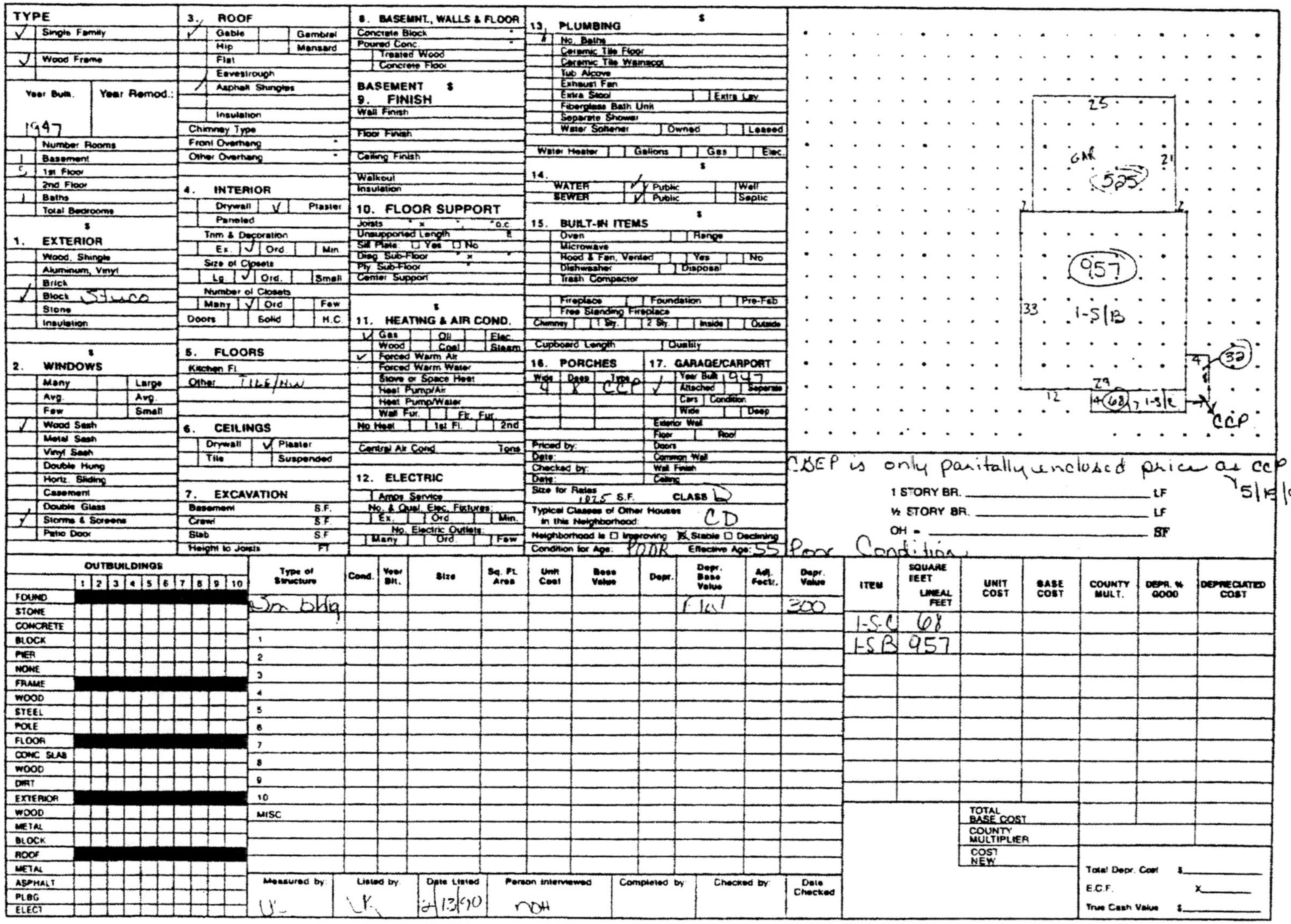

TYPE
✓ Single Family
✓ Wood Frame
Year Built: 1947 | Year Remod.:
Number Rooms
1 Basement
5 1st Floor
2nd Floor
1 Baths
Total Bedrooms
$

1. EXTERIOR
Wood, Shingle
Aluminum, Vinyl
Brick
✓ Block Stucco
Stone
Insulation
$

2. WINDOWS
Many | Large
Avg. | Avg.
Few | Small
✓ Wood Sash
Metal Sash
Vinyl Sash
Double Hung
Horiz. Sliding
Casement
Double Glass
✓ Storms & Screens
Patio Door

3. ROOF
✓ Gable | Gambrel
Hip | Mansard
Flat
Eavestrough
✓ Asphalt Shingles
Insulation
Chimney Type
Front Overhang
Other Overhang

4. INTERIOR
Drywall ✓ Plaster
Paneled
Trim & Decoration
Ex. ✓ Ord Min
Size of Closets
Lg ✓ Ord. Small
Number of Closets
Many ✓ Ord Few
Doors | Solid | H.C.

5. FLOORS
Kitchen Fl.
Other: TILE/HW

6. CEILINGS
Drywall ✓ Plaster
Tile | Suspended

7. EXCAVATION
Basement S.F.
Crawl S.F.
Slab S.F.
Height to Joists FT

8. BASEMNT., WALLS & FLOOR
Concrete Block
Poured Conc.
Treated Wood
Concrete Floor
BASEMENT $
9. FINISH
Wall Finish
Floor Finish
Ceiling Finish
Walkout
Insulation

10. FLOOR SUPPORT
Joists " x " " o.c.
Unsupported Length ft
Sill Plate ☐ Yes ☐ No
Diag. Sub-Floor " x "
Ply. Sub-Floor "
Center Support
$

11. HEATING & AIR COND.
✓ Gas | Oil | Elec.
Wood | Coal | Steam
✓ Forced Warm Air
Forced Warm Water
Stove or Space Heat
Heat Pump/Air
Heat Pump/Water
Wall Fur. | Flr. Fur.
No Heat | 1st Fl. | 2nd
Central Air Cond. Tons

12. ELECTRIC
Amps Service
No. & Qual. Elec. Fixtures:
Ex. | Ord | Min.
No. Electric Outlets:
Many | Ord. | Few

13. PLUMBING $
1 No. Baths
Ceramic Tile Floor
Ceramic Tile Wainscot
Tub Alcove
Exhaust Fan
Extra Stool | Extra Lav.
Fiberglass Bath Unit
Separate Shower
Water Softener | Owned | Leased
Water Heater | Gallons | Gas | Elec.

14. $
WATER ✓ Public | Well
SEWER ✓ Public | Septic

15. BUILT-IN ITEMS $
Oven | Range
Microwave
Hood & Fan, Vented | Yes | No
Dishwasher | Disposal
Trash Compactor
Fireplace | Foundation | Pre-Fab
Free Standing Fireplace
Chimney | 1 Sty. | 2 Sty. | Inside | Outside
Cupboard Length | Quality

16. PORCHES
Wide | Deep | Type
4 | 8 | CCP

17. GARAGE/CARPORT
✓ Year Built 1947
Attached | Separate
Cars | Condition
Wide | Deep
Exterior Wall
Floor | Roof
Doors
Common Wall
Wall Finish
Ceiling

Priced by:
Date:
Checked by:
Date:
Size for Rates 1025 S.F. CLASS D
Typical Classes of Other Houses in this Neighborhood: CD
Neighborhood is ☐ Improving ☒ Stable ☐ Declining
Condition for Age: POOR Effective Age: 55

GAR 25 × 21 (525)
1-S/B 33 × 29 (957)
4 × 8 (32)
CCP
12 (68) 1-S/C

CCEP is only paritally enclosed price as CCP 5/15/90
Poor Condition

1 STORY BR. ______ LF
½ STORY BR. ______ LF
OH = ______ SF

OUTBUILDINGS	1	2	3	4	5	6	7	8	9	10
FOUND										
STONE										
CONCRETE										
BLOCK										
PIER										
NONE										
FRAME										
WOOD										
STEEL										
POLE										
FLOOR										
CONC SLAB										
WOOD										
DIRT										
EXTERIOR										
WOOD										
METAL										
BLOCK										
ROOF										
METAL										
ASPHALT										
PLBG										
ELECT										

	Type of Structure	Cond.	Year Blt.	Size	Sq. Ft. Area	Unit Cost	Base Value	Depr.	Depr. Base Value	Adj. Fectr.	Depr. Value
	Dn bldg								Flat		300
1											
2											
3											
4											
5											
6											
7											
8											
9											
10											
MISC											

Measured by	Listed by	Date Listed	Person Interviewed	Completed by	Checked by	Date Checked
UL	UK	2/13/90 5/15/90	NOH			

ITEM	SQUARE FEET / LINEAL FEET	UNIT COST	BASE COST	COUNTY MULT.	DEPR. % GOOD	DEPRECIATED COST
1-SC	68					
1-SB	957					

TOTAL BASE COST
COUNTY MULTIPLIER
COST NEW
Total Depr. Cost $______
E.C.F. X______
True Cash Value $______

Sample #2

TYPE
- ✓ Single Family
- ✓ Wood Frame
- Year Built: 1996 · Year Remod.:
- Number Rooms · Basement · 1st Floor · 2nd Floor · Baths · 3 Total Bedrooms

1. EXTERIOR $
- ✓ Wood, Shingle
- ✓ Aluminum/(Vinyl)
- ✓ Brick
- Block · Stone · Insulation

2. WINDOWS $
- ✓ Many · Avg · Few | ✓ Large · Avg · Small
- ✓ Wood Sash · Metal Sash · Vinyl Sash · Double Hung · Horiz. Sliding · ✓ Casement · Double Glass · Storms & Screens · Patio Door

3. ROOF
- ✓ Gable · ✓ Hip · Gambrel · Mansard · ✓ Flat
- ✓ Eavestrough · ✓ Asphalt Shingles
- Insulation · Chimney Type · Front Overhang · Other Overhang

4. INTERIOR
- ✓ Drywall · Plaster · Paneled
- ✓ Trim & Decoration: Ex. · Ord. · Min.
- Size of Closets: Lg · ✓ Ord. · Small
- Number of Closets: Many · ✓ Ord. · Few
- Doors: Solid · ✓ H.C

5. FLOORS
- Kitchen Fl. Hardwood
- Other Hardwood, Carpet

6. CEILINGS
- ✓ Drywall · Plaster · Tile · Suspended

7. EXCAVATION
- Basement S.F. · Crawl S.F. · Slab S.F. · Height to Joists FT.

8. BASEMNT., WALLS & FLOOR
- Concrete Block · Poured Conc. · Treated Wood · ✓ Concrete Floor

BASEMENT $ 9. FINISH Ø
- Wall Finish · Floor Finish · Ceiling Finish · Walkout · Insulation

10. FLOOR SUPPORT
- Joists " x " " o.c. · Unsupported Length · Sill Plate: [ ] Yes [ ] No · Diag. Sub-Floor · Ply. Sub-Floor · Center Support

11. HEATING & AIR COND. $
- ✓ Gas · Oil · Elec. · Wood · Coal · Steam
- ✓ Forced Warm Air · Forced Warm Water · Stove or Space Heat · Heat Pump/Air · Heat Pump/Water · Wall Fur. · Flr. Fur.
- No Heat · 1st Fl. · 2nd
- Central Air Cond. ✓ Tons

12. ELECTRIC
- Amps Service · No. & Qual. Elec. Fixtures: Ex. · Ord. · Min. · No. Electric Outlets: Many · Ord · Few

13. PLUMBING $
- 2½ No. Baths MB Jacuzzi
- Ceramic Tile Floor · Ceramic Tile Wainscot · ✓ Tub Alcove · Exhaust Fan · Extra Stool · ✓ Extra Lav. · Fiberglass Bath Unit · Separate Shower · Water Softener · Owned · Leased
- Water Heater · Gallons · Gas · Elec.

14. $
- WATER ✓ Public · Well
- SEWER ✓ Public · Septic

15. BUILT-IN ITEMS $
- Oven · ✓ Range · ✓ Microwave · Hood & Fan, Vented · Yes · No · Dishwasher · ✓ Disposal · Trash Compactor
- Fireplace · Foundation · ✓ Pre-Fab · Free Standing Fireplace
- Chimney ✓ 1 Sty. · 2 Sty. · Inside · ✓ Outside
- Cupboard Length · Quality

16. PORCHES
- Wide · Deep · Type

17. GARAGE/CARPORT
- Year Built [illegible] · ✓ Attached · Separate · Cars · Condition · Wide · Deep · Exterior Wall · Floor · Roof · Doors -1L 1-9 · Common Wall · Wall Finish DW · Ceiling DW

- Priced by: · Date: · Checked by: · Date:
- Size for Rates S.F. · CLASS B+5
- Typical Classes of Other Houses in this Neighborhood:
- Neighborhood is [ ] Improving [ ] Stable [ ] Declining
- Condition for Age: · Effective Age:

- 1 STORY BR. 101 LF
- ½ STORY BR. ______ LF
- OH = ______ SF

OUTBUILDINGS	1	2	3	4	5	6	7	8	9	10
FOUND.										
STONE										
CONCRETE										
BLOCK										
PIER										
NONE										
FRAME										
WOOD										
STEEL										
POLE										
FLOOR										
CONC. SLAB										
WOOD										
DIRT										
EXTERIOR										
WOOD										
METAL										
BLOCK										
ROOF										
METAL										
ASPHALT										
[illegible]										

Type of Structure	Cond.	Year Blt.	Size	Sq. Ft. Area	Unit Cost	Base Value	Depr.	Depr. Base Value	Adj. Factr.	Depr. Value
1										
2										
3										
4										
5										
6										
7										
8										
9										
10										
MISC										

Measured by · Listed by · Date Listed · Person Interviewed · Completed by · Checked by · Date Checked

ITEM	SQUARE FEET / LINEAL FEET	UNIT COST	BASE COST	COUNTY MULT.	DEPR. % GOOD	DEPRECIATED COST

TOTAL BASE COST · COUNTY MULTIPLIER · COST NEW · Total Depr. Cost $ · E.C.F.

Dwelling Specifics

Sample #2

Type: Indicates whether it is a single-family house, and if it is a wood frame.

Year Built and Year Remodeled: This can give you a very accurate data source rather than believing the homeowner or sales representative who is indicating that the actual house is 10 or 20 years newer than the Assessor Card indicates. Following that is the number of rooms, whether it has a basement, how many rooms are on the first floor, second floor, the total amount of bedrooms and baths.

Exterior: This tells the type of exterior of the house, whether it has aluminum, brick, stucco or even wood siding.

Windows: Basically, these are generalized categories which indicate if they are wood or metal sashed, if there are very few, if there are many windows in the house, or an average amount. Sometimes storm windows and doors and screens are indicated.

Roof: The style and slope are identified, whether it be gable, hip or flat, along with eave troughing. Also the type of roofing is indicated as being asphalt shingles. An area for insulation and overhangs, as well as chimneys, is also provided.

Interior: This gives an idea of whether it is plaster, drywall, or paneled, and the extensive amount of trim, along with the number of closets and the types of doors.

Floors: This indicates the type of floor covering, such as hardwood floors, or if linoleum, carpet or ceramic tile exists.

Ceilings: This indicates whether drywall, plastered or suspended ceilings exist.

Excavation: This gives information on a basement, its size, whether it has a crawl space or a slab, and its size. This is important because a house could have a combination crawl space and basement. If you can't inspect the size of the basement, for whatever reason, the Assessor Card should indicate the square footage, how much of it is on a crawl space and how much is on a slab.

Basement Walls/Floors: This indicates the type of construction material used, be it concrete block, poured concrete, or even wood basements could be noted here in the newer homes.

Basement Finish: This goes into detail if the basement is finished, the percentage of area, the number of rooms, if it is a walkout basement, and perhaps if it is an insulated basement.

Floor Support: This gives the type of dimensional lumber and if there is a diagonal sub-flooring or plywood sub-flooring which would indicate the quality of material and the craftsmanship used in the home.

Heating and Air Conditioning: This indicates the type of fuel used and the type of system, and if it is a gas-fueled forced warm air furnace. If it is a heat pump or a space heater, this will be indicated, too. It will note if no heat source is available to certain parts of the house, such as the lack of heat ducts. Also found here is information on central air conditioning and the size of the unit.

Electric: The size of the electric service with the various types of amperage (100, 125, 150, or 200 amp service) could be noted. And it also gives an indication of the number of outlets.

Plumbing: Specified here are the number of bathrooms, the number of lavatories, stools, fiberglass enclosures, separate showers, and water softeners. Number 14 indicates if there is public water and sewer, or a well and septic.

Built-In Items: Built-ins are very common in newer homes (ovens, microwaves, hood fans, dishwashers, garbage disposals and trash compactors). Also, there can be notations for fireplaces or freestanding fireplaces and wood stove inserts, and if the chimney is a one or two story. Some Assessor Cards are so specific they mention the type, length, the quality of materials, and the type of wood for the interior cabinets, which can be very important in customized construction.

Porches: The porch size by width and depth and type can be specified as noted on this sample, CCP (concrete covered porch). Wood decks, enclosed decks, enclosed porches sometimes are specified, and whether they are heated or not.

Garage/Carports: The year built can be specified, together with whether it is attached or detached, the number of cars it holds, its condition, its width and depth, along with exterior walls, the type of flooring, roofing, and the type of doors. A common wall may be specified, which could be very important in small city lots where the garages may have a common wall on the property line for two houses. The wall finish, and if there is a ceiling, is noted as well.

Neighborhood Stability: There is a notation as to if the neighborhood is stable, improving, or declining, **a very important factor to consider in home investment**. (See District Trend.)

The Overall Condition for the Age of the Property: The Effective Age can reflect in the Assessor's mind not only the condition, but also can give consideration to the possible life span of the house. As an example, a house may be 30 years of age, but having poor construction quality and materials, the lack of proper maintenance and neglect, the house may have an Effective Age of 50 years. Very much like a person who is 25 years of age but who has neglected their health, may effectively have the health of a 50-year-old person. Vice versa, a 60-year-old house may have been gutted and renovated with wiring, plumbing, and interior finish to make its effective age 30 years.

The condition could be noted as good, average, or poor.

Building and Sketch: This can be an actual sketch with dimensions of the house, porches, and garage as indicated by the Assessor and anyone making an inspection. Please note that these are general dimensions as Assessors round their numbers. Therefore, looking at an example, a house that may actually be 32 1/2 feet in length, the Assessor may round that up to 33 feet. And a house that may be 28 1/2 feet in length may be rounded up to 29 feet. Their actual square footage may be larger or smaller than it really is. In two-story houses, especially the modern houses, many times the Assessors do not actually measure the second floor area. It would be good to have access to diagrams, blueprints or other documents to verify this size.

Outbuildings: It is quite common in this area for people to build pole barns. These are often used to store motor homes, recreational vehicles, boats, off-road vehicles, or act as an extra garage. Often the Assessor Card has notations of the size of the outbuilding, when it was actually built and the type of construction that was noted when it was inspected. Sometimes outbuildings, such as old barns and old sheds, are noted to contribute no value to the property. This could be a very good clue as to their condition if you are not able to inspect the property or have doubts.

Sample #3

PARCEL NUMBER 3·26·556·009

ADDRESS

YEAR	LOSS	ADJUST	NEW	CURRENT AV	TAXABLE VALUE
95		1500		38200	37650
96		4600		42800	38700
97		3800		46600	39780

3-26-556-009
SMITH, JOHN
1809 NORTH ST ,MI
PROP ADR.. 1809 NORTH RD
, MI
LOT 19 NORTH ESTATES

01/01/76
CLASS 401 RI
TAXUNIT 5301
SCH
DDA
TIFA

LAND AND LAND IMPROVEMENTS

TOPOGRAPHY: HIGH, LOW, LEVEL ✓, ROLLING, ROUGH, SWAMP, LAKEFRONT

IMPROVEMENTS: WATER ✓, DIRT, SEWER-SANITARY ✓, GRAVEL, SEWER-STORM, SOIL CEMENT, GAS ✓, ASPHALT ✓, ELECTRICITY ✓, CONCRETE, WELL, CURB ✓, SEPTIC TANK, SIDEWALK ✓, LANDSCAPED, PAVED DRIVE ✓, SHADE TREES, FENCING

DISTRICT TREND: IMPROVING, DECLINING, STABLE ✓

PROPERTY CLASSIFICATION: RESIDENTIAL ✓, ACREAGE, RESORT, PLATTED ✓, RURBAN, IMPROVED ✓, SUBURBAN, VACANT

MAP NO. | BOOK NO. | PAGE NO. | PARCEL CODE NO.

PROPERTY ADDRESS 1809 North Road

SALES RECORD

YEAR OF SALE	SALE PRICE	TYPE OF SALE	DOWN PAYMENT	MONTHLY PAYMENT	NAME OF BROKER
11/78	$ 41,900		$	$	

LAND VALUE COMPUTATIONS

FRONTAGE	DEPTH	DEPTH FACTOR	EQUIV. FRONT.	RATE	BASE VALUE
70	107	55	60	$ 75	$ 4500

EXTRAS: (WELL, SEPTIC TANK, FENCING, ETC.)

70 | 107 | 95

ENHANCING OR DETRACTING INFLUENCE

CAUSE	BASE VALUE	-%	+%	TRUE CASH VALUE
Traffic	$ 100	5		$

SUMMARY OF APPRAISAL

TOTAL LAND	$ 4500
TOTAL BUILDINGS	$ 31,180
TOTAL APPRAISAL 1979	$ 35,680

RECORD OF ASSESSMENT

YEAR	LAND ASSESSMENT	BUILDING ASSESSMENT	TOTAL ASSESSMENT	DEPARTMENT APPRAISAL	
74	$	$	$ 15525	$ 30200	89
76			14575	31,700	90
76			15100	33000	91
79			17850	33,000	92
[illegible]			26,200	35,300	93
[illegible]			27,400	36,700	94

Enhancing or Detracting Influences

Sample #3

In this sample, we see a cause, a base rate and a percentage, minus or plus, as effective value. This particular house is on a very high traffic volume street in this city. The assessor recognized this factor and decreased the assessment by 5 % of the value compared to comparable houses on side streets that don't have this heavy traffic situation.

Sample #4

* 5-C8-537-003

01/C1/96

CLASS 401 RI
AXUNIT 1503
SCH
DDA
TIFA

SMITH, ROBERT & MARY
5260 WYNDWOOD
SWARTZ VALLEY, MI 48422

PROP ADR. - 5260 WYNDWOOD

LOT 154 WYNDWOOD NO 4 (96)

MAP NUMBER	|	PROPERTY NUMBER	|
CLASS OF PROPERTY: RSA	NBHD NO.: 630	BLDG TYPE: ---	

PROPERTY ADDRESS 5260 WYNDWOOD

SALES RECORD

YEAR OF SALE	SALE PRICE	TYPE OF SALE	DOWN PAYMENT	NAME OF BROKER
10-14-97	$287,500	WD	$	

TOPOGRAPHY

- ✓ Level
- High
- Low
- Rolling
- Rocky
- Swampy
- Wooded
- ✓ Landscaped
- ✓ Building Site

LAND IMPROVEMENTS

- ✓ Water
- ✓ Sanitary Sewer
- ✓ Storm Sewer
- ✓ Electric
- ✓ Gas
- ✓ Curb & Gutter
- ✓ Paved
- Dirt Street
- Sidewalk
- Well
- Septic System

OGR (E)

CLASSIFICATION

- Improved
- Vacant

REMARKS:

10% 12-5-95
95% 12-31-96 (pq)
High ceilings - in one bedroom also
Ceiling A.B.
Exceptional trim (pq)

LAND VALUE COMPUTATIONS

FRONTAGE OR LAND CLASS	DEPTH FACTOR OR # ACRES	EQUIV. FRONTAGE	RATE	BASE VALUE
125 x 175	1.06	132		

WELL $	SEPTIC $	$

SUMMARY OF APPRAISAL

TOTAL LAND	
TOTAL BUILDINGS	
TOTAL APPRAISAL	

RECORD OF ASSESSMENT

YEAR	TOTAL ASSESSMENT	YEAR	TOTAL ASSESSMENT
	$		$

LAND SKETCH

N

175.61

125

WYNDWOOD SQ

Sales Record

Sample #4

A sales record indicates the year and the date that it actually sold, the sale price and the type of sale, being WD (warranty deed). Noted are neighborhood numbers and the classification of property, which is a residential single-family property.

Appeals

Sample #5

In the section entitled "Appeals," often the initials BOR with a date (March 1970) are listed (Board of Review, in March 1970). A comment is made, such as denied, granted, or reduced.

Remarks and Building Permits: This Assessor Card is from a very sophisticated metropolitan assessing department. The records and notations on this house date back to 1938 when it was built. **Study the Remarks paragraph and the Building Permit paragraph.** The house was built in 1938, and sometimes noted will be the permit number, date, month, and the amount of money that was applied for to build the house. Updates in 1949 added two dormers and an attic, making four more rooms. Also noted is the history of adding on a garage and tearing down a garage. Noteworthy was a fire to this property and the amount of damages estimated. Sometimes there will even be a notation of how much the insurance company paid out on the repairs. Further on it is noted that in 1978 the furnace was replaced. Also noted are facts on when the roof was replaced, and when the air conditioner was added. This is quite important, and an excellent document if someone says that the furnace is five or 10 years old and the records indicate that actually the furnace is 20 years old. It may be necessary in the next year, five years, or 10 years to replace the furnace. Often the Remarks Section will tell about property inspections and, in talking with renters, the progress of repairs and the various stages of construction and how far along it is, or what is complete.

Sample #5

IST. NO. / ESC. NO. 1-060 255 412 007 4

DESCRIPTION

10735 Smith, o-Allen & wf Mary
11311 Bishop Avenue
7 B Oldberry, Michigan

Urban Gardens
Lot 707 and the W 1/2 of lot 708

SALES DATA

RENTAL DATA

REMARKS

[illegible]

APPEALS

3170 B.O.R. Denied

ASSESSMENT SUMMARY

YEAR	19	19 87	19 90	19 90	19 93	19 95	19 95	19 96	19 97
LAND									
BLDGS.		.90		.94		.85			
TOTAL		20000	20600	19400	19400	16400	2000	2000	2000

TYPE	CLASS C-5	NO. 1969	TYPE	CLASS C	NO. 1971	TYPE	CLASS C	NO. 77
STY. / SQ. FT. / Unit Rate / Net Rate	AMOUNT		STY. / SQ. FT. / Unit Rate / Net Rate	AMOUNT		STY. / SQ. FT. / Unit Rate / Net Rate	AMOUNT	
1½ 988 13.03 −5%	12870 / 640 / 12230		1½ 988 15.40	15215		1½ 988 16.94	16737	

ADDITIONS AND DEDUCTIONS

ITEM	RATE +	RATE −	FLAT +	FLAT −	ITEM	RATE +	RATE −	FLAT +	FLAT −	ITEM	RATE +	RATE −	FLAT +	FLAT −
E-6			1210		E-6			1210		E-6			1210	
O-13 14			300		O-13 14			300		O-13-14			300	
P-1			320		P-1			315		P-1			315	
Total / Net			1830		Total / Net			1825	−	Total / Net			1825	−

	Column 1	Column 2	Column 3
Net	+1830	+1825	+1825
REPLACEMENT COST	14060	17040	18562
DEPR'N % / Residual Value	74% / 105%	68 / 106%	67 / 112%
PRESENT VALUE	10920	12286	13921
Roll Factor / Garage	1400 / 12320	438 / 12724	2200 / 16121
APPRAISED BY	AJC	[illegible]	JH
DATE	5-2-69	[illegible]	6/22/[illegible]

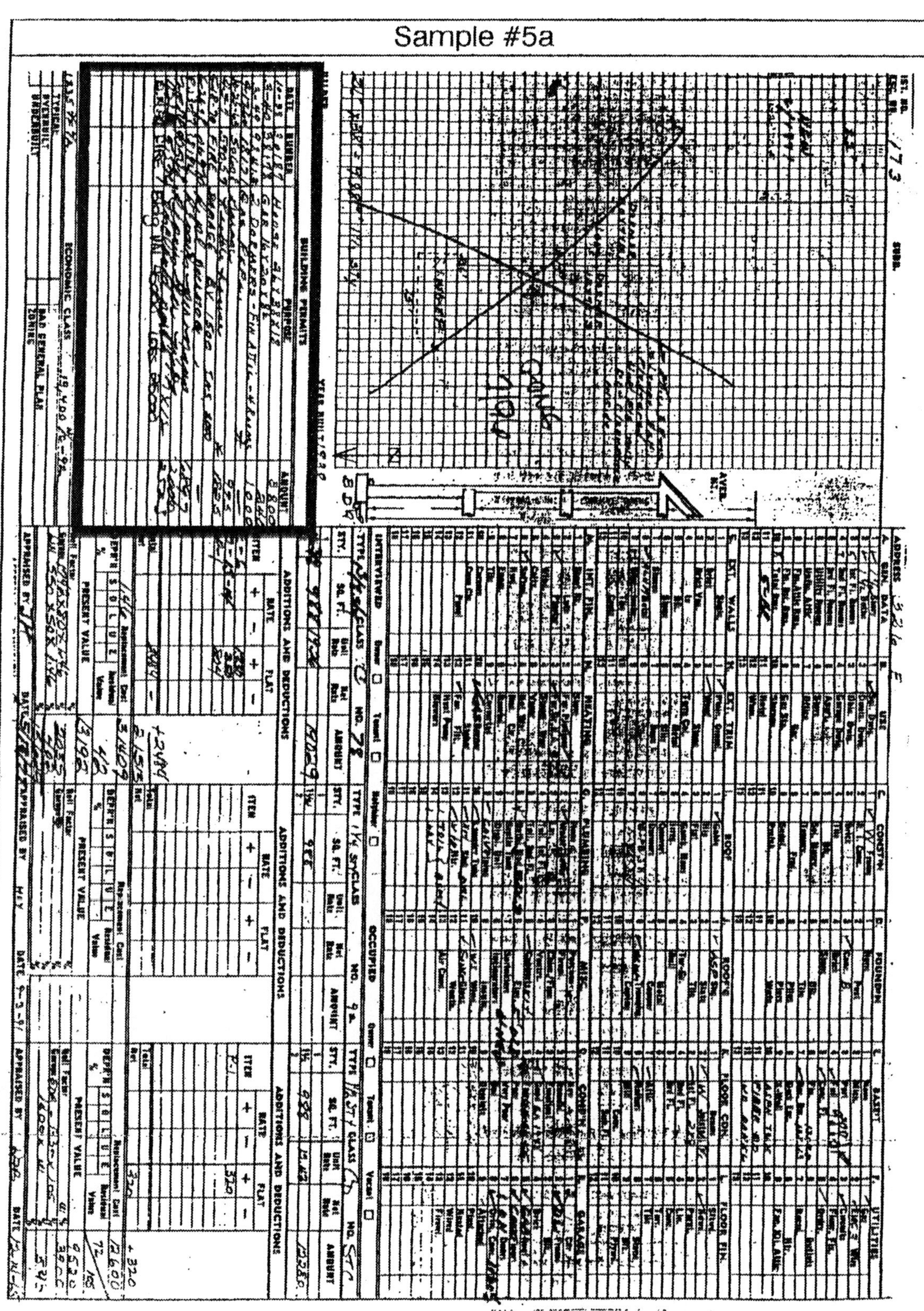

Sample #5a

Sample #5b

AS-55

LOCATION S. SIDE AVE BETWEEN HARVARD AND SUMMIT

DESCRIPTION

10735

7 B

308640

Smith, o-Allen & wf Mary
11311 Bishop Avenue
Oldberry, Michigan

Urban Gardens
Lot 707 and the W 1/2 of lot 708

60 × 117.70 / 117.52

Slightly Irregular Lot Dimensions

LAND SKETCH

SCALE 1" =

LAND	UTILITIES	PAVEMENT
LEVEL	✓ WATER	✓ ASPHALT-BRICK
LOW	✓ SEWER	✓ BLACKTOP 76-79
HIGH	✓ GAS	FOUNDATION
SWAMPY	✓ ELECTRICITY	CONCRETE
	✓ SIDEWALK	✓ CURB & GUTTER
		DIRT-GRAVEL ST.

EFFECTIVE FRONTAGE: [(a x) + (a x)] + 2

DEPTH	% OF ACT. UNIT	ACTUAL UNIT	DEPTH VALUE	EFFECTIVE FRONTAGE	TOTALS
117.70 / 117.12	106.65	9	9.60	60	576 –
C. I. SIDE ST. DEPTH	% OF C. I. UNIT	SIDE ST. UNIT	C. I. VALUE PER FT.	SIDE ST. FRONTAGE	
___ SQ. FT. @ ___ PER SQ. FT. =					
___ ACRES @ ___ PER ACRE =					
19 -/ Grand Total					576 –

DEPTH	% OF ACT. UNIT	ACTUAL UNIT	DEPTH VALUE	EFFECTIVE FRONTAGE	TOTALS
117.70 / 117.12	106.63	40	42.65	60	2559
C. I. SIDE ST. DEPTH	% OF C. I. UNIT	SIDE ST. UNIT	C. I. VALUE PER FT.	SIDE ST. FRONTAGE	
___ SQ. FT. @ ___ PER SQ. FT. =					
___ ACRES @ ___ PER ACRE =					
1964 Grand Total					2560

DEPTH	% OF ACT. UNIT	ACTUAL UNIT	DEPTH VALUE	EFFECTIVE FRONTAGE	TOTALS
117.70 / 117.12	106.63	45	47.98	60	2879
C. I. SIDE ST. DEPTH	% OF C. I. UNIT	SIDE ST. UNIT	C. I. VALUE PER FT.	SIDE ST. FRONTAGE	
___ SQ. FT. @ ___ PER SQ. FT. =					
___ ACRES @ ___ PER ACRE =					
1971 Grand Total					2879

Additional Enhancing or Detracting Influences

Sample #6

Enhancing or Detracting Influence: The Assessor indicates that approximately five acres of this total six acres of property, is in swampland and in a flood plain. In this case, a negative value adjustment was given. Most people know what swampland is. However, in this situation with six acres, part of the appraisal was trying to determine without benefit of a detailed survey how much of the land was actually in the swamp and how much was in a building site. The site would have "real value" to the property. The Appraiser has given a value based upon one acre of building site plus the other five acres a "marginal value."

Comments: Studying and reviewing the Assessor Cards can be extremely helpful in really understanding the unique features of a house or property. The Assessor Card sometimes will mention that a house has been moved to that lot from another area. The homeowner may say, "Well, the house has only been here 20 years," but what they failed to mention is that the house was 20 years old before it was moved there from another lot.

Sometimes it is difficult to determine on a modular home if in fact it **is** a modular home, because of the good quality of construction that now is available. The Assessor Card can tell that. Also interesting to know when dealing with a manufactured home is that it may be listed on the Assessor Card. The different quality levels and price levels of manufactured homes (without knowing the actual model number and the manufacturer) can be difficult to determine. Many times an Assessor Card will give the actual sales price of the manufactured home as being, for example, $50,000, but the homeowner may inflate that and say, "Oh yeah, I paid $65,000 for this home before having it placed on the lot." The Assessor Card may give you more accurate information per a bill of sale, often included in the folder.

Sample #6

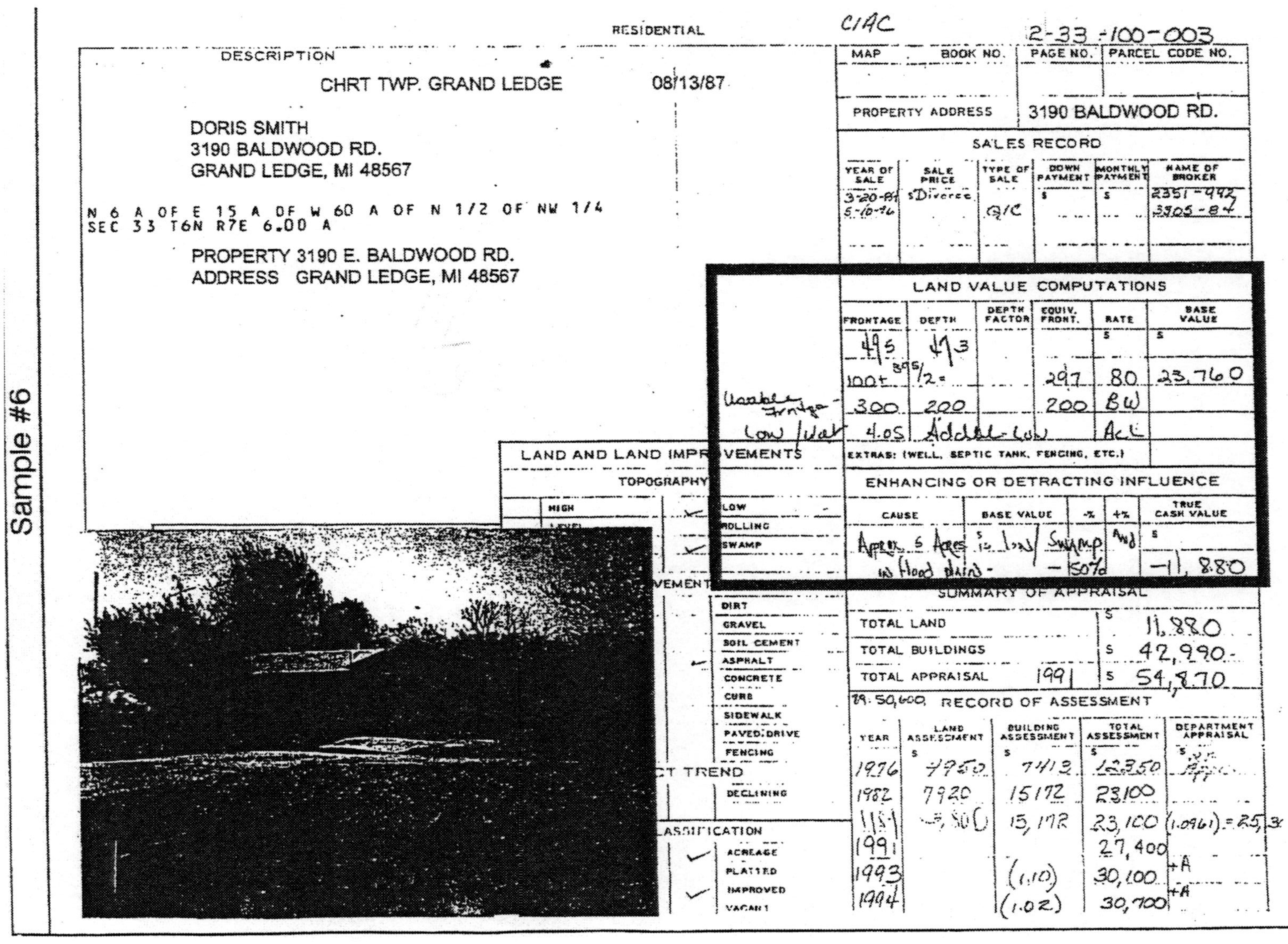

RESIDENTIAL

CIAC

MAP	BOOK NO.	PAGE NO.	PARCEL CODE NO.
			2-33-100-003

PROPERTY ADDRESS 3190 BALDWOOD RD.

DESCRIPTION

CHRT TWP. GRAND LEDGE 08/13/87

DORIS SMITH
3190 BALDWOOD RD.
GRAND LEDGE, MI 48567

N 6 A OF E 15 A OF W 60 A OF N 1/2 OF NW 1/4
SEC 33 T6N R7E 6.00 A

PROPERTY 3190 E. BALDWOOD RD.
ADDRESS GRAND LEDGE, MI 48567

SALES RECORD

YEAR OF SALE	SALE PRICE	TYPE OF SALE	DOWN PAYMENT	MONTHLY PAYMENT	NAME OF BROKER
3-20-81	$ Divorce		$	$	2351-442
5-10-76		Q/C			3305-84

LAND VALUE COMPUTATIONS

	FRONTAGE	DEPTH	DEPTH FACTOR	EQUIV. FRONT.	RATE	BASE VALUE
					$	$
	495	473				
	100 + 395/2 =			297	80	23,760
Usable Frntge -	300	200		200	BW	
Low/Wet	4.05	Addtl-Low			Ac	

EXTRAS: (WELL, SEPTIC TANK, FENCING, ETC.)

ENHANCING OR DETRACTING INFLUENCE

CAUSE	BASE VALUE	-%	+%	TRUE CASH VALUE
Aprox. 5 Acres is low/ Swamp and in flood plain -	$	- 50%		$ -11,880

LAND AND LAND IMPROVEMENTS

TOPOGRAPHY

HIGH		LOW
LEVEL		ROLLING
	✓	SWAMP

IMPROVEMENTS

DIRT
GRAVEL
SOIL CEMENT
✓ ASPHALT
CONCRETE
CURB
SIDEWALK
PAVED DRIVE
FENCING

[...]CT TREND

DECLINING

[CL]ASSIFICATION

✓ ACREAGE
PLATTED
✓ IMPROVED
VACANT

SUMMARY OF APPRAISAL

TOTAL LAND	$ 11,880
TOTAL BUILDINGS	$ 42,990
TOTAL APPRAISAL 1991	$ 54,870

89. 50,600 RECORD OF ASSESSMENT

YEAR	LAND ASSESSMENT	BUILDING ASSESSMENT	TOTAL ASSESSMENT	DEPARTMENT APPRAISAL
	$	$	$	$
1976	4950	7412	12350	
1982	7920	15172	23100	
1989	7,900	15,172	23,100	(1.0961) = 25,3[...]
1991			27,400	
1993		(1.10)	30,100	+A
1994		(1.02)	30,700	+A

Review Assessor Cards for Permits, or remarks involving the roof, the age of the roof, age or replacement of the furnace, and age or replacement of the central air conditioning.

Check this Permit and Remark section for any natural catastrophes such as fire, floods or vehicle damage. Note indications of the extent of damage, the dollar amount of permits, and if the repairs were actually made.

Review of the Assessor Card on a house that exploded and burned showed that there had been a previous fire two or three years prior to this calamity. The insurance company that ordered this appraisal contended that possibly the house was in a non-repaired or half-burned state prior to this fire. The assessor records showed in the history of the assessment that after the fire a couple of years earlier, the assessment was actually reduced. A notation a year later indicated that the assessment value was raised back to its previous level because the repairs ***had*** *been made. This was noted in the Remark section. So when the appraisal was done, it was done assuming the house was in a repaired condition rather than a half-repaired condition. (The homeowner was not available to ask.) This can also apply to other calamities, such as tornadoes or windstorms.*

One house that had been totally destroyed in a tornado was challenging to appraise. By using the Assessor Card, plus picking through the debris, the appraiser was able to reconstruct the house on paper and replace its value. The homeowner was out of the country and not available for communication. As an interesting side note, there was a small barn that was not on a foundation, which was totally taken away in the tornado. The value of the barn was not approved until the homeowners questioned the appraisal with their insurance adjuster. Review of the Assessor Card revealed some brief notations that enabled a more accurate appraisal for an accurate insurance settlement.

Note: Check for Remarks on the card about permits for garages, pole barns, remodeling, etc. Many times no permits are obtained, and the construction is done by the homeowner. Who knows if the garage has the proper depth of footings, or was properly wired to code without permits/inspections? Don't get fooled -- don't let your guard down.

Caution: Many computer-generated assessor records delete vital details. Ask for/insist on seeing the original hard copies. Some (not all) government offices attempt to discourage people by saying the records are in storage, etc. Firmly ask for the long versions, even if you have to file a Freedom of Information Request. (Some government offices require it for these "public" records.)

MICHIGAN DEPARTMENT OF NATURAL RESOURCES
FOREST, MINERAL AND FIRE MANAGEMENT

INFORMATION ON HOW TO READ LEGAL LAND DESCRIPTIONS

Issued as a courtesy under Authority of the Michigan Department of Natural Resources

The state is divided into townships which are identified by their Town (N or S) and Range (E or W) location in respect to Michigan's Meridian and Base lines.

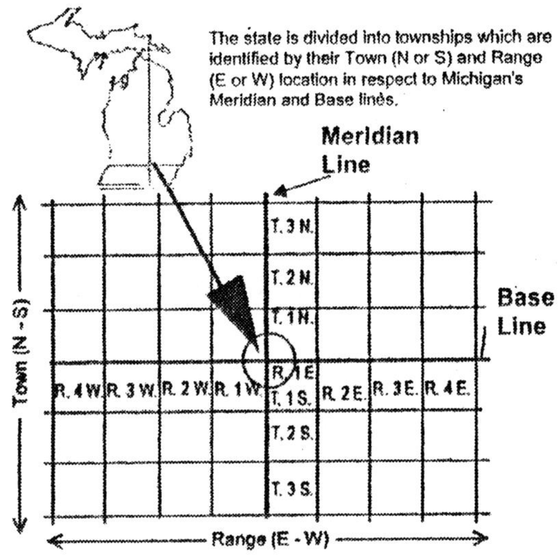

A township is normally a quadrangle approximately 6 miles on a side which contains thirty-six (36) sections. As shown below in some townships corrections for the earth's curvature will show up on it's northern and western boundary lines. Also, note the way in which sections are numbered within a township.

6	5	4	3	2	1
7	8	9	10	11	12
18	17	16	15	14	13
19	20	21	22	23	24
30	29	28	27	26	25
31	32	33	34	35	36

Sections are typically divided into quarters (ex: NW 1/4) and sometimes halves (ex: W1/2), which are then divided again into quarter-quarters (ex: NW1/4 of NW1/4) and so on. It is best to remember to read a land description backwards.

Section broken down into 40 Acre parcels.

(NW 1/4)	NW 1/4 NW 1/4	NE 1/4 NW 1/4	NW 1/4 NE 1/4	NE 1/4 NE 1/4	(NE 1/4)
	SW 1/4 NW 1/4	SE 1/4 NW 1/4	SW 1/4 NE 1/4	SE 1/4 NE 1/4	
(SW 1/4)	NW 1/4 SW 1/4	NE 1/4 SW 1/4	NW 1/4 SE 1/4	NE 1/4 SE 1/4	(SE 1/4)
	SW 1/4 SW 1/4	SE 1/4 SW 1/4	SW 1/4 SE 1/4	SE 1/4 SE 1/4	

Typical example showing distances, acreages and land descriptions within a section.
1 Mile = 5280 Feet = 320 Rods = 80 Chains

1/2 Mile = 2640 Feet
2640 Feet
NE 1/4
160 Acres
W 1/2
320 Acres
W 1/2
SE 1/4
80 Acres
1320 Feet
NE 1/4
SE 1/4
40 Acres
660Ft
W 1/2
SE 1/4
SE 1/4
20 Ac
10 Ac
NE 1/4
SE 1/4
SE 1/4
10 Ac
SE 1/4
SE 1/4
SE 1/4

Typical example of a section containing Government Lots (fractional part of a section designated on the township plat).

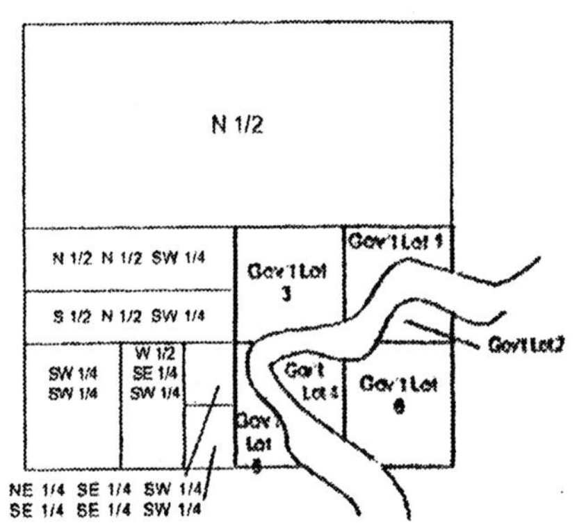

IC4008 (Rev. 10/16/2002)

This information was provided by and is the property of the Michigan Department of Natural Resources.

GENESEE COUNTY - PARCEL NUMBERING SYSTEM

N.W. CORNER	N.E. CORNER
(100) 501 - 525 601 - 625	(200) 526 - 550 626 - 650
(300) 551 - 575 651 - 675	(400) 576 - 599 676 - 699
S.W. CORNER	S.E. CORNER

100 - 400	Metes & Bounds
501 - 599	Subdivisions
601 - 699	Condo's

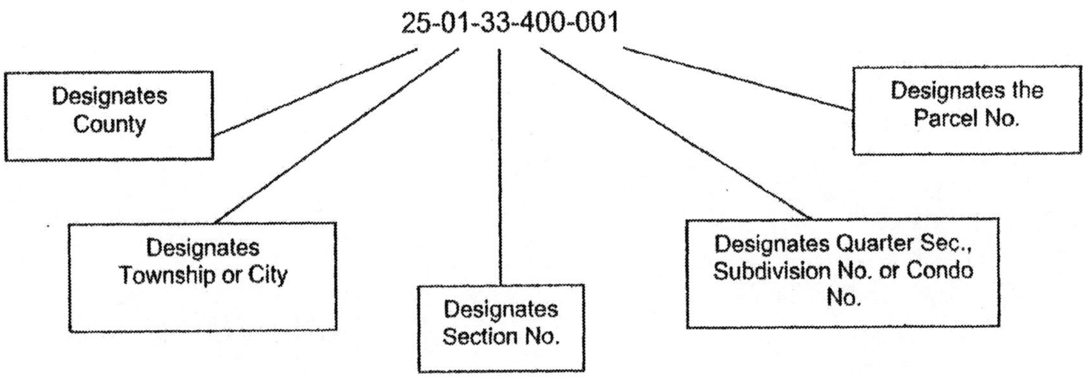

Authorized for use by the Genesee County Equalization Department.

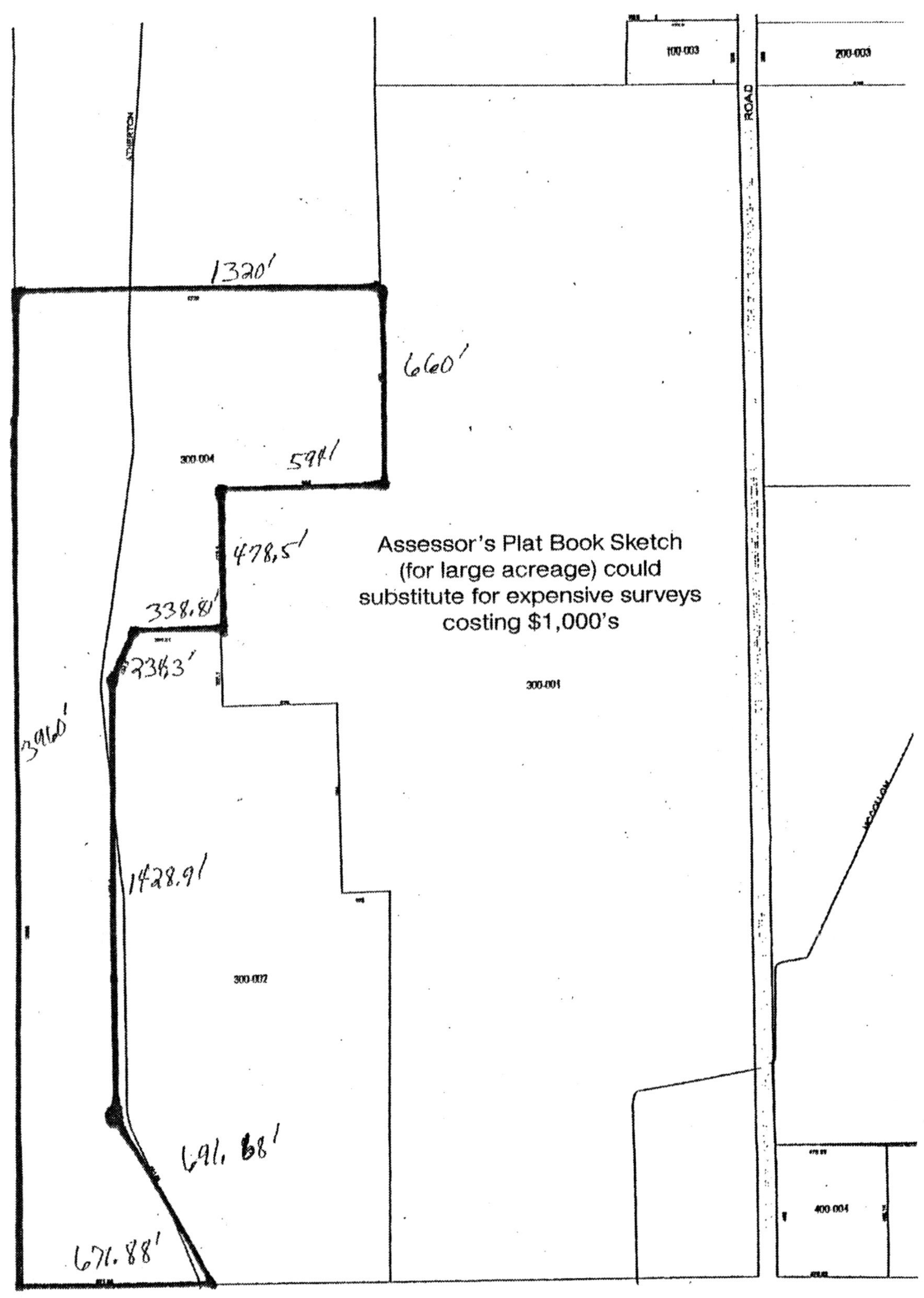
100-003
200-003
ROAD
ATHERTON
1320'
660'
300-004
591'
478.5'
338.8'
300-001
3960'
1428.91'
300-002
691.88'
671.88'
400-004
Assessor's Plat Book Sketch
(for large acreage) could
substitute for expensive surveys
costing $1,000's

LESSON #18:
REAL ESTATE ATTORNEY INTERVIEW

This is a special chapter which could be worth at least $200 or more of legal advice to your home-buying education (assuming $175-$200/hour attorney fees).

Don't believe it, hire a local real estate attorney for one or two hours. That's what was involved in this interview.

Read it, make notes, and save your wallet (thousands of dollars in legal fees) and your sanity (avoid headaches and heartaches).

Today we're having the opportunity of speaking with Attorney Jeffrey Birrell of 1203 Beach Street, Flint, Michigan, about home buying. (Phone 810-341-1400)

Dick Smith (DS): Isn't it amazing how some homebuyers take action without thinking of the consequences ... get themselves into trouble ... then they come running to an attorney to bail them out? I'm sure you've seen this happen many times over the years.

Jeffrey Birrell (JB): Well, I can't tell you how many times people have come to me after signing a purchase agreement, or even scarier, after signing all of the closing documents, then they call me and make an appointment, they bring the paperwork in, and they say, "Look what I've signed!" And, "What do you think of this deal I've gotten myself in?" And I usually just say,

"Well, whatever you've signed, you're stuck with. You should have come to me first." But it does happen quite a bit, unfortunately.

DS: Right. It would probably be better for homeowners to develop a plan before getting themselves into or even before doing their serious home shopping. Would that be right?

JB: Oh, there's no question. The biggest investment in most people's lives is their home. That may not be quite true for Donald Trump or Ted Turner or some others who have huge investments in other places. But for most people, working class people, if they're going to spend anywhere between $50,000 to $500,000, that's the biggest investment they make in their lives, and it absolutely makes no sense to spend that much money on your biggest investment, and not have a plan.

DS: It seems to me like if they first chose and develop a relationship with a real estate attorney for counseling, that would be one of their first steps, and then maybe secondly getting involved in doing home buying homework, such as reading home buying books. Sunday newspapers have special sections on home buying and real estate that provide how-to articles, real estate firms, listings, there's even articles about appraisals, home inspectors, surveyors, and things like that. So it's pretty easily accessible. It isn't like people have to knock themselves out to get information. In fact I believe the local Board of REALTORS® have magazines available at restaurants and stands, where a person can even get those for free. Have you seen some of those around town?

JB: I have, and those are all great ideas. And again, the very first thing they need to do is develop a relationship with a real estate attorney as part of the plan, and then all of that other information you mentioned are all great ideas, especially with the advent of the Internet now, most people have so much information available at their fingertips. And even for the people that don't have a computer yet, I know at least in Flint you can go to the Flint Public Library for free and get on the Internet. And there's just mountains of information available through the Internet, and all of the other sources you mentioned are also really good.

DS: Right. Well I know that the National Association of REALTORS® even has their own web site of REALTOR.com, and then there's even a web site forsalebyowner.com where people can even do some shopping around, get some tips on what to look for and that sort of thing. So it's out there. One of the things that might also be a good idea is for people to see what fits in their budgets. Mortgage brokers and bankers offer a free service of sitting down with people and get them pre-qualified to see what they can afford before they even go home shopping.

JB: Yes, definitely. Anytime you make a purchase, you have to determine if you can afford it or not. And I also urge people to look beyond just the principal and interest, taxes, and insurance. You will have utilities, there's upkeep and maintenance associated with the home. In other words, if someone were to buy a home, and they're looking at something that has a five-acre yard, they have to realize that that's like a part-time job to mow that yard. It's going to take about from 2 to 5 hours a week just doing that, and are you going to hire that out? Well, if you hired that out, that's probably going to be $50 to $150 a week that you're going to have to pay someone to do it, and I mean just all the associated costs of a home, not just the mortgage. They're got to think of their utilities. If they're looking at a 3,500-square-foot home, that's going to cost more to heat than a 1,200-square-foot ranch. So certainly all of the costs have to be considered before they purchase.

DS: They've got to really look at it from the real world, rather than what they would like to have. Within the last several years we've been getting involved with home buyer representatives and home buyer agents. A lot of REALTORS® or real estate people are acting as agents for the buyers. I seem to find that to be very helpful. Have you had any experience dealing with that?

JB: I have. That's a very usable source for the people who need the assistance of real estate brokers and real estate agents. A number of agents are making themselves available to assist people in finding a home, and I think that's one of the things they do ... we were talking about the budget ... they sit down with someone to determine their budget, and what they can afford, and then they go to the multi-listing book and they find homes that are in their price range. Maybe also geographically, someone may be looking for a home in a certain school district for example, within a certain price range. And a real estate agent can go to a multi-listing book and help them find whatever is listed in the multi-listing book.

DS: And it would seem like the next step would be then to consult with a real estate attorney to review the offers and seller's disclosure statements, which are required in many states, before they even sign them. Would that be a good plan?

JB: Definitely. It goes back to your very first question. In my opinion, before anyone buys or sells real estate, their first step would be to consult with a competent real estate attorney to help develop the plan, and then if they're selling, if an offer comes in the attorney is already prepared and can assist the seller in preparing a purchase agreement. They also can assist in at least providing the seller's disclosure statement ... the seller would have to develop that themselves, but they could at least assist in that and explain it. And there's also the lead paint disclosure for homes that were built prior to 1978.

DS: Right. Well, a lot of this could be done either by phone or fax or mail or e-mail or in person. I mean there's so many ways that this could be facilitated.

JB: It really can. In our information age now with computers and e-mail being so prevalent, and of course telephones and fax machines being available, you really could do that without having to make a trip.

DS: Most of the purchase agreements that I've seen strongly suggest, or there's a word of caution at the top, that people seek competent legal advice before signing, so it isn't like people aren't seeing this. They perhaps just need to be told two or three times to get it through their heads.

JB: Well, whenever you enter into that type of a transaction, spending that much money, the last thing you want to think of is that something is going to go wrong. I think most people are optimistic, that they're buying a dream home let's say, or they're buying an investment, or they're buying a home that they're going to raise their family in, the last thing that they want to think about is that something is going to go wrong. But unfortunately, the people that don't think about the possible consequences are the ones that end up in trouble.

DS: What would be a good way to pick out a real estate attorney? You know, there's so many different fields of law, many types of attorneys. What would be a good way? Should people get referrals from their bankers or real estate agents?

JB: I think the very best way that people have found me in my practice is by word of mouth. In other words, speaking with friends or relatives, or bankers and real estate agents. But getting an opinion of someone who had already hired that attorney, their word is the best. You know, it doesn't matter what service industry you're in, and attorneys are in a service industry; they either make or break themselves by the quality of service that they give. And the best way to find out what type of quality service they give is to speak to people who have hired them in the past.

DS: After a person gets the name or names ... I'm just thinking of what questions they should ask the attorney. Should they ask what percentage of their practice is devoted to residential real estate?

JB: Yes, I think that's a great question. I think you can start with asking how long they've been an attorney, for one thing. What year were you admitted to the Bar Association? What percentage of your practice do you devote to real estate? Do you do any "For Sale by Owner" assistance, which is a big area of my personal practice? I assist a lot of people who are selling or buying without the assistance of a real estate broker, and if they're trying to do it on their own, you're going to want to know whether that attorney has assisted people without having brokers or agents involved.

DS: The other question would be how much they represent buyers, or how much they represent sellers.

JB: Yes, you could determine if they have practices devoted to buyers or sellers, I suppose would be a good question. You could also ask them what percentage of their practice is devoted to commercial versus residential, because there are a lot of differences between the two, commercial real estate being much more technical.

DS: Okay. And I guess you could have an attorney who has been practicing for 50 years but maybe that person has only been in the area for two years. I think I'd feel a lot more comfortable with someone who is ... how would I say it ... a local, or at least been around here for many years. I guess that would be another question to ask, is how long they've actually been in this area.

JB: Yes, how long they've practiced in this area, and how long they've been an attorney, and how long they've been practicing in the area of real estate law.

DS: Going along with that is if that attorney is familiar with the town or the neighborhood in which the person is really home shopping, because if it was in your own general area, you know a lot of peculiarities about that area or neighborhood.

JB: That's true, and one of the reasons that it's important to have a local attorney is because there may be local ordinances that can play a role in real estate sales. For example, the city of Flint has a local ordinance that says that any real estate sold within the city limits has to be inspected by a city inspector. That's just one example. So if you're asking an attorney who is practicing in Detroit about real estate that's being sold in Lansing, the Detroit attorney would not be familiar with Lansing's local ordinances, or whether local ordinances apply or not.

DS: Does an attorney personally review, research, and counsel the individual in the documents, or do they have assistants that do this work?

JB: Any time you hire anyone who is going to provide a service, whether it's cleaning your carpets, building a garage, or assisting you with a sale or purchase of real estate, you want to know whether that service provider is personally going to provide the service, or whether they're going to subcontract the work out or hand the file or hand the work off to an assistant. Because you can do all the background checks in the world and ask all the right questions of that person that you're hiring, but if they turn around and have someone else do the work, all those questions you ask may not be relative to the actual person who is doing the work.

DS: I've seen it done and people won't 'fess up that they had an assistant who makes $5 an hour do this or that, who really wasn't competent or whatever. How would an attorney usually charge? Would they charge by the hour, and what would be the normal rate at this time?

JB: There are a number of different ways that an attorney would charge, and it depends on the type of work. If the person is hiring an attorney to just draft a purchase agreement, let's say, that likely would be charged by a flat fee, the attorney would just charge a flat fee, somewhere in the neighborhood of $175. But then if a person or a buyer or seller were to say, "You know, I need assistance with the entire project all the way through," the attorney would either charge hourly or at a flat rate, and it would vary from attorney to attorney and it would be very important for any potential buyer or seller to discuss that in detail with their attorney and get the employment agreement in writing.

DS: What would be a normal rate at this time? Would this be like a $150 or $200 rate, or what would be typical would you think, in this area?

JB: Something in the range of $175 to $200 per hour for a real estate attorney would be reasonable for 2004.

DS: Would you, in your process of doing this, recommend names of home inspectors, appraisers, surveyors, real estate buyer representatives, contractors, or title insurance companies?

JB: I certainly can. I recommend, for example, home inspection. Any time any buyer comes to me and says, "I'm interested in purchasing this home. I'm looking at it. Can you help me?" the first thing I do is recommend that they hire a licensed home inspector. If they want the name of a home inspector, I'll certainly help them find someone. But I always let them know that the Yellow Pages are a great source for home inspectors, surveyor or engineering companies, or real estate appraisers or real estate agents. I have a number of people that I work closely with in my practice, because I've been doing this for a number of years now. I've been an attorney since 1987, and I've developed some relationships with a number of other people associated with real estate that I can recommend clients to, but they're certainly welcome to use whoever they like.

DS: From a buyer's point of view, when you review a purchase agreement ... I have several things that you might suggest to review ... do you get involved in suggesting a time of possession?

JB: Definitely. That is one of the elements of every purchase agreement. The first thing would be what day they are planning on closing this transaction, and then how long does the seller intend on remaining on the property. A lot of times sellers are moved out of the property before the closing, but there are other times when sellers are waiting on, let's say, their next home to be built, and they may need 30 or 60 or 90 days before they can move out. And if they do, then the buyer is certainly entitled to charge the seller monthly rent in an amount equal to their monthly mortgage, principal and interest, tax, insurance, etc.

DS: How about a written listing or personal property addendum that would specify things like if a stove, refrigerator, drapes, satellite dish, or storage shed or even a portable dishwasher, if those things are going to be left behind. Is that a big issue also?

JB: That absolutely has to be in writing. That is a very big area of dispute at times, and the way to resolve the dispute in advance is to place it in writing, and also in detail. In other words, if you just say, "I am purchasing the home and the stove," there are homes that could have more than one stove, or there could be a brand new stove in that home when the buyer walks through it, and he signs the purchase agreement thinking he's buying that stove, when in reality the seller says, "Well, I didn't say which stove. I said I'd leave you a stove." And they removed that brand new stove and they replaced it with a used stove. So I think it's a good idea to not only say a stove, but I would detail it and say even the model number, the make, and color so there is no question later of what's going to stay.

DS: Good point. What about the closing costs? Is that an item of who pays for what and who shares what?

JB: Yes, that's another item that should be in every purchase agreement. Normally the seller pays the closing costs associated with the transaction including the mandatory transfer tax.

DS: I've heard in competitive markets that there is even a right of first refusal in the purchase agreements, where if a person can either raise or improve on any offer that is received during the time of the negotiations ... do you ever see that sort of thing?

JB: Yes, I see that quite a bit. Normally what would happen is the buyer offers to purchase the home, let's say for $50,000, and then the seller says, "Well, we're not going to close on this deal for let's say 60 days. During that 60 days if someone comes up and offers $60,000 or $70,000 for this home, I will give you the first opportunity to match that $60,000 or $70,000 offer, and I'll give you 48 hours to match it, but if you're unable to match it, then I'm going to sell it to this new buyer." And as long as that's in writing, it's enforceable.

DS: And then obviously some things like the pro-ration of property taxes, that would just be a routine thing that's always checked on?

JB: Yes. That's a standard part of every purchase agreement that is sometimes overlooked by parties. If the seller has prepaid property taxes, they certainly would be entitled to reimbursement for a portion of the taxes that accrue after the closing.

DS: Going along with that is verifying that the taxes were actually paid, because sometimes people say things that aren't the truth.

JB: They definitely should do that, and that's a very easy check. You just go to the township (local government office) to make sure that all of the property taxes are current.

DS: And I guess along with that would be checking on utility bills, such as gas, water, and sewer, because sometimes those things are paid quarterly rather than monthly, to know if there are outstanding bills, and so forth.

JB: Yes, you're certainly entitled to have all of the utilities paid current up to the day of closing. A lot of times buyers will require an escrow account be established to make sure that any bills that come in after closing are paid from the escrow account. For example, they'll say we're going to hold the $500 of your payment in a separate account, and we're going to hold that for 60 days, and during that time if any utility bills or water or sewer bills come in that cover a time period prior to closing, we're going to pay that from that escrow account. Any balance is refunded to the seller.

DS: How about checking for local government assessments that there may be a sewer or a road assessment that is not discussed but will come up and haunt somebody later on. I would think that would be pretty important.

JB: Every buyer should check for special assessments. It's a simple check. Just contact your local government with the property address just to make sure if any assessments are due. And then usually what most purchase agreements will say is that if there is a local assessment pending, the assessment is paid off at closing. This will also be discussed in the title insurance commitment.

DS: What about a title search? Are those routinely done, like to search for liens by a state, or an IRS lien for unpaid taxes or title problems?

JB: At one time title searches were the only way a seller provided evidence of title. Now, title insurance has taken the place of the old-fashioned title search. What happens now is the seller provides the title insurance policy to a buyer that, number one, provides evidence of title, proves that the seller owns the property. But over and above that, the title insurance company will do their own title search and that will disclose any liens or other title problems.

DS: When people are buying vacant land or building sites, how about perk or percolation tests? Are those something that would be a very big item?

JB: That's a very big item. If the property does not have city sewer, then the buyer is going to have to build their own septic system, and that's something that should be in every purchase agreement where a buyer plans to install a septic system. The health department will test the soil and issue a report on what it will take to satisfy them when the septic system is built. The purchase agreement could be contingent upon this "perk test" and what it will cost to build a system that will satisfy the local authorities.

DS: Do you actually review home inspection reports? I have an additional chapter about home inspectors, but do you ever review those, too?

JB: I can, and I have from time to time where the home inspection has developed a problem. But that's not quite really in the mandatory category. I think most of the home inspection reports are very plain and very easy to understand, and most people can read them and understand them on their own. But I have gotten involved and I've had to go back and review some home inspection reports where they discovered major problems that caused an interruption in the transaction.

DS: You mentioned earlier about the lead paint testing for houses built before 1978. A lot of the REALTORS® in this area are very professional in mentioning that. Is that something that is routinely checked into, or is it just an item that you're aware of that should be checked into?

JB: Oh, that's mandatory by law. Every home in every state built before 1978 requires a lead paint disclosure.

DS: How about reviewing the appraisal, like checking for accuracy or validity? Do you ever get involved in that?

JB: I have done that, because a lot of the appraisals are subjective, and they're prepared according to comparisons to other property that is sold in the area. But a lot of times the comparable properties used are not really comparable to the home being appraised. I suggest that everyone use a licensed real estate appraiser and not a market analysis. Once that licensed appraiser has looked at a property and given their opinion of value, there's really nothing that I can do to change that, whether it's valid or accurate. We have to take their opinion.

DS: I know you mentioned earlier about sellers' disclosure statements, and those are required in so many states. Are those something that are checked out routinely, or are they pretty much straightforward for a person to look over?

JB: Absolutely mandatory in the state of Michigan, and I recommend that they be provided in every case. The whole idea there is to prevent fraud concerning the condition of the property.

DS: Is there often a provision for a final walk-through suggested before the closing, because many times I've heard horror stories of people going to the house that's been stripped or trashed. Is that a common provision?

JB: It is a common provision, and it is another one that I would recommend be placed in every purchase agreement, especially if there's going to be personal property left behind as mentioned earlier where we described that stove, for example. Whenever there is personal property, you have the right before the closing to go back and make sure that property is still there, and not only that, you have the right to make sure that that property and the home is in the same condition as it was in when you looked at it initially.

DS: How about deposits? I know sometimes there are deposits made, and is there any specification as to who keeps what or who forfeits what under what circumstances?

JB: Yes. Deposits are routinely used in real estate transactions and every purchase agreement should contain a provision dictating how the deposit is dealt with in the event of the default of either party, so if the seller were to default, this is what happens, or if the buyer were to default, this is what happens to the deposit.

DS: In this state, flood insurance is required in some areas. Sometimes the property can be in a flood zone with only part of it, like a rear lot line being in a flood zone, and people are told they have to have flood insurance. Do you ever ask who actually checks to determine this, if it's done by an appraiser or if it's done by a surveyor or by a certification company? Because sometimes people could be forced to buy flood insurance and the house would never be affected and would never be flooded. Does that issue ever come up?

JB: That comes up quite a bit, although in Michigan in this area, luckily we're not subject to floods like other parts of the country. But we do have flood zones in Michigan and it's very important that a homebuyer be aware of whether their home is located in a flood zone. A lot of times mortgage companies, when they loan money, will require the buyer to obtain an additional flood insurance policy.

DS: How about homeowner and condo association dues and fees and unusual rules and regulations. Are those something that should be considered also?

JB: They definitely should be considered in advance. That's part of the question about whether a buyer can afford that property. Not only do they have to pay for the mortgage, principal and interest, taxes and insurance, but if there are homeowner or condo association dues and fees that are due every month, that's another item that they have to be aware of when they put it in their budget to make sure they can afford that property. And as far as condo association rules, if someone were to buy property that's in a condo association, they have the right to review all of those rules prior to the closing, and I would suggest they have an attorney review them with them because at times they are quite technical. But at the very least they should read them themselves because it will dictate things like whether your garage door can be left open or whether you're allowed to leave a garden hose in your front yard. Very small details like that are often covered in your homeowners association. I've heard of people buying condos or real estate that is included in a condo association, and not realize these things, that they can't leave a garden hose in their front yard or they can't leave their garage door open for more than 30 minutes without violating the rules. So they should know those types of things.

DS: Now obviously when a person is buying a house, they're going to have to buy homeowners insurance or some type of an insurance. One of the things that should be specified is when it actually goes into effect and if there are any special or local circumstances that need to be addressed when they buy that homeowners insurance. And one of the biggest predicaments I've heard about is so many people buy homeowners insurance based on the sale of the total house and the lot. They don't even realize this, *so they buy a house for $150,000 and they get a $150,000 homeowners' policy because they were told to by their banker or whoever. When in fact the value of the lot may be $50,000 and the house may be worth $100,000, and they should have insurance for $100,000 on the house. Have you ever run into situations like that?*

JB: I have, and it's part of any plan to purchase real estate, a buyer should align themselves with their insurance agent to make sure they have adequate insurance in place. They want to make sure that their insurance is effective the date of the closing and that they are adequately covered.

DS: How about review of the survey or subdivision plat from the local government office to check for discrepancies on the sizes or easements or encroachments. Is that something to be concerned with?

JB: Yes it is. I recommend that every buyer obtain a stake survey of the property that they're buying, and what would happen is an engineering company would come out and place a clear marker at the four corners of the property, assuming it's a rectangular or a square lot ... some of them are irregularly shaped ... and that definitely needs a stake survey if they're irregularly shaped. But even for the standard square lots or rectangular lots, I recommend that everyone obtain a stake survey just so that there is no questions later about where your lot line is and whether there are any encroachments. For example, we see a lot of garages or pole barns that are built right on the line or over the line or that are built in a way that violates set-off provisions. And again, if you get a stake survey, at least a stake survey of the four corners before you close, you can take a look and see exactly where your lot lines are. I have a number of cases where fences are built and the parties treat that fence as the lot line, because that's where the fence was for all these years.

When in reality, the true lot line is something different than where that fence was built. And if you go to buy property and you look out and you see a fence, and if you think, well there's that fence, that must be the lot line, you could be sadly mistaken.

DS: Should one refer to local building department rules and regulations for future additions or garages, or even subdivision rules and deed restrictions, which might even restrict not only what you're talking about, the setbacks and how far from the lines? It may even restrict whether they could even build one.

JB: Yes. Any time that you're going to buy property in an area, again you want to know what the local ordinances are or the local building codes. If you have plans to do future additions or build a pole barn or another garage or things like that, that should be checked in advance prior to the closing.

DS: Okay. I know we talked briefly about the title insurance and the need for it. I had been told recently that title insurance does not guarantee surveys. Is that something you've ever run into?

JB: Title insurance is really evidence of title. In other words, the seller must prove that they own the real estate. And the way that the seller proves that they own the property that they're trying to sell, is by providing the buyer title insurance. If it turns out that the seller does not have clear title to the property, then the buyer is able to collect his purchase money back from the title insurance company. So my point is that title insurance is absolutely necessary in every transaction, although there is no law that I'm aware of that makes it mandatory. You can buy property without title insurance, but I think it would be a mistake.

DS: Recently I saw a provision in a purchase agreement that said, "To maintain premises, the seller agrees to maintain the premises in the same condition as existed at acceptance of the contract until possession is delivered to buyer. Upon vacating, seller will clear house of all rubbish, debris and personal belongings." And maybe it would even be a good deal to set up some kind of a deposit or fine to enforce that. Have you ever seen that provision?

JB: I haven't. That's not a bad idea at all. If the buyer has any inclination that the seller may not be able to maintain that property in the same condition that they looked at the very first time, I think that it's mandatory that be in writing. If it's in writing, then it's enforceable.

DS: Another item to consider is when there are legal descriptions with metes and bounds, which is usually out in a rural setting, are those ever checked for accuracy? You know, somebody says they've got 10 acres, and then somebody sets down with a metes and bounds legal description and draws it out and they've actually got 5 acres. Is that ever checked?

JB: Oh yes, and that's why I recommend the stake survey be prepared by a licensed engineering company. That would avoid the whole problem. If you have an engineering company come out and stake your corners of your property or stake your lot line for you, you will know whether the legal description matches the purchase agreement.

DS: I recently heard of somebody buying property in a rural area. They did it themselves without benefit of either a real estate company or an attorney, and they didn't even have right of way for the utilities to come into that property. They had to buy an adjacent property to get the utilities to come back in there.

JB: What a horror story. That's the type of thing that could have been discovered in advance of the closing, and then the buyer could have either backed out of the closing or made adequate preparation.

DS: I've seen a lot of sloppy documentation, such as unsigned and undated purchase agreements that are sent to a bank when they start the mortgage process, and my question is, are those documents even valid?

JB: No, a purchase agreement is not valid unless it's been signed. Every real estate transaction has to be in writing to be enforced according to the Statute of Frauds. And in addition to being in writing, it has to be signed by the parties who are entering into the transaction.

DS: And it has to be dated, also, doesn't it?

JB: I don't believe a date would be necessary to satisfy the Statute of Frauds, although I would always recommend it.

DS: By understanding a buyer's individual needs, their assets, and understanding their situation, it would seem a real estate attorney could actually counsel or tailor make those persons' situations to fit the real estate that they are interested in buying.

JB: Those are almost the very words that I use with my clients. I try to tailor make every transaction, because every deal is a little bit different. Every buyer is a little different, every seller is a little different, every property is a little bit different, and therefore every transaction is just a little bit different. There's not one purchase agreement, for example, that will satisfy every real estate transaction. A lot of people try to do transactions on their own, for example they'll go to an office supply store and buy a blank real estate purchase agreement form, and they'll fill in the blanks and sign it, and although that contract is valid and is binding, it often leaves major things out, and it also leads to misunderstandings later. So I think it's best if you have an attorney present at the beginning to draft a contract, to tailor make that individual purchase agreement, make sure that it accomplishes both the buyer's and the seller's goals.

DS: So in the long run, a buyer is actually paying hundreds of dollars up front for counseling versus thousands of dollars for a messy lawsuit or on a bad real estate deal in the future. They're really saving themselves big money to pay it up front then.

JB: That's a good way to put it. Again, the buyer is making probably the biggest investment they're ever going to make in their life by buying that real estate, it just makes sense to spend a few hundred dollars on an attorney to make sure that everything is done right.

DS: Any last words of advice? It's better to get a plan ahead of time and pay hundreds of dollars, than to get involved in a big mess later.

JB: Yes, there's no question that anyone that is going to buy or sell real estate needs the assistance of a real estate attorney, title insurance company, engineering company to do surveys, the homeowners insurance agent, and a home inspector. They're all like a team and they all play a significant role in the real estate transaction. But of course, the first place to start is with a competent real estate attorney.

DS: Okay. Well, I think we've pretty much covered everything. I do thank you for your time.

Author's comment: Please note that local customs often dictate if the buyer or seller pays the costs. The wording of the purchase agreement should control this.

Specific instructions/wording in the purchase agreement should/could dictate if the buyer or seller pays for title insurance, transfer tax, special assessments, taxes owed, or prorated-forward, home inspections, pest inspections, appraisal, points, recording fee, mortgage policy, etc.

Get expert legal advice to avoid misunderstandings and problems.

THIS IS A LEGALLY BINDING CONTRACT,
IF NOT UNDERSTOOD, SEEK LEGAL COUNSEL

PURCHASE AGREEMENT

1. OFFER TO PURCHASE: The undersigned, hereinafter known as "Purchaser" hereby agrees to purchase the property commonly known as: and legally described as: LOT 39 Maplewood Subdivision (Property size and square footage of all structures located thereon are approximate and not guaranteed.) Tax I.D.# 5935576050 and located in the City Village Township of Burton County of Genesee Michigan. Subject to all existing building and use restrictions, easements and zoning ordinances, if any, and to pay the sum of ONE HUNDRED FORTY THOUSAND + 00/100 Dollars ($140,000).

2. TERMS OF PURCHASE: As indicated by "X" below, (choose A, B, C. or D below). Payment of the cash portion of the purchase price is to be a cashier's check issued by a federally regulated financial institution.

[ ] **A. CASH SALE:** The full purchase price upon the delivery of a recordable Warranty Deed conveying title in the condition provided for herein.

[X] **B. NEW MORTGAGE:** The full purchase price upon the delivery of a recordable Warranty Deed conveying title in the condition provided for herein, contingent upon Purchaser's ability to obtain a Con mortgage amortized for no less than 30 years, in the amount of 100 % of purchase price on or before the date the sale is to be closed, which Purchaser agrees to apply for financing by (Date) 11/5/04

Purchaser agrees to use his or her best efforts to obtain such financing. Purchaser agrees to pay any and all costs that are a condition of financing, unless otherwise agreed therein. **IF SAID MORTGAGE FINANCING IS NOT APPROVED BY** (Date) 11/15/04 At 6 PM **AM/PM, SELLER HAS OPTION TO DECLARE PURCHASER'S DEFAULT AND TO TERMINATE THIS AGREEMENT BY WRITTEN NOTICE TO PURCHASER.** A certificate of pre-approval presented by the Purchaser, does not necessarily guaranty financing.

[ ] **C. SALE TO EXISTING MORTGAGE OR LAND CONTRACT:** Upon execution and delivery of [ ] a recordable Warranty Deed and subject to existing mortgage.

[ ] Assignment of vendee interest in land contract. Purchaser to pay the difference (approximately $) between the purchase price and the balance as of day of closing, of said mortgage or land contract bearing interest at % per annum and with monthly payments of $ which do do not include tax and/or insurance, which Purchaser assumes and agrees to pay. Purchaser agrees to reimburse Seller for any funds held in escrow. Purchaser to pay all taxes and insurance costs if not included in the monthly payment stated above. **SELLER UNDERSTANDS THAT THE SALE OR TRANSFER OF THE PROPERTY DESCRIBED IN THIS AGREEMENT MAY NOT RELIEVE THE SELLER OF ANY LIABILITY THAT SELLER MAY HAVE UNDER THE MORTGAGE(S) OR LAND CONTRACT(S) TO WHICH THE PROPERTY IS SUBJECT, UNLESS OTHERWISE AGREED TO BY THE LENDER OR VENDOR OR REQUIRED BY LAW OR REGULATION.**

[ ] **D. LAND CONTRACT:** The down payment of ($) Dollars and the execution of land contract, acknowledging payment of that sum and calling for the payment of the remainder of the purchase money of $ in payments of $ or more, which (SHALL) (SHALL NOT) include interest payment at the rate of percent per annum, and which (SHALL) (SHALL NOT) include prepaid taxes and insurance. The contract shall be paid in full on or before years from date of sale. Purchaser agrees to provide Seller a recent credit report acceptable to the sellers.

3. PURSUANT TO THE ABOVE IDENTIFIED TERMS OF PURCHASE, SELLERS AND PURCHASERS AGREE TO CLOSE BY (Date) 12/10/04 **BUT NOT PRIOR TO** (Date) 12/1/04 **UNLESS MUTUALLY AGREED OTHERWISE. IF SALE IS NOT CLOSED AS SET FORTH ABOVE, SELLER HAS OPTION TO DECLARE PURCHASER'S DEFAULT AND TO TERMINATE THIS AGREEMENT BY WRITTEN NOTICE TO PURCHASER.**

4. FIXTURES AND IMPROVEMENTS: All improvements and fixtures are included in the purchase price including, if now in or on the property, the following: all buildings; landscaping; lighting fixtures and their shades and bulbs; ceiling fans; drapery and curtain hardware; window coverings, shades and blinds; built-in kitchen appliances, including garbage disposal, drop-in ranges and range hood; wall to wall carpeting, if attached; all attached mirrors; all attached shelving; attached work benches; stationary laundry tubs; water softener (unless rented); water heater; incinerator; sump pump; water pump and pressure tank; heating and air conditioning equipment (window units excluded); attached humidifiers; heating units, including add-on wood stoves and wood stoves connected by flue pipe; fireplace screens; inserts and grates; fireplace doors, it attached; liquid heating and cooking fuels in tank(s) at time of transfer of possession (tanks will not be empty unless now empty); liquid heating and cooking fuel tanks if owned by Seller; TV antenna and complete rotor equipment; all support equipment for in ground pools; screens and storm windows and doors; awnings; basketball backboard and goal; mailbox; fences; detached storage buildings; underground sprinkling, including the pump; installed outdoor grills; all plantings and bulbs; garage door opener and control(s); and any and all items and fixtures permanently affixed to the property.
Exceptions:

5. TITLE: As evidence of title, Seller agrees to furnish Purchaser at sellers cost, a title commitment, issued by Centennial Title Insurance Agency, Inc, and after closing, a policy of title insurance, issued by Centennial Title Insurance Agency, Inc, in an amount not less than the purchase price, bearing date later than the acceptance hereof and insuring the title in the condition as required herein. Title Objections: If objection to the title is made, based upon a written opinion of the Purchaser's attorney that the title is not in the condition as required for performance hereunder, the Seller shall have thirty (30) days from the date he is notified in writing of the particular defects claimed, either (1) to remedy the title, or (2) if unable to remedy the title to refund the deposit in full termination of this agreement. If the Seller remedies the title within the time specified, the Purchaser agrees to complete the sale.

6. **POSSESSION:** to be given as indicated by "X" [X] immediately following closing; [ ] days after closing by 12:00 noon; subject to rights of tenants, if any. Seller agrees to pay Purchaser rent (which commences the day of closing), during time of Sellers occupancy after closing as indicated by "X" [ ] $ per day [X] at an amount prorated per day equal to Purchaser's monthly payment including principal, interest, taxes and insurance. Purchaser and Seller hereby agree to settle the above rent proration, if any, between themselves, subsequent to closing. Purchaser acknowledges responsibility of transferring all utilities the day possession is given: Further, Seller and Purchaser agree to prorate for water and sewer usage to date of possession.

6a. **OTHER PRORATIONS:** Interest rents, water/sewer bills, condominium dues and association dues shall be prorated and adjusted as of the date of closing, if applicable.

6b. At the time of possession the Seller will have the property free and clear of trash and debris.

6c. If Seller's Tenants occupy the property, then:
[ ] Seller will have the tenants vacate the property before closing
[ ] Purchaser will be assigned all Landlord rights and security deposit and rents prorated to date of closing, with Purchaser assuming Landlord rights and obligations after date of closing.

7. **TAXES:** Seller agrees to pay all taxes, fees and assessments that are a lien against the premises as of the time of closing. Further, the immediately previous December and July, if any, tax bills will be prorated as paid in advance based upon the current year of January 1st through December 31st and July 1st through June 30th respectively, unless otherwise agreed to herein. Purchaser(s) acknowledge that they are responsible for all real estate tax bills due after date of closing.

Other

8. **SELLER'S ACCEPTANCE:** Seller's signature to the written acceptance of this Purchase Agreement shall constitute a binding agreement between Purchaser and Seller, and Purchaser herewith deposits the sum of Two thousand & 00/100 ——→ Dollars ($2,000.00) in the form of Personal Check, as good will or earnest money that Purchaser will comply with the terms and conditions hereof and within the time limited therefore, which sum is to be credited on the purchase price in the event the sale is completed. In the event Seller or Purchaser refuses to complete this transaction, seller or purchaser may pursue his or her legal equitable remedies and in the event of Purchaser(s) default the deposit shall be forfeited.

9. **ACCEPTANCE TIME:** The Purchaser agrees that this offer is irrevocable until (Date) 11/3/04, at 6 AM/PM, and if it is not accepted by the Seller within that time, the deposit shall be refunded forthwith to the Purchaser and this agreement shall be null and void.

10. **PURCHASER AGREES** that he has examined the before identified property, Seller's property disclosure, if applicable and agrees to accept the same as it now is unless otherwise hereafter specified.

11. **FACSIMILE AGREEMENT:** The Purchaser(s) and the Seller (s) agree that a facsimile transmission of any original document shall have the same effect as an original. Any signature required on an original shall be completed when a facsimile copy has been signed. The parties agree that originally signed facsimile copies of documents shall be appended to the originals thereof, and given full effect as if an original

12. **THE PURCHASER AND SELLER** agree that they have read this document and understand thoroughly the contents herein and agree that there are no different or additional written or verbal understandings. The covenants herein, shall also bind the heirs, personal representatives, administrators, executors, assigns and successors of the respective parties. THE PARTIES FURTHER ACKNOWLEDGE THAT "TIME IS OF THE ESSENCE." CENTENNIAL TITLE INSURANCE AGENCY, INC. RECOMMENDS THAT YOUR ATTORNEY EXAMINE ALL PAPERS NECESSARY TO CLOSE THIS TRANSACTION. CENTENNIAL TITLE INSURANCE AGENCY, INC. FURTHER RECOMMENDS PURCHASER OBTAIN A SURVEY OF THE PROPERTY.

13. **INSPECTIONS/SERVICES:** By signing this agreement, Purchaser is representing that Purchaser is aware that inspection/services are available at a fee. The Purchaser has elected to arrange and pay for the following, as indicated by their initials, and must be completed by no later than (Date) 11/12/04 at 6 AM/PM. This transaction X IS ____ IS NOT contingent on the below initialed items. If this IS contingent, the contingencies must be removed in writing by no later than (Date) 11/15/04, at 6 AM/PM; provided, however, if contingencies are not removed in writing by the aforementioned date, property is accepted "as is" and contingencies are considered automatically removed.

Purchaser Initials ____ ____ No Inspection ____ ____ Wood Destroying Insects ____ ____ Radon

_____ _____ Well & Septic RJ SJ Home Inspection _____ _____ Other

14. DISCLOSURES REQUIRED BY LAW:

X Lead Based Paint X Sellers Disclosure _____ Land Division Act, P.A. 87 (See attachments, if any)
[Meets & Bounds]

15. OTHER PROVISIONS: Seller to pay $5,000 in prepaids & closings fees.

16. ACKNOWLEDGMENT: Purchaser, by signing this offer, further acknowledges receipt of a copy of this written offer

(Date) 11/1/2004

Richard Jones
Purchaser: Print Name

M
Marital Status

Richard Jones
Purchaser: Signature

362-82-2442
Social Security No.

Sally Jones
Purchaser: Print Name

M
Marital Status

Sally Jones
Purchaser: Signature

363-87-5212
Social Security No.

Address: 123 Primrose Lane City: Flushing State: MI Zip: 48433 Phone: 732-9399

Denise Anatouk
Witness

17. SELLER'S ACCEPTANCE: Seller's hereby accept the purchaser's offer and acknowledges receipt of a copy of this agreement on (Date) 11/1/2004, and further acknowledges receipt from Purchaser of the amount of earnest money herein before mentioned.

Sam Brown
Seller: Print Name

M
Marital Status

Sam Brown
Seller: Signature

392-43-1212
Social Security No.

Mary Brown
Seller: Print Name

M
Marital Status

Mary Brown
Seller: Signature

362-52-9349
Social Security No.

Paulette Chandrow
Witness

PERSONAL PROPERTY

IN CONNECTION WITH THE SALE OF: Address 1245 Maple St
City Grand Blanc
State Mi Zip 48439

THE FOLLOWING DESCRIBED PERSONAL PROPERTY IS INCLUDED IN THE SALE PRICE AND IS HEREBY CONVEYED TO THE PURCAHER(s) AT **NO MONETARY VALUE** or **COST**. THERE SHALL BE **NO WARRANTY** EITHER EXPRESSED OR IMPLIED.

GE Stove Model 124 Serial # 12345
Whirlpool Washer + Dryer

Paulette Chandnois — WITNESS
Sam Brown — SELLER — DATE 11/1/04
Mary Brown — SELLER — DATE 11/1/04
Denise Hnatuik — WITNESS
Sally Jones — PURCHASER — DATE 11/1/2004
Richard Jones 11/1/2004

DISCLOSURE OF INFORMATION AND ACKNOWLEDGMENT LEAD-BASED PAINT AND/OR LEAD-BASED PAINT HAZARDS

Date: 9/20/04

Our Home Located At: 1245 Maple ST. Grand Blanc Mi 48439

Was built in: 1959

SELLER: Sam Brown And Mary Brown

BUYER: Richard Jones And Sally Jones

Lead Warning Statement:

Every purchaser of any interest in residential real property on which a residential dwelling was built prior to 1978 is notified that such property may present exposure to lead from lead-based paint that may place young children at risk of developing lead poisoning. Lead poisoning in young children may produce permanent neurological damage, including learning disabilities, reduced intelligence quotient, behavioral problems and impaired memory. Lead poisoning also poses a particular risk to pregnant women. The seller of any interest in residential real property is required to provide the buyer with any information on lead-based paint hazards. A risk assessment or inspection for possible lead-based paint hazards is recommended prior to purchase.

NOTE: YOU DO NOT HAVE TO FILL OUT, THE REMAINDER OF THIS FORM IF THE HOUSING BEING LISTED OR SOLD WAS BUILT IN 1978 OR AFTER

Seller's Disclosure (initial)

(a) Presence of lead-based paint and/or lead-based paint hazards (check one below:)

_____ Known lead-based paint and/or lead-based paint hazards are present in the housing
Explain:

SB MB Seller has no knowledge of lead-based paint and/or lead-based paint hazards in the housing

(b) Records and Reports available to the seller (check one below):

_____ Seller has provided the purchaser with all available records and reports pertaining to lead-based paint and/or lead base hazards in the housing (list documents below):

SB MB Seller has no reports or records pertaining to lead-based paint and/or lead-based paint hazards in the housing

Purchaser's Acknowledgment (initial)

SJ RJ (c) Purchaser has received copies of all information listed above.

SJ RJ (d) Purchaser has received the pamphlet ***Protect Your Family From Lead in Your Home***

(e) Purchaser has (check one below):

____ Received a 10-day opportunity (or mutually agreed upon period) to conduct a risk assessment or inspection of the presence of lead-based paint or lead-based paint hazards, OR

SJ RJ Waived the opportunity to conduct a risk assessment or inspection for the presence of lead-based paint and/or lead-based paint hazards.

Agent's Acknowledgment (initial)

PC (f) Agent has informed the seller of the seller's obligations under **42 U.S.C. 4852 d** and is aware of his/her responsibility to ensure compliance.

Certification of Accuracy

The following parties have reviewed the information above and certify, to the best of their knowledge, that the information they have provided is true and accurate.

Seller Sam Brown **Date** 9-20-04

Seller Mary Brown **Date** 9-20-04

Purchaser Sally Jones **Date** 11/01/04

Purchaser Richard Jones **Date** 11/01/04

Seller's Agent Paulette Chambrois **Date** 11-01-04

Purchaser's Agent Denise Hnatiuk **Date** 11/1/2004

Note: Intact lead-based paint that is in good condition is not necessarily a hazard. See EPA Pamphlet *Protect Your Family From Lead in Your Home* for more information.

Seller's Disclosure Statement

Property Address: 1245 Maple St

City: Grand Blanc, MI., Zip: 48433

Purpose of Statement: (1) This statement is a disclosure of the condition of the property in compliance with the Seller Disclosure Act, effective January 8, 1994. (2) This statement is a disclosure of the condition and information concerning the property, known by the Seller. Unless otherwise advised, the Seller does not possess any expertise in construction, architecture, engineering or any other specific area related to the construction or condition of the improvements on the property or the land. Also unless otherwise advised, the Seller has not conducted any inspection of generally inaccessible areas such as the foundation or roof. This statement is not a warranty of any kind by the Seller or by any Agent representing the Seller in this transaction and is not a substitute for any inspections or warranties the Buyer may wish to obtain.

Seller's Disclosure: The Seller discloses the following information with the knowledge that even though this is not a warranty, the Seller specifically makes the following representations based on the Seller's knowledge at the signing of this document. Upon receiving this statement from the Seller, the Seller's Agent is required to provide a copy to the Buyer or the Agent of the Buyer. The Seller authorizes its Agent(s) to provide a copy of this statement to any prospective Buyer in connection with any actual or anticipated sale of property. The following are representations made solely by the Seller and are not the representations of the Seller's Agent(s), if any. This information is a disclosure only and is not intended to be part of any contract between Buyer and Seller.

Instructions to the Seller: (1) Answer ALL questions. (2) Report known conditions affecting the property. (3) Attach additional pages with your signature if additional space is required. (4) Complete this form yourself. (5) If some items do not apply to your property, check N/A (non-applicable). If you do not know the facts, check UNKNOWN EFFECTIVE JANUARY 8, 1994, FAILURE TO PROVIDE A PURCHASER WITH A SIGNED DISCLOSURE STATEMENT WILL ENABLE PURCHASER TO TERMINATE AN OTHERWISE BINDING PURCHASE AGREEMENT.

Appliances/Systems/Services: The items below are in working order:

	Yes	No	Unknown	N/A
Range/oven	✓			
Dishwasher				✓
Refrigerator				✓
Hood/fan	✓			
Disposal	✓			
TV antenna, TV rotor & controls				✓
Electrical System	✓			
Garage door opener & remote control	✓			
Alarm system				✓
Intercom				✓
Central vacuum				✓
Attic fan	✓			
Pool heater, wall liner & equipment				✓
Microwave				✓
Trash compactor				✓
Ceiling fan	✓			
Sauna/hot tub				✓

	Yes	No	Unknown	N/A
Lawn sprinkler system				✓
Water heater	✓			
Plumbing System	✓			
Water Softener/ conditioner				✓
Well & Pump				✓
Septic tank & drain field				✓
Sump Pump				✓
City Water System	✓			
City Sewer System	✓			
Central air conditioner	✓			
Central heat system	✓			
Furnace	✓			
Humidifier			✓	
Electronic air filter				✓
Solar heating system				✓
Fireplace & chimney	✓			
Wood burning system				✓

Explanations (attach additional sheets, if necessary):

UNLESS OTHERWISE AGREED, ALL HOUSEHOLD APPLIANCES ARE SOLD IN WORKING ORDER EXCEPT AS NOTED, WITHOUT WARRANTY BEYOND DATE OF CLOSING.

Property conditions, improvements & additional information:

1. **Basement:** Has there been evidence of water? yes X no ____
If yes, please explain: ____

2. **Insulation:** Describe, if known: ____
Urea Formaldehyde foam insulation (UFFI) is installed? unknown____ yes____ no X

3. **Roof:** Leaks? yes____ no X
Approximate age, if known: Roof 2yrs old

4. **Well:** Type of well (depth/diameter), age and repair history, if known: Na
Has the water been tested? yes____ no ____
If yes, date of last report/results: ____

5. **Septic tanks/drain fields:** Condition, if known: Na

6. **Heating system:** Type/approximate age: Gas furnace 3yrs old

7. **Plumbing system:** Type: copper X galvanized X other ____
Any known problems? All plumbing has been upgraded with exception of Hobby Room.

8. **Electrical system:** Any known problems? none

9. **History of infestation,** if any,: (termites, carpenter ants, etc.) None

10. **Environmental problems:** Substances, materials or products which may be an environmental hazard such as, but not limited to, asbestos, radon gas, formaldehyde, lead-based paint, fuel or chemical storage tanks and contaminated soil on the property.
unknown ____ yes ____ no X
If yes, please explain: ____

Other items: Are you aware of any of the following:

1. Features of the property shared in common with adjoining landowners, such as walls, fences, roads, driveways or other features whose use or responsibility for maintenance may have an effect on the property?
unknown ____ yes ____ no X
2. Any encroachments, easements, zoning violations or nonconforming uses?
unknown ____ yes ____ no X
3. Any "common areas" (facilities like pools, tennis courts, walkways or other areas co-owned with others) or a homeowners association which has any authority over the property?
unknown ____ yes ____ no X
4. Structural modification, alterations or repairs made without necessary permits or licensed contractors?
unknown ____ yes ____ no X
5. Setting, flooding, drainage, structural or grading problems?
unknown ____ yes ____ no X
6. Major damage to the property from fire, wind, floods or landslides?
unknown ____ yes ____ no X
7. Any underground storage tanks? unknown ____ yes ____ no X
8. Farm or farm operation in the vicinity; or proximity to a landfill, airport, shooting range, etc?
unknown ____ yes ____ no X

If the answer to any of these questions is yes, please explain. Attach additional sheets, if necessary:

The most recent State Equalized Valuation of the property provided by the local taxing unit to the Seller was $ 60,000 as of 12/30/03 (date).

The Seller has lived in the residence on the property from 3/1/82 (date) to present (date).

The Seller has owned the property since 3/1/82 (date) and makes representation only since that date.

The Seller has indicated above the history and condition of all items based on that information known to the Seller. If any changes occur in the structural/mechanical/appliance systems of this property from the date of this form to the date of closing, Seller will immediately disclose the changes to Buyer. In no event shall the parties hold the Broker liable for any representations not directly made by the Broker or Broker's Agent.

Seller certifies that the information in this statement is true and correct to the best of the Seller's knowledge as of the date of seller's signature.

BUYER SHOULD OBTAIN PROFESSIONAL ADVICE AND INSPECTIONS OF THE PROPERTY TO MORE FULLY DETERMINE THE CONDITION OF THE PROPERTY.

Seller Sam Brown Date 9-20-04

Seller Mary Brown Date 9-20-04

Buyer has read and acknowledges receipt of this statement.

Buyer Sally Jones Date 11/01/04 Time 3 45 pm

Buyer Richard Jones Date 11/01/04 Time 345 pm

LESSON #19: HOME INSPECTOR INTERVIEW

Today we're having the opportunity of interviewing Tim Cook of Pillar to Post Home Inspections of Flint, Michigan. (Phone: 810-577-3502)

Dick Smith (DS): Tim, thank you very much for this opportunity. First of all, could you give us your name and company?

Tim Cook (TC): The company is Pillar to Post Professional Home Inspections. My name is Tim Cook.

DS: Are you licensed, or do you belong to any type of association such as a national association of inspectors?

TC: In the state of Michigan there is no licensing for home inspections. There are some things going on right now within the legislature where hopefully they will be doing licensing, but right now there is no licensing. I am a Certified Home Inspector through the international franchise that I own, Pillar to Post down in Florida and Canada, and I am also a member of the American

Society of Home Inspectors (ASHI), and there are a couple of the others that we're considering joining.

DS: Obviously you had to go through training and education to get into those organizations. Do you also have to go through ongoing training and continuing education for that?

TC: Yes sir, you do.

DS: How much ... is that on a yearly basis?

TC: It's by credit. You have to get a certain number of credits per year and as far as for the franchise, the training is yearly and it's mandatory. You must go to or basically you cannot have a franchise.

DS: And you mentioned that right now in Michigan there is no licensing of home inspectors.

TC: Yes, that's true.

DS: What would you describe about your personality that makes you an easy home inspector to deal with?

TC: Well, I'm honest and I basically will call it like I see it as far as performing a home inspection. And also I've been around people all of my life so I am a people type of person, and that's very important because you're going to be dealing with a wide variety of people.

DS: A couple of things I've noticed in dealing with you is that you seem to be a pretty patient person and able to communicate verbally and also in a report fashion. Would that be a pretty good analysis of your personality?

TC: Yes. In this particular business, communication is everything.

DS: Okay. How long have you been in the home inspection business, Tim?

TC: Nearly five years.

DS: Has this been just in the Michigan area?

TC: Yes sir.

DS: How long have you actually lived in the Michigan area? Have you lived and worked here for some time?

TC: Yes. Actually I was born in Flint, Michigan and I still live here.

DS: Oh, so you're a native of this area then, which gives you lot of background information on the particular situations and problems of the real estate and housing market here. What would be a normal volume that a home inspector would do in a week or a month or a day or a year? I've heard some outrageous claims of people saying they're doing 10 home inspections in a day, or something. Is that unrealistic, or what would be reasonable volume that a home inspector would do?

TC: Ten home inspections in a day would be unrealistic, it would be impossible ... 10 home inspections in one day, one working day, if you put in even 12 hours ... and do it properly. An average home inspection is going to take you two to two and a half hours, that would be for an average size home, that would be around 1,400 square feet with a basement. Generally two a day is comfortable, three a day is kind of on the heavy side. If you do four a day you're really pushing yourself. If you were to do five in a day, which I've done before in a bind, it's physically and mentally exhausting. Around 400 to 500 home inspections a year, in my personal opinion, would be a maximum one inspector can do by himself.

DS: What other related experience do you have, like in construction or remodeling or real estate? What background would you have in any of those areas?

TC: Well, I actually as a youngster started out being mechanical. My dad always gave me tools to play with, even when I was just a couple of years old, and classes I had in high school, auto mechanics and things like that, added to that. In machine shop I was always doing mechanical things. When I was a senior in high school I began a job doing building maintenance in a large apartment complex, so you know I was around everything, like plumbing, heating, electrical, mechanical, construction, carpentry, and also after I did that for several years I decided I wanted to move up and I went to one of the local universities and I did receive a degree in refrigeration, heating and air conditioning, an associates degree. And I pursued that field for some time. I was actually in the houses a lot, because when I got out of college I started my own company doing residential refrigeration, so I was dealing with the public a lot. And then I gradually moved up into supermarket refrigeration, doing plumbing and heating, refrigeration, air conditioning and some controls and what not, again dealing with mechanical and things that are in a house, but it did expose me to the public tremendously, you know with problems and making repairs. There were other large contractors that I have worked for doing similar jobs, and I really believe that background really helped me a lot in doing the home inspection industry.

DS: Why should buyers get a professional home inspection done? What is the biggest reason?

TC: I would say the biggest reason is that you want to know what you're purchasing. Even though you may have an aunt or an uncle, or somebody that you feel is knowledgeable in that area, they don't do it every day and they do not see things that professional home inspectors see. They don't know exactly what to look for. And that's of course not putting down your uncle, it's just that that's not his full-time career. There could be anything from a sump-pump not working to a leaky roof and holes in the attic that in the purchaser's mind would make it worthwhile for him to get a home inspection.

DS: Do you identify only the immediate problems? What I'm thinking is like when an FHA appraisal is done, the appraiser is required to indicate if a roof has a minimum of a 2-year life remaining but nothing more than that. Would you be going into detail and to indicating that the roof may have to be replaced in the near future, such as four or five years?

TC: Yes, generally we will, if it's that close to the end of its life expectancy, we will rate the roof either as typical, middle, and exceeded, or if there's an area of the roof that's in bad condition, that would also be documented.

DS: Do you estimate repair costs on some of these items?

TC: We will, somewhat. But many repairs, honestly, you're not going to be able to tell until you get a contractor in there and go into some great detail as to what is going to need to be done.

DS: What's the basic cost of a home inspection? Is it based on the size of the house or the number of outbuildings?

TC: Generally the outbuilding aren't included. If they want them, we'll of course inspect them, but as a rule we don't include outbuildings. The home inspections begin at $260 to $275 and that would cover up to a 2,000-square-foot house.

DS: And then obviously if a person got into a huge mansion, a 5,000 square foot house, they're going to have to pay more because you're going to have to spend more time there.

TC: Yes, 5,000, 7,000, 8,000-square-foot houses, they can take one home inspector all day, depending on the way it's set up.

DS: Are there additional tests that you perform in addition to the basic home inspection, and I'm wondering how expensive they may be. On the additional tests, here's the things that are running through my mind. Are there tests for termite inspections too?

TC: Yes, for all wood destroying insects, are grouped into one inspection. A lot of people will call them a pest inspection. But it's termites, carpenter ants, power post beetles, wood-boring bees, any wood destroying insects.

DS: How about well tests? There are a lot of areas in this county, where there still are private wells. Do you do those that would test for the quality and volume of the flow?

TC: Yes sir, we do well testing. We actually include functional flow with the home inspection, so as far as if the well is functioning properly, we do include that in our home inspection. Water quality testing, we have a wide variety of tests that we can perform from a basic analysis, with nitrates and bacteria right through to arsenic and tripidity, sodium, we can even go so far as having water tested for VOCs or volatile organic compounds

DS: How about septic? Are there septic tests done too, Tim?

TC: Yes sir. We do perform septic evaluations. Again anywhere from a basic evaluation to a complete deluxe evaluation, where risers are installed to make it easier to get to the septic tank, and observation ports installed in the drain field.

DS: That would be a pretty thorough and expensive test, I would imagine.

TC: It's not actually as much as what you might think. Even to include pumping the tank, you're still looking at well under $500 for that septic evaluation.

DS: Whereas some of these engineered septic systems now, they can run anywhere from $10,000 to $15,000, so it might be a very good investment before getting into a big, big investment.

TC: Yes sir.

DS: How about radon? Do you do any testing for that or is there any on-site equipment for something like that?

TC: Yes sir, we do use continuous radon monitors, which is a type of equipment where you place it in the basement of the home if there is a basement, and we leave it there for 48 hours minimum, and we do have an on-site report that we print out right on site as far as radon levels.

DS: How about mold testing? Is that something that's done?

TC: Yes sir, we also do complete mold evaluation, where the house has a visual inspection for molds and if there's any found we will take a sample and send it off for EPA certified tests. We also will do indoor air quality testing if necessary to find out what airborne molds are in the air. We can also do a test similar to that for bacteria.

DS: Many years ago there was insulation called UFFI. Are there any tests done for that? That's the urea foam insulation. I'm just wondering if that's something that is of particular concern anymore.

TC: Generally it's not, because the gases that were in that foam have already dissipated by now. So most of the time when I run into an issue like that, there is a type of test that can be done to verify it, but generally that's not an issue anymore.

DS: How about asbestos testing? Is there anything like that, or is that just a very remote thing? There used to be a lot of wrapping around the old octopus-type furnaces, you know in those old 100-year-old homes and so forth, with the asbestos wrapped around it, but obviously you don't see a lot of those anymore, I would imagine.

TC: No, we do asbestos testing all the time, from tiles right through the insulation.

DS: Is it true that right now, under FHA financed sales, that home inspection costs are rolled into the closing, so basically these are no out-of-pocket costs for the home buyer?

TC: Yes sir. FHA will allow up to I believe it's $300 if they haven't raised it, to be rolled into the closing.

DS: Are inspections used as a negotiating tool? I don't know if you're put in the middle of the negotiations, or is that something, you know, you do your thing, or do people use the report as a negotiating tool, or maybe just use it to walk away from a deal?

TC: Well, to make it clear, the way the purchase agreement is set up in the state of Michigan, the purchaser has X number of days to get a home inspection after they sign the purchase agreement, whatever the REALTOR® puts in there, five, seven to 10 is common. Very seldom will we have more than 10 days to give a home inspection after the purchaser signs the purchase agreement. The purchase agreement is contingent on an acceptable home inspection in the purchaser's eyes, okay? So is it a negotiating tool? It shouldn't be, unless we find a major deficiency.

DS: So as you say, it's basically the buyer accepting the property and accepting the report accordingly, before he completes the sale, is what it amounts to.

TC: That's right.

DS: Bankers and real estate agents often tell me that the three biggest areas of buyer complaints they get after a sale are furnace problems, leaky roofs, and wet basements. How can these areas be checked out, starting with number one, furnace problems?

TC: Well as for the furnace, we do a very thorough inspection of the furnace, from the furnace filter right through to running the furnace, checking mechanical operation, and actually physically seeing if there is any carbon monoxide being discharged out of the furnace with the carbon monoxide detector. The home inspection is not an exhaustive inspection, so the furnace is not disassembled to see if there are any cracks in the heat exchanger, but we do test for carbon monoxide, which would be the leading indicator if there were any cracks.

DS: Oh, I see. How about leaky roofs? How are those checked out?

TC: Well, the roof is generally walked, unless it is too tall or too steep, and in that case it's looked at from the roof's edge or with binoculars, so the roof gets a thorough going over from the outside. And then on the inside, the roof is looked at from the attic. So if there's any leaks, generally they're going to be revealed.

DS: Okay. So you do it from the outside and the inside both.

TC: Yes sir.

DS: How about wet basements? How are those addressed?

TC: Well the house is looked at completely, so we address even landscaping, which could be an issue in drainage away from the house, so if the land is sloping toward the house or whatever the case may be, that is documented. Gutters are inspected, so if they're plugged and full of leaves, or there's no extension from the downspout, all those types of things are noted, documented, and recommendations are made. If there's any cracking of the foundation, if there are any floor drains that possibly are plugged up, if the sump-pump is just discharging outside the wall, things like that ... there's a wide variety of things that could lead to a leaky basement.

DS: Do you ever take photos to document these things, or do people specifically ask you to take photos, or do you do that on your own?

TC: No, we do have a deluxe inspection where we can take photos and insert them in the inspection report, or for documentation if there is a major deficiency as we talked about previously. Generally we will take a digital photo of it.

DS: I heard you give a recent radio interview telling about the more common defects that you find in your inspections. I just wondered if maybe I could mention some of those and you could just comment on them a little bit. You mentioned Number One is a cracked heat exchanger. What is it, and how is that normally checked?

TC: Okay, that goes right in with what we were just talking about as far as the furnace inspection. The heat exchanger is the part of the furnace where the flames are, okay? So the burners burn up inside the heat exchanger and the gases from that combustion go directly outside, okay? So if there's a crack in that heat exchanger and the furnace is not burning 100 percent efficiently, which generally they're not, there will be carbon monoxide created and it could leak through that crack and go into the house, because on the outside of the heat exchanger is where we pick up the heat with a fan to blow into the house.

DS: Okay, so with your detection or monitor device you're picking that up, is that correct?

TC: Yes sir. We use Monoxor Three, made by Bacarac Corporation, which is the state-of-the-art carbon monoxide detector.

DS: I've heard of some people actually doing a visual inspection of the heat exchanger, but with the poor lighting conditions and so forth I would think there would be a good possibility of overlooking that, just doing a visual inspection sometimes.

TC: Yes. You know, if you can see anything visual on the front of the furnace, you know, definitely we will be shining our lights looking in there, but as far as using a fluoroscope or anything like that in the furnace compartment, generally unless you disassemble the furnace and physically look at it, you're only looking at a portion of it.

DS: Okay. How about leaking water heaters? That was something that you talked about when I heard the interview.

TC: A water heater can rust out and leak through on the bottom or the top. If there are no dielectric unions installed on them they can actually corrode out. There's pressure relief valves on water heaters that can leak and drip. There are also drain valves that can leak. That is definitely another issue.

DS: I know we talked briefly about foundation deficiencies and you mentioned that you're checking them on the inside and the outside, and we talked about negative drainage. So you're looking in back of the bushes and the landscaping, too.

What about sump-pumps? I know you talked about that. It sounds like a minor issue, but obviously if it comes to flooding the basement, it's not a minor issue. One of the things you mentioned was it can be as minor as not having the float set properly on a sump-pump, and just checking that.

TC: Sump-pumps are actually a major issue.

DS: Are they really?

TC: They are much overlooked by most people. As you said, if a sump-pump malfunctions you could end up with a wet basement, and with a wet basement you could end up with a mold issue, so sump-pump function is actually a top priority in a basement. Backup sump-pumps are always recommended in the event the main sump-pump fails, and low level settings are very critical, because if they leave standing water in the drain tiles, they could be asking for more wet basements and even structural problems.

DS: So you actually check them to make sure they're working then, is what you're doing. How about ground fault circuit interrupters? Maybe you could just briefly tell me what they are, and maybe explain the wet areas or the areas where there should be ground fault circuit interrupters.

TC: Yes sir. Ground fault circuit interrupter protectors are the reset-style electrical outlets that are placed within six feet of any potential wet area. They're designed to trip in the event that a human begins to become shocked, so theoretically the way they work is they should trip before we're even shocked. Of course the reason is if Mom's making a cake in the kitchen and she flips her electric mixer into a sink of water, we want that power shut off before she can get electrocuted.

DS: Right. What areas of the house should they be in? I know you mentioned six feet from a water source. Would that include like a kitchen, bathroom, laundry, basement, porches, wood decks, outside and garage areas?

TC: Yes sir, exactly. Outside within eight feet of the ground, and inside within six feet of any sink, which could mean laundry, kitchen, bath, you know, areas like that.

DS: When we're talking about electrical problems, do you actually disassemble or look inside the fuse or breaker box? How is that inspection done?

TC: Yes sir, we will pull the electrical panel cover whenever possible, which is 90 percent of the time, and we will physically look at where the wires terminate into the circuit breakers or fuses. We're looking for things like scorching if there were bad connections, if the wire is aluminum or copper, or maybe if it's an old house with knob and tube wiring, we want to make sure there's a ground connected to it, and there's many other things you can see as far as the workmanship when you pull the panel cover.

DS: Okay. Do you check for proper wire size, or is that something that an electrician should be doing?

TC: No, that is included in the home inspection.

DS: I've heard the phrase about "double tapping" and what exactly is double tapping?

TC: That's where more than one wire is connected to one circuit breaker. So you're basically going to set yourself up for nuisance trips if you have that much on one circuit. Usually what's going to be needed is another circuit breaker should be added, so that the wires can be moved to their own circuit breakers.

DS: You mentioned aluminum wiring. Why is that important that you would be checking for aluminum wiring?

TC: Well, if aluminum wiring is present in the house, the buyer definitely needs to know that. With aluminum you need to have proper receptacle plugs, which is outlets, connected to it, so they are designed just for aluminum wiring, and maintenance is recommended every few years when you have aluminum wiring at these connections. There's a special paste that's used to help the connection with heat transfer and to reduce the chance of arcing or shorts.

DS: I've even heard in an electrical class that a person should go around every year or two and tighten up all the wiring on their outlets, because it will gradually loosen up.

TC: That's correct. From expansion and contraction.

DS: You mentioned that when you're checking the furnace you're even checking the air filters, and how about on the blower motor? Are you checking for dust and dirt on the blower motors, too?

TC: Yes sir. That is looked at. That and if the ductwork is very dirty, that would be documented also. The air conditioning is also tested for proper temperature difference across the air conditioning coil.

DS: Would a furnace man be able to do any evaluation, like projecting what it would cost yearly or determining the indoor quality? Is that something that a furnace man would do rather than a home inspector?

TC: Not generally, no.

DS: And it was also mentioned in the previous interview that a lot of people have humidifiers attached to the furnace, and I guess it would just be part of your inspection to be seeing if it actually is functional. Would that be correct?

TC: Yes sir, we do. We do test the humidifiers. We also will be looking at the humidifier element to make sure that it is intact and not in need of replacement.

DS: One of the things I heard you mention in regards to plumbing is sometimes homeowners will use flex connections rather than copper on water heaters, which obviously can break and flood a basement. I'd never heard or seen such a thing. Do you run into that very often?

TC: Yes sir, I have. I've heard stories about these particular flex connectors that you and I were talking about. They are generally used for a handyman do-it-yourselfer, where someone replaces a water heater and they don't know how to do piping, so the flex connector can eliminate the need of them having to put any 90 degree elbows or whatever it may be on the heater, but we have had reports of those splitting, so we don't recommend them.

DS: Do you ever use levels on the floors of a house? I've heard of home inspectors carrying them. Do you do that sort of thing?

TC: Well, it kind of depends on the home. If the floor is un-level it's going to be documented. As far as putting a level on the floor or rolling a marble across it, now most of the time that's not going to be necessary. If the floor is un-level, generally it's going to be obvious. If it's a new build and it's un-level, then we would be coming in and putting a level on it.

DS: How about safety issues such as handrails or rails on porches and steps, and safety reverse operators on garage doors? Do you make note of those sort of things?

TC: Yes sir, we do. Garage doors openers are tested for proper function and the handrails definitely are recommended and that issue is documented all the way through the entire house. Handrails on porches, spindle spacing, all of those issues are attended to.

DS: When you mention spindle spacing, I guess you're talking about the distance so that a youngster wouldn't be able to stick their head in there and hang themselves. Is that what you're talking about?

TC: Yes sir.

DS: A lot of people won't think of that, but it can be a real tragedy if they do that. How about testing of windows and doors? Is that done on a sample basis, or do you check all of them to see if they open and latch properly?

TC: It's a random basis. It depends on the house again. If it's a new build, generally we're going to check every single one of them.

DS: How about doing any humidity tests inside of a structure? Do you do anything like that, or is there such a test?

TC: You could do a humidity test in a structure if there is something that would indicate that there was a problem with moisture and humidity, but generally that is not included in the home inspection. That would be a more invasive test.

DS: Does it matter what time of the day or the season that an inspection is done? Does that kind of flavor the whole inspection?

TC: Well, we do them all year long and our inspections we've done as early as 6 in the morning or as late as an hour before it gets dark. So February or August, it does make a little bit of a difference because we want to have enough light to see the outside of the house to begin with, and you know wintertime, roofs are concealed by snow cover. There are different limitations for different times of the year, but obviously people can't wait 'til summer to buy a house.

DS: I've heard in other areas of the country there's some big challenges, and I'll just run these by you. Obviously you said most of your experience has been here in Michigan, but I've heard about fire ants, especially in some of the southern states and Virginia, and snakes and scorpions, mice, termites, earthquake design, mudslide problems, and even flooding problems. Are those the type of things that I guess would just be addressed on a regional to regional basis by home inspectors?

TC: Yes sir, but again the house placement, even here in Michigan, we do have some areas that are low, some areas that are high, if the house is built into a hill or the house is down on a lower level towards a swamp, all those areas are looked at when you first begin a home inspection.

DS: So you're looking at the orientation of the house on the property, even probably which way it situates to the sun or to the south or to the east to get the sun exposure to the north or whatever. So you're taking all of that into consideration then.

TC: That is correct.

DS: What would be a very brief overview of your routine? What do you do when you do a home inspection? Do you start any particular place, or I'm just wondering if you have an organized routine, or do you just go from here to there to whatever?

TC: No, it's very systematic, and generally it's going to be that way through every home inspection, the same way. We begin the home inspection on the exterior, then we would come inside and begin on the lower level if there is one, and work our way all the way up through the house. So in the basement we would be doing all the mechanical downstairs, and then work our way up through the whole house and end up in the attic.

DS: So you would almost be looking at the house from the way that it was built in the beginning then, from the ground up?

TC: Yes sir.

DS: Here are just some additional questions, and I think you've answered some of them. Number one, I was just wondering if you test the electrical outlets? Do you actually put a tester in there to see the polarity on them, if they're wired correctly?

TC: Yes sir, we do a random check of the electrical outlets for proper polarity, reverse ground, open neutral, etc.

DS: You already mentioned the orientation on the property, so we don't need to talk about that, and the general lay of the land. How about adjacent trees? Are those taken into consideration, if they would do damage to roofs or foundations or sidewalks or driveways?

TC: Yes sir, that would go into the landscaping page, like trimming trees back away from the home. That's definitely a big issue.

DS: How about checking or probing the soffits or checking caulking around windows and so forth? Is that something that's done?

TC: Generally as I've said it's not an exhaustive inspection, but if there is rot we will probe it to see if it is indeed soft, and if there is loose caulking that would be documented, and if re-caulking would be necessary.

DS: You mentioned that you look behind the bushes and the landscaping where you can. What about underground storage tanks, like underground fuel oil tanks? Is that something you would make note of or would check, or how do you address something like that?

TC: Well, if there is any evidence that there's something there, we would document it and recommend further investigation, but if there's no evidence, obviously there would be no way to know that.

DS: And we were talking about the cracking of masonry and basement walls. I understand there are different types, like step cracking and horizontal cracking. Maybe you can just tell me what's the difference, and what's the one to be most concerned about.

TC: Okay. It's not really uncommon here in Michigan to have some step cracking on occasion on basement walls, and generally that's going to be due to inadequate drainage away from the house, as we discussed landscaping, downspouts, gutters, things like that. Most of the time those kinds of cracks can be repaired. When they're an issue is when they start leaking.

DS: So they would obviously look like a step of stair steps on a wall, then.

TC: Yes sir, and providing that that step crack did not have any shifting in it where the blocks were actually moving from their original location. Where an issue comes in is when you get horizontal cracks, long cracks from left to right, and the wall begins to bow. That could be a major structural issue where the wall may even need to be completely rebuilt.

DS: Wow. So that's the thing to be looking out for. How about chipping or flaking paint? Is that a major item, both on the inside and the outside, or do you just make note of that?

TC: Well it is noted, but in an older home it can be a major item with the fact that back then many houses were painted with lead paint, and if children are moving into the house, the buyer needs to know that.

DS: How about fogging up of insulated glass windows? Is that something that's noted or recommended for replacement or repair?

TC: Yes sir. Every bedroom, every room in the entire house is documented so if there are any windows that have broken thermal seals, that would be documented and recommendations would be made for repair.

DS: Probably you would make note on settling or cracking of lentils by windows or door areas -- that would be the support member up above them, for people who aren't aware of what a lentil is -- but I would imagine that would be a major foundation concern or something to be checked out further then.

TC: Yes it would.

DS: Along with probably, just as you say, the bowing of walls and that sort of thing. One of the things that I've run into personally at my house, with chimneys obviously it would be a big concern if they're leaning and that would be something I'm sure you would check on, but many times there are varmints that get into these ... we have a lot of raccoons ... do you make note if there's a lack of chimney guards or things like that to keep out a lot of the pests?

TC: Yes, we do recommend ... actually they call many of those spark arresters for chimneys to keep the sparks from flying out, but what they do is keep the pests from coming in, and we do recommend those many times. We have found raccoons in fireplaces during our inspections.

DS: Oh, gee. That's no fun! And you mentioned that you check also the gutters and downspouts. How about on the roof and roof vents, do you check to see if there are actually vents up, so there is proper circulation/ventilation up there?

TC: Yes sir. Insulation, ventilation, all those areas are documented and recommendations made.

DS: One thing that a lot of people don't realize is that with an attached garage the garage floor actually should be lower than the house so that the gas fumes do not seep down into the house. I've actually seen a couple of houses where the garage floor has been higher than the house. In my opinion, that's a real serious safety issue. Is that something that you've run into, with the idea that the gas fumes from a car could actually seep down into a house?

TC: Yes sir, we run across that. We also have seen them where there would be a basement entry from the garage into the home with actual stairs from the garage going down into the home which would just allow the carbon monoxide to basically fall down into the living area.

DS: Right. And obviously, with the presence of a water heater and a flame, that could be a disastrous situation. Do you check any appliances, Tim, like dishwashers or garbage disposals or jet tubs or ovens?

TC: Yes sir, we check all of those, including the refrigerator.

DS: So you would actually turn them on then?

TC: Generally we want them running at the time of the inspection.

DS: Okay. How about leaking shower pans? That seems to be a problem with upstairs showers in a lot of the 30- and 40-year-old houses because they start to give out and leak down in the first floor. Is that something that you've found fairly often?

TC: Yes, we've found that quite often, we've even found leaking shower pans in new builds.

DS: Oh really? I'll be darned. How about fireplaces? Do you look down the flue? How are those checked out?

TC: If there is access to the top of the chimney, depending on the pitch of the roof, we will look down them, the entire chimney is documented, the fireplace, firebricks, hearth, fascia, everything is documented on the fireplace that is visually available to inspect.

DS: Wow! How about looking under the sinks? I would imagine you would probably do that to see if there's any leakage or floors rotting or anything under there, or cabinetry rotting.

TC: Yes sir, and also improper piping is noted, if that's the case.

DS: I've also seen some toilets in houses that were so wobbly that it looked unsafe for anybody to even use them, to sit on the toilet. Is that something that is just a normal part of the inspection?

TC: Yes it is.

DS: And you mentioned that you check the attics on the outside and the inside. Probably one of the big areas of leakage would be any pipe protrusions that would come through there. Is that where you find a lot of problems?

TC: Yes, we've seen everywhere from plumbing stacks with torn roof boots to flashing around chimneys, and cases where there's just been a manufacturer's defect in the shingles, and the roof has begun to leak.

DS: Do you check to see if there is insulation and how much there might be in a ceiling area?

TC: Yes sir, we do the type and the amount documented on every report.

DS: When you're checking some of the basement areas, is there a big red flag that goes up when you see freshly cleaned and freshly painted basements in areas that haven't been maintained and so forth? My meaning is that all of a sudden there is a lot of maintenance and care given to the basement, and it makes you wonder why somebody is paying all that attention, unless there has been a serious problem. Is that something that would be noted on the report? Obviously you're not a clairvoyant to know what went on before you got there, but do you see that type of situation?

TC: Well, we do see it and it is documented whenever there's fresh paint in the basement on the walls or the floor. We do document that. But generally we will find high moisture levels if someone is trying to keep it concealed.

DS: The same thing if there are stacked boxes or shelving or paneling that you can't really even see behind those in a basement to know what's going on.

TC: Yes. Excessive stored items would be documented also.

DS: Do you check for the age on a water heater, would that come from the identification plate?

TC: Yes sir, the age is documented, and safety devices as far as pressure relief, if there is no di-electric unions, flue pipe connection, all those areas are documented.

DS: So would you, on a water heater, turn the thermostat up and down to see if it operates?

TC: Yes sir.

DS: And would you look inside the heating chamber on the water heater also?

TC: Yes.

DS: I guess just in the basement area, or some of the general areas you would really be checking out would be for staining or rotting or pest infiltration or asbestos I guess would be the main big areas of concern down in the basement. With new built houses and houses under construction, do you ever do any progress inspections while that house is being built?

TC: Yes sir, we do. We do what is called a pre-concealment inspection where from the time the house is built we make a couple of visits over to the home. We will do an inspection and take photographs before the drywall is up, and then we will come in after the drywall is up and all the appliances are installed and we will complete the home inspection.

DS: Okay. So you would be checking for things like nailing patterns and the general workmanship there, and if they are complying with the plans and specs then, I take it.

TC: Yes.

DS: And one of the big issues I've heard horror stories about is when a basement is put in, checking before the back filling, I've heard of everything from beer cans to roadway signs being put down there and then filled over. I mean I've heard of some really weird, weird stuff, because basically nobody checked them, or the government inspector was too late or sat out in his car from the street and never checked anything.

TC: That is definitely an issue, and it is just great when a homeowner can get a pre-concealment inspection and have somebody basically watching as his house is built.

DS: Well, basically, what is the advantage of using you, Tim?

TC: Well I do I think have one of the most thorough home inspections in the area. We have a 1,600-item checklist that we use to perform all of our home inspections, but I think what my clients would tell you is that I'm honest, and I'm going to tell you that to the best of my knowledge what you're purchasing, and we're not going to sugarcoat anything, yet we're not going to alarm you for no reason either.

DS: Have you ever considered doing a photograph or videotaping on a roof or in a crawl space so that people can see a problem area if they are not able to be there?

TC: Yes sir, we actually have done that when we've been in a crawl space where the buyers could not get in there to see the issues and we've done it on occasion when we've had purchasers from out of the state or even out of the country and they could not attend the home inspection.

DS: Which brings up another question. Do you encourage people to be there when you do the inspection?

TC: Oh, most definitely.

DS: If people wanted you to diagram or measure up the roof I assume you probably would do that but probably would have to charge them for it, I would imagine, is that correct?

TC: Yes. Generally if they're going to need new shingles we're not going to do any measuring for them as far as so they can get a price on the roof. We're going to more encourage them to get a roofer out there, but if we're up there already, by all means we'd be happy to do it.

DS: If people ask you for copies of your errors and omissions insurance, do you provide that for people if they ask for something like that?

TC: Yes sir.

DS: And like you said, here in Michigan we don't have licensing laws yet, so that's not something that you would be able to provide, because we don't even have those, but I would imagine where that is an issue, I would imagine a home inspector would be glad to provide a copy of the license.

TC: Yes. The way the laws are written in other states is you cannot perform inspections without a license. That's what we're pushing for in Michigan.

DS: I think we've covered a lot of ground here. Is there anything else you want to add on, or explain in a little more detail before we draw this to a conclusion?

TC: Sure. A couple of things. Number one, Pillar to Post is an international home inspection franchise, so we have a network of over 400 inspection franchises across North America, United States and Canada, and we have a wealth of knowledge where if there's an issue we come up to in a home that is something way out of the ordinary we do have a bank, so to speak, of knowledge that we can rely on to find some answers. And also as you said earlier we are insured home inspectors, we are backed by ASHI standards, and we truly do give you a thorough inspection of your home. We give you a very objective view of what you're purchasing in an honest way.

DS: Very good. So if you run into trouble you can always call somebody and get a second opinion over the phone, or whatever, of something unusual. That's wonderful. That's great! Well I thank you very much. Anything else you would like to add on Tim, or have we pretty much covered everything?

TC: No sir, but I do appreciate you calling me today.

DS: Okay. Very good.

How to Pick a Home Inspector

Ask your potential home inspector these questions:

1. Do you personally do the whole inspection? Or send out assistants? Or do part of the inspection and have assistants do other parts of the inspection?

2. How would you describe your personality? Are you patient, courteous, friendly, able to communicate verbally and in reports, are you a people-type person? (This may be an area that you will not be able to ask directly, but maybe you should keep in the back of your mind after interviewing the inspector to see if these questions are answered by their behavior. If they are not fully answered, ask them directly.)

3. Are you licensed or do you belong to an association?

4. If so, are you a full member of that organization or just a probationary or introductory member?

5. How long have you been involved in that association?

6. Please describe your home inspection training.

7. Are you current in your continuing education classes?

8. Do you have other areas of expertise such as construction, remodeling, or real estate?

9. Would you care to share with me references such as names and phone numbers that I could call?

10. Are you a full-time or part-time inspector?

11. How many inspections do you do in this area in a year's time?

12. How long have you lived in this area?

13. How long have you been in business?

14. Do you carry insurance in case anything is missed? (Many home inspectors do not carry Errors and Omissions insurance because it is too expensive.)

15. Would you mind providing a copy of your insurance certificate, along with the name, address, and telephone number of your insurance agent and company?

16. Have you worked in other areas of the country?

17. Where do you get most of your customers? (Referrals, advertising?)

18. Do you allow buyers to inspect the house while you are there?

19. What are the advantages of that?

20. What areas of the property are inspected, such as electrical, furnace, plumbing, etc., and how many questions are covered in the report?

21. Are the reports written or computer generated?

22. How quickly are they available?

23. What types of inspections do you do besides the basic inspection?

    a. Well? Does this have to do with quality and volume?

    b. Septic?

    c. Radon?

    d. Termites?

    e. Mold?

    f. Lead paint?

24. Is there a written agreement between the customer and the inspector before the inspection is started?

25. What are the fees?

26. Are they in writing?

27. Is there a dispute resolution agreement/clause in your contract?

28. How does that work?

29. What is your turn-around time for me to schedule an inspection and expect to get the report?

30. Do you preview MLS listing sheets and local government assessor records to get background information?

(Note: A California inspector routinely checks the local government assessor records and MLS listing sheets prior to inspections. In one case, something seemed strange. The MLS sheets indicated a 1,500 square foot stick-built home. The city records showed a 900 square foot manufactured home! The house had an addition, built without permits. A complete exterior makeover to the roof and siding disguised the style and grade of construction. The inspector estimated the value to be inflated by $50,000-$100,000 due to the house being a hybrid!)

Nothing beats the referrals of satisfied customers -- ask real estate friends, appraiser friends, and banker friends for names of good home inspectors.

Home Inspection Report

The detailed, thorough home inspection reports are often in bound manuals of 10-40 pages. This style, with definitions and explanations, allows for easy understanding by the homebuyer. There are E-mail/electronic versions.

Request a sample report or page(s) to be e-mailed or sent. The quality and ease of reading of the reports varies greatly. Some reports need a magnifying glass. Get one that has reader-friendly organization and is easily understood.

Ask if there is a Spanish version if that is an issue.

Following is a sample home inspection report courtesy of and with the permission of American Home Inspectors Training Institute. (14100 W. Cleveland Ave, New Berlin, WI 53151 – Phone: 262-754-3744 and 25229 DeQuindre, Madison Hts., MI 48701)

D

HOME INSPECTION REPORT

1234 Main St. My Town, Michigan 48439

INSPECTION DATE:

5/25/05

PREPARED FOR:

Robert Brown

PREPARED BY:

Smittys Inspection Service
1234 Cook Rd.
Grand Oak, Michigan
999-654-1234

INSPECTION NUMBER:

1782

INSPECTOR:

Richard Smitty

BUILDING DATA / RECEIPT INFORMATION

RECEIPT

Inspection Date:
Inspection Number:
Client Name:
Inspected by:

Inspection:		$270.00
	Total:	**$ 270.00**

Paid by: Check

BUILDING DATA

Approximate Age:	53 Years old
Style:	Ranch
General Appearance:	Satisfactory
Main Entrance Faces:	For sake of the report the house faces North
Weather Condition:	Clear
Temperature:	30-50°F
Ground cover:	Snow cover

GROUNDS

Service Walks ☐ None ☐ Public sidewalk needs repair
☑ Concrete ☐ Flagstone ☐ Brick ☐ Other
Condition: ☑ Satisfactory. ☐ Marginal ☐ Poor ☐ **Trip Hazard**
☐ Pitched towards home ☐ Settling cracks ☐ Not visible

Driveway ☐ None
☐ Concrete ☑ Asphalt ☐ Gravel ☐ Other
Condition: ☐ Satisfactory ☑ Marginal ☐ Poor ☐ **Trip hazard**
☑ Fill cracks and seal ☐ Pitched towards home ☑ Settling cracks ☐ Not visible

Patio/Lanai ☑ None
☐ Concrete ☐ Flagstone ☐ Brick ☐ Kool-Deck® ☐ Other
Condition: ☐ Satisfactory ☐ Marginal ☐ Poor ☐ **Trip Hazard**
☐ Pitched towards home **(See Remarks page)** ☐ Settling cracks ☐ Not visible

Deck ☑ None ☐ Wood ☐ Other
☐ Treated ☐ Painted/Stained ☐ **Railing/balusters recommended**
Condition: ☐ Satisfactory ☐ Marginal ☐ Poor ☐ Not visible

Deck/Patio/Porch Covers ☑ None ☐ Earth to wood contact ☐ Moisture/insect damage
Lacks: ☐ Metal straps/bolts/nails ☐ Improper attachment to house

Porch *(covered entrance)* ☑ None ☐ **Railing/balusters recommended**
Support Pier: ☐ Wood ☐ Concrete ☐ Other ☐ Not visible
Condition: ☐ Satisfactory ☐ Marginal ☐ Poor
Floor: ☐ Satisfactory ☐ Marginal ☐ Poor ☐ **Safety Hazard**

Balcony *(2nd floor platform)* ☑ None ☐ Wood ☐ Metal ☐ Other
Railing: ☐ Yes ☐ No ☐ **Railing/balusters recommended**
Condition: ☐ Satisfactory ☐ Marginal ☐ Poor ☐ **Safety Hazard**

Stoops/Steps ☐ None ☐ Uneven risers ☐ **Safety Hazard**
☑ Concrete- right side ☑ Wood-rear ☐ Other ☐ **Railing recommended**
Condition: ☑ Satisfactory- rear ☑ Marginal- right side ☐ Poor ☐ **Recommend baluster**
☑ Chipped concrete ☐ Settled ☐ Damaged wood

Fencing ☑ None ☐ Type: ☐ Not evaluated

Landscaping Affecting Foundation **(See Remarks page)**
Negative grade at: ☐ East ☐ West ☐ North ☐ South ☑ Satisfactory
☐ Recommend additional backfill ☐ Recommend window wells/covers
☐ Trim back trees/shrubberies ☐ Wood in contact/too close to soil
☐ Yard drains observed - not tested ☐ N/A

Retaining Wall: ☐ Yes ☑ No
☐ Concrete ☐ Wood ☐ Other ☐ **Safety Hazard**
Visual Condition: ☐ Satisfactory ☐ Marginal ☐ Poor

Hose Bibs ☑ Yes ☐ No ☐ No anti-siphon valve
Operates: ☐ Yes ☐ No ☑ Not tested ☐ Not on

General Comments

Approx. 1/3 of the driveway was covered with snow and not visible. Viewable areas of the driveway had some cracks and slight heaving, but usable, recommend repair as needed. Side concrete steps has some spalling, flaking concrete, however appears structurally sufficient, recommend repair as needed.

GROUNDS REMARKS

Service Walks/Driveways

Spalling concrete cannot be patched with concrete because the new will not bond with the old. Water will freeze between the two layers, or the concrete will break up from movement or wear. Replacement of the damaged section is recommended. Walks or driveways that are close to the property should be properly pitched away to direct water away from the foundation. Asphalt driveways should be kept sealed and larger cracks filled so as to prevent damage from frost.

Patios that have settled towards the structure should be mudjacked or replaced to assure proper pitch. Improperly pitched patios are one source of wet basements.

Exterior Wood Surfaces

All surfaces of untreated wood need regular applications of paint or special chemicals to resist damage. Porch or deck columns and fence posts which are buried in the ground and made of untreated wood will become damaged within a year or two.

Decks should always be nailed with galvanized or aluminum nails. Decks that are not painted or stained should be treated with a water sealer.

Grading and Drainage

Any system of grading or landscaping that creates positive drainage (moving water away from the foundation walls) will help to keep a basement dry. Where negative grade exists and additional backfill is suggested, it may require digging out around the property to get a proper pitch. Dirt shall be approximately 6" below the bottom sill and should not touch wood surfaces.

Flower beds, loose mulched areas, railroad ties and other such landscaping items close to the foundation trap moisture and contribute to wet basements. To establish a positive grade, a proper slope away from the house is 1" per foot for approximately 5-6 feet. Recommend ground cover planting or grass to foundation.

Roof and Surface Water Control

Roof and surface water must be controlled to maintain a dry basement. This means keeping gutters cleaned out and aligned, extending downspouts, installing splashblocks, and building up the grade so that roof and surface water is diverted away from the building.

Window Wells

The amount of water which enters a window well from falling rain is generally slight, but water will accumulate in window wells if the yard is improperly graded. Plastic window well covers are useful in keeping out leaves and debris.

Retaining Walls

Retaining walls deteriorate because of excessive pressure buildup behind them, generally due to water accumulation. Often, conditions can be improved by excavating a trench behind the retaining wall and filling it with coarse gravel. Drain holes through the wall will then be able to relieve the water pressure.

Retaining walls sometime suffer from tree root pressure or from general movement of topsoil down the slope. Normally, these conditions require rebuilding the retaining wall.

Railings

It is recommended that railings be installed for any stairway over 3 steps and porches over 30" for safety reasons. Balusters for porches, balconies, and stairs should be close enough to assure children cannot squeeze through.

ROOF COVERING

General Information

Roof Visibility ☑ All ☐ Percent ☐ None ☐ Limited By:

Inspected From ☑ Roof ☐ Ladder at eaves ☐ Ground w/binoculars

Style of Roof

Type: Combination: ☑ Gable ☐ Hip ☐ Mansard ☑ Shed ☐ Flat ☐ Other

Pitch: Combination: ☑ Low ☑ Medium ☐ Steep ☐ Flat

Roof Covering

Roof #1: Type: Asphalt Estimated Layers: 2+ Layers Approximate age of cover: 8-12 years

Roof #2: Type: Rubber Single Ply Membrane Estimated Layers: 1+ Layers, Approximate age of cover: 10-12+ years

Ventilation System

Combination: ☐ Soffit ☐ Ridge ☑ Gable ☐ Roof
☐ Powered ☐ Eaves ☐ Other

Flashing Material

Combination: ☐ Galv./Aluminum ☐ Asphalt ☐ Lead ☐ Rubber ☑ Not visible
☐ Copper ☐ Other

Valley Material

Combination: ☑ Galv./Aluminum ☑ Asphalt ☑ Tarred over rubber ☐ N/A
☐ Not visible ☐ Other

Apparent Condition of the Following at Time of Inspection (conditions reported reflect visible portion only)

Roof Covering ☑ Satisfactory-asphalt ☐ Marginal ☑ Poor-rubber

Condition: ☐ Curling ☐ Cupping ☐ Missing tabs/shingles/tiles
☐ Moss Buildup ☐ Nail Popping ☐ Ponding ☐ Burn Spots
☑ Extensive network cracking -rubber ☐ Other

Ventilation **(See Remarks page)** **(See Attic page)**

Flashings ☑ Not visible ☐ Satisfactory ☐ Marginal ☐ Poor
☐ Rusted ☐ **Recommend Sealing** ☐ Pulled away from chimney/roof

Valleys ☑ Satisfactory-asphalt,alum. ☐ Marginal ☑ Poor=rubber tarred over
☐ Not visible ☐ N/A ☐ Rusted
☐ Holes ☑ **Recommend Sealing-rubber**

Skylights ☐ Yes ☑ No ☐ Satisfactory ☐ Marginal ☐ Poor

Plumbing Vents ☑ Yes ☐ No ☑ Satisfactory ☐ Marginal ☐ Poor

General Comments

Main asphalt roof coverings appeared overall satisfactory. Rubber single ply membrane roof has network cracks, spongy spot in one area where water has appeared to penetrate the roof, some cracks in tar at valleys and appears to be nearing end of its useful life, recommend filling in any cracks with tar and budgeting to replace soon.

ROOF COVERING REMARKS

Valleys & Flashings

Valleys and flashings that are covered with shingles and/or tar or any other material are considered not visible and are not part of the inspection.

Stone Roofs - Coverings

This type of covering on a pitched roof requires ongoing annual maintenance. We recommend that a roofing contractor evaluate this type of roof. Infra-red photography is best used to determine areas of potential leaks.

Flat Roofs

Flat roofs are very vulnerable to leaking. It is very important to maintain proper drainage to prevent ponding of water. We recommend that a roofing contractor evaluate this type of roof.

ROOF TYPE	LIFE EXPECTANCY	SPECIAL REMARKS
Asphalt Shingles	15-20 years	Used on nearly 80% of all residential roofs; requires little maintenance
*Asphalt Multi-Thickness Shingles**	20-30 years	Heavier and more durable than regular asphalt shingles
*Asphalt Interlocking Shingles**	15-25 years	Especially good in high-wind areas
Asphalt Rolls	10 years	Used on low slope roofs
Built-up Roofing	10-20 years	Used on low slope roofs; 2 to 3 times as costly as asphalt shingles
*Wood Shingles**	10-40 years[1]	Treat with preservative every 5 years to prevent decay
*Clay Tiles** *Cement Tiles**	20 + years 20 + years	Durable, fireproof, but not watertight, requiring a good subsurface base
*Slate Shingles**	30-100 years[2]	Extremely durable, but brittle and expensive
*Asbestos Cement Shingles**	30-75 years	Durable, but brittle and difficult to repair
Metal Roofing	15-40 + years	Comes in sheets & shingles; should be well grounded for protection from lightning; certain metals must be painted
Single Ply Membrane	15-25 years (mfgr's claim)	New material; not yet passed test of time

* Not recommended for use on low slope roof

[1] Depending on local conditions and proper installation
[2] Depending on quality of slate

Roof covering should be visually checked in spring and fall for any visible missing shingles, damaged coverings or other defects. Before re-roofing, the underside of the roof structure and roof sheathing should be inspected to determine that the roof structure can support the additional weight of the shingles.

Wood shakes and shingles will vary in aging, due to quality of the material, installation, maintenance, and surrounding shade trees. Ventilation and drying of the wood material is critical in extending the life expectancy of the wood. Commercial preservatives are available on the market, which could be applied to wood to impede deterioration.

CHIMNEY / GUTTERS / SIDING / TRIM

Chimney(s) ☐ None Location(s): rear middle of roof

Viewed from: ☑ Roof ☐ Ladder at eaves ☐ Ground w/binoculars

Chase: ☐ Brick ☐ Stone ☐ Metal ☐ Framed ☐ Blocks ☑ Weatherproof wallboard

Evidence of: ☐ Cracked chimney cap ☐ Loose mortar joints ☐ Loose brick ☐ Holes in metal ☐ Rust ☐ Flaking

Flue: ☐ Tile ☑ Metal ☐ **Unlined** ☐ Not visible

Evidence of: ☐ Scaling ☐ Cracks ☐ Creosote

☑ **Have flue(s) cleaned and re-evaluated** ☑ **Not evaluated (See Remarks page)**

☐ Recommend cricket/saddle flashing ☐ Spark arrestor/rain cap recommended

Gutters & Downspouts ☐ None **(See Remarks page)**

☐ Insides need to be cleaned ☐ Ponding

☑ Galvanized/Alum. ☐ Copper ☐ Vinyl ☐ Other

Condition: ☐ Satisfactory ☑ Marginal ☐ Poor ☐ Rusting

☐ Hole in main run Leaking: ☐ Corners ☐ Joints

Extension needed: ☑ Front left ☑ Rear left ☑ Front right loose connection

Siding

☐ Brick ☐ Wood ☐ Metal ☑ Vinyl ☐ Stucco ☐ Fiber-cement

☐ Stone ☐ Slate ☐ Asphalt ☐ EIFS **(See Remarks)** ☐ Other

Condition: ☑ Satisfactory ☐ Marginal ☐ Poor ☐ **Recommend repair/painting**

Window Frames

☐ Wood ☑ Aluminum covered ☐ Vinyl ☐ Metal ☐ Other

Condition: ☑ Satisfactory ☐ Marginal ☐ Poor

☐ **Recommend painting** ☐ **Damaged wood**

Storms & Screens ☐ N/A

☐ Wood ☐ Clad comb. ☐ Wood/metal comb. ☑ Insulated glass-most ☐ Other

Putty: ☐ Satisfactory ☑ Needed-older windows ☐ N/A

Screens: ☐ Satisfactory ☑ Torn- few spots ☐ Missing

Storms: ☑ Satisfactory ☐ Broken/cracked ☐ **Damaged wood** ☐ Not installed

1 - Trim, 2 - Soffit, 3 - Fascia

☐ Wood ☑ Metal -3 ☑ Vinyl-1,2 ☐ Other

Condition: ☑ Satisfactory-1,3 ☑ Marginal-2 ☐ Poor

☐ **Recommend painting** ☐ **Damaged wood**

Caulking

Condition: ☐ Satisfactory ☑ Marginal ☐ Poor

☑ **Recommend around windows/doors/masonry ledges/corners/utility penetrations**

General Comments

Flashing around chimney is completely covered with tar and could not be inspected, recommend checking tar periodically and sealing any gaps if needed as the tar will dry and crack over time. Chimney flue was not accessible and not inspected, recommend having flue cleaned and re-evaluated . Siding appeared to be all intact and in overall satisfactory condition. Soffit is missing vinyl capping (gap) in the rear left of home, recommend filling in gap with vinyl as needed. Chimney chase appears to be covered with some type of waterproof wallboard. Leader and downspout extension missing on rear left of home, recommend adding leader and downspout extension as necessary. Downspout extension needed on front left of home, 6-8 ft extension recommended. Front right downspout extension has come unfasted to connecting pipe, recommend re-securing connection as needed.

CHIMNEY / GUTTERS / SIDING / TRIM REMARKS

Chimneys

Chimneys built of masonry will eventually need tuckpointing. A cracked chimney top that allows water and carbonic acid to get behind the surface brick/stone will accelerate the deterioration. Moisture will also deteriorate the clay flue liner. Periodic chimney cleaning will keep you apprised of the chimney's condition. The flashing around the chimney may need resealing and should be inspected every year or two. Fireplace chimneys should be inspected and evaluated by a chimney professional before using. Chimneys must be adequate height for proper drafting. Spark arrestors are recommended for wood burning chimney and chimney caps for fossil fuels

Unlined Chimney - should be re-evaluated by a chimney technician.

Have flue cleaned and re-evaluated. The flue lining is covered with soot or creosote and no representation can be made as to the condition.

NOT EVALUATED- ***The flue was not evaluated due to inaccessibility such as roof pitch, cap, cleanout not accessible, etc.***

Cricket Flashing

Small, sloped structure made of metal and designed to drain moisture away from a chimney. Usually placed at the back of a chimney.

Gutters and Downspouts

This is an extremely important element in basement dampness control. Keep gutters clean and downspout extensions in place (4' or more). Paint the inside of galvanized gutters, which will extend the life. Shortly after a rain or thaw in winter, look for leaks at seams in the gutters. These can be recaulked before they cause damage to fascia or soffit boards. If no gutters exist, it is recommended that they be added.

Siding

Wood siding should not come in contact with the ground. The moisture will cause rotting to take place and can attract carpenter ants.

EIFS - This type of siding has experienced serious problems and requires a certified EIFS inspector to determine condition.

Brick and stone veneer must be monitored for loose or missing mortar. Some brick and stone are susceptible to spalling. This can be caused when moisture is trapped and a freeze/thaw situation occurs. There are products on the market that can be used to seal out the moisture. This holds true for brick and stone chimneys also.

Metal sidings will dent and scratch. Oxidation is a normal reaction in aluminum. There are good cleaners on the market and it is recommended that they be used occasionally. Metal siding can be painted.

Doors and Windows

These can waste an enormous amount of energy. Maintain the caulking around the frames on the exterior. Check for drafts in the winter and improve the worst offenders first. Windows that have leaky storm windows will usually have a lot of sweating. Likewise, well-sealed storms that sweat indicate a leaky window. It is the tighter unit that will sweat (unless the home has excess humidity to begin with.)

Wood that exhibits blistering or peeling paint should be examined for possible moisture sources: roof leaks, bad gutters, interior moisture from baths or laundry or from a poorly vented crawl space. Some paint problems have no logical explanation, but many are a symptom of an underlying problem. A freshly painted house may mask these symptoms, but after you have lived in the home for a year or two, look for localized paint blistering (peeling). It may be a clue.

New glazing will last longer if the raw wood is treated with boiled linseed oil prior to glazing. It prevents the wood from drawing the moisture out of the new glazing.

Caulking

Many different types of caulk are available on the market today. Check with a paint or hardware store for the kind of application you need.

EXTERIOR / ELECTRICAL / AC / GARAGE

Exterior Wall Construction

☑ Not visible ☐ Wood frame ☐ Masonry ☐ Log ☐ Other

Exterior Doors ☐ Entrance (1); Storm (2); Side Door (3) Side Storm (4);

Weatherstripping: ☑ Satisfactory-2 ☑ Marginal-1 ☑ Poor-3,4

Condition: ☑ Satisfactory-1,2 ☐ Marginal ☑ Poor-3,4

Exterior Electrical Service

☑ Overhead ☐ Underground Service drop: ☑ Satisfactory ☐ Needs service

Exterior outlets: ☐ Yes ☑ No *Operate*: ☐ Yes ☑ N/A

GFCI protected: ☐ Yes ☑ N/A *Operate*: ☐ Yes ☑ N/A

Reverse polarity: ☐ Yes ☑ N/A Open ground: ☐ Yes ☑ N/A

Overhead wires: ☐ Low ☐ Less than 3' from balcony/deck/window ☐ Extension cord/exposed Romex

Potential safety hazard: ☐ Yes ☑ No **(See Remarks page)**

A/C Condenser/Heat Pump ☑ None Approximate age: Max breaker/fuse:

Brand: Model #: Shutoff: ☐ Yes ☐ No

Condition: ☐ Satisfactory ☐ Marginal ☐ Poor ☐ Rusted/dirty *Level*: ☐ Yes ☐ No

Garage ☑ None

☐ Attached ☐ Detached ☐ 1-car ☐ 2-car ☐ 3-car

Automatic opener: ☐ Yes ☐ No ☐ Operable ☐ Inoperable

Safety reverse: Present: ☐ Yes ☐ No Operates: ☐ Yes ☐ No ☐ **Safety Hazard**

Electric sensor: Present: ☐ Yes ☐ No Operates: ☐ Yes ☐ No ☐ **Safety Hazard**

Roofing: ☐ Same as house Type: ??? Approx. age: ??? Approx. layers: ???

Condition: ☐ Satisfactory ☐ Marginal ☐ Poor

Gutters: ☐ Satisfactory ☐ Marginal ☐ Poor ☐ None

Siding: ☐ Same as house ☐ Wood ☐ Metal ☐ Vinyl

☐ Stucco ☐ Masonry ☐ Slate ☐ Fiberboard

Trim: ☐ Same as house ☐ Wood ☐ Aluminum ☐ Vinyl

Floor: ☐ Concrete ☐ Gravel ☐ Asphalt ☐ Dirt

Burners less than 18" above garage floor: ☐ N/A ☐ Yes ☐ No ☐ **Safety** hazard

Condition: ☐ Satisfactory ☐ Typical cracks ☐ Large settling cracks

Overhead door: ☐ Wood ☐ Fiberglass ☐ Masonite ☐ Metal ☐ Other

Condition: ☐ Satisfactory ☐ Marginal ☐ Poor ☐ **Repair, replace, paint**

Service door: ☐ Satisfactory ☐ Marginal ☐ Poor ☐ None

Sill plates: ☐ Elevated ☐ Floor level ☐ Both ☐ Not visible ☐ Rotted

Electricity present: ☐ Yes ☐ No **GFCI Protected:** ☐ Yes ☐ No *Operates*: ☐ Yes ☐ No

Reverse polarity/open ground: ☐ Yes ☐ **Safety Hazard** ☐ No ☐ Handyman/ext. cord wiring

Firewall: (Between garage & living area) ☐ N/A ☐ Present ☐ Missing ☐ Damaged

Fire door: ☐ Not verifiable ☐ Not a fire door ☐ Needs repair ☐ Satisfactory

Auto closure: ☐ N/A ☐ Satisfactory ☐ Inoperative ☐ Missing ☐ Needs repair

General Comments

Side storm door is damaged-dented , has no weatherstripping and side main wood door is delaminated and also Has no weatherstripping, recommend adding weatherstripping and repair or replacement of doors as needed. Tear on front door weatherstripping noted, replace as needed.

EXTERIOR / ELECTRICAL / AC / GARAGE REMARKS

Exterior Doors

The exposed side of exterior doors needs to be painted or properly stained and varnished to prevent discoloring and delamination. Weatherstripping is a must to prevent drafts.

Electrical

Overhead wires from the mast to the main panel that are exposed to the weather may fray and crack. If this occurs, wires should be replaced by a licensed electrician.

Any outdoor overhead service conductor wires should have adequate clearance above the ground (10 feet) and from balcony and windows (3 feet), for safety reasons.

Underground system - Some exterior boxes that are at ground level have a grade line on them. You should insure that the grade remains below this line to prevent moisture from entering the main panel.

Overhead Door Openers

We recommend that a separate electrical outlet be provided. Openers that do not have a safety reverse are considered a safety hazard. Small children and pets are especially vulnerable. We recommend the operating switches be set high enough so children cannot reach them. If a electric sensor is present, it should be teste occasionally to ensure it is working.

Garage Sill Plates

Sill plates within the garage should be elevated or treated lumber should be used. If this is not the case, try to direct water away to prevent rotting.

A/C Compressors

They should not become overgrown with foliage. Clearance requirements vary, but 2' on all sides should be considered minimal with up to 6' of air discharge desirable. If a clothes dryer vent is within five to ten feet, either relocate the vent or do not run when the A/C is running. The lint will quickly reduce the efficiency of the A/C unit.

Burners

Any appliance such as a water heater, furnace, etc. should have the flame a minimum of 18" above the floor. Any open flame less than 18" from the floor is a potential safety hazard. The appliance should also be protected from vehicle damage.

KITCHEN

Countertops	☐ Satisfactory	☑ Marginal	☐ Poor	

Cabinets				
Condition:	☐ Satisfactory	☑ Marginal	☐ Poor	☐ **Recommend repairs**

Plumbing Comments					
Faucet leaks:	☐ Yes	☑ No	Pipes leak/corroded:	☐ Yes	☑ No
Drainage:	☑ Adequate	☐ Poor	Water pressure:	☑ Adequate	☐ Poor

Walls & Ceiling					
Condition	☐ Satisfactory	☑ Marginal	☐ Poor	☑ Typical cracks	☐ Moisture stains

Heat Source Present	☐ Yes	☑ No

Floor					
Condition	☑ Satisfactory	☐ Marginal	☐ Poor	☐ Sloping	☐ Squeaks

Appliances			**(See Remarks page)**			
Disposal:	☐ Yes	☑ No	*Operates*:	☐ Yes	☐ No	☑ N/A
Dishwasher:	☑ Yes	☐ No	*Operates*:	☑ Yes	☐ No	☐ N/A
Range:	☑ Yes	☐ No	*Operates*:	☑ Yes	☐ No	☐ N/A
Oven:	☑ Yes	☐ No	*Operates*:	☑ Yes	☐ No	☐ N/A
Trash compactor:	☐ Yes	☑ No	*Operates*:	☐ Yes	☐ No	☑ N/A
Exhaust fan:	☑ Yes	☐ No	*Operates*:	☑ Yes	☐ No	☐ N/A
Refrigerator:	☑ Yes	☐ No	*Operates*:	☑ Yes	☐ No	☐ N/A
Other:	☐ Yes	☑ No	*Operates*:	☐ Yes	☐ No	☑ N/A

Electrical					
Outlets present:	☑ Yes	☐ No	*Operates*:	☑ Yes	☐ No
GFCI protected:	☐ Yes	☑ No	*Operates*:	☐ Yes	☐ No **(Remarks)**
Open ground/reverse polarity within 6' of water:			☐ Yes	☐ **Safety Hazard**	☑ No

General Comments:

Countertops have some stains. Cabinets have wear. Some stains on walls and ceiling noted. There were no visible active piping leaks at the time of the inspection. Drain lines had no visible leaks or signs of backup at the time of inspection.

LAUNDRY / UTILITY ROOM

Room Components						
Laundry sink:	☑ N/A	Faucet leaks:	☐ Yes ☐ No		Pipe leaks:	☐ Yes ☐ No
Cross connections:	☐ Yes	☑ N/A	Heat source present:	☐ Yes	☐ No	
Room appears vented:	☑ Yes	☐ No	☐ Not visible			
Dryer vented:	☐ N/A	☑ Wall	☐ Ceiling	☐ Not vented		
Electrical: Open ground/reverse polarity within 6' of water:			☐ Yes	☐ **Safety Hazard**	☑ No	
Appliances present:	☑ Washer	☑ Dryer	☐ Water heater	☐ Furnace	☐ Other	
Gas pipe:	☑ N/A	Valve shutoff:	☐ Yes ☐ No	☐ Cap Needed	☐ **Safety Hazard**	

General Comments

Recommend replacing rubber washer hoses with steel braided hoses to prevent rupturing and replacing plastic dryer hose with aluminum, plastic hose presents a potential fire hazard.

KITCHEN / LAUNDRY / UTILITIY ROOM REMARKS

Plaster on Wood Lath

Plaster on wood lath is an old technique and is no longer in general use. Wood lath shrinks with time and the nails rust and loosen. As a result, the plaster may become fragile and caution is needed in working with this type of plastering system. Sagging ceilings are best repaired by laminating drywall over the existing plaster and screwing it to the ceiling joists.

Plaster on Gypsum Lath (Rock Lath)

Plaster on gypsum lath will sometimes show the seams of the 16" wide gypsum lath, but this does not indicate a structural fault. The scalloping appearance can be leveled with drywall joint compound and fiberglass mesh joint tape or drywall can be laminated over the existing plaster on the ceiling.

Wood Flooring

Always attempt to clean wood floors first before making the decision to refinish the floor. Wax removers and other mild stripping agents plus a good waxing and buffing will usually produce satisfactory results. Mild bleaching agents help remove deep stains. Sanding removes some of the wood in the floor and can usually be done safely only once or twice in the life of the floor.

Nail Pops

Drywall nail pops are due to normal expansion and contraction of the wood members to which the drywall is nailed, and are usually of no structural significance.

Carpeting

Where carpeting has been installed, the materials and condition of the floor underneath cannot be determined.

Appliances

Dishwashers are tested to see if the motor operates and water sprays properly (full cycles are not run). Stoves are tested to see that burners are working and oven and broiler get hot. Timer and controls are not tested. Refrigerators are not tested.

No representation is made to continued life expectancy of any appliance.

Asbestos and Other Hazards

Asbestos fibers in some form are present in many homes, but are often not visible and cannot be identified without testing.

If there is reason to suspect that asbestos may be present and if it is of particular concern, a sample of the material in question may be removed and analyzed in a laboratory. ***However, detecting or inspecting for the presence or absence of asbestos is not a part of our inspection.***

Also excluded from this inspection and report are the possible presence of, or danger from, radon gas, lead-based paint, urea formaldehyde, toxic or flammable chemicals and all other similar or potentially harmful substances and environmental hazards.

Windows

A representative number of windows are inspected.

BATHROOMS

Bath: First floor bath

Sinks Faucet leaks: ☐ Yes ☑ No Pipes leak: ☐ Yes ☑ No
Tubs- N/A Faucet leaks: ☐ Yes ☐ No Pipes leak: ☐ Yes ☐ No
Showers Faucet leaks:. ☐ Yes ☑ No Pipes leak: ☐ Yes ☑ No
Toilet: Bowl loose ☐ Yes ☑ No *Operates*: ☑ Yes ☐ No ☐ Cracked bowl ☐ Toilet leaks
Whirlpool: ☐ Yes ☑ No *Operates*: ☐ Yes ☐ No
Shower/Tub area: ☑ Ceramic/Plastic ☐ Fiberglass ☐ Masonite ☐ Other
Condition: ☐ Satisfactory ☑ Marginal ☐ Poor ☐ Rotted floors
Caulk/Grouting needed: ☐ Yes ☑ No Where:
Drainage: ☑ Satisfactory ☐ Marginal ☐ Poor
Water flow: ☑ Satisfactory ☐ Marginal ☐ Poor
Moisture stains present: ☑ Yes ☑ Walls ☑ Ceilings ☐ No
Window/doors: ☐ Satisfactory ☐ Marginal ☑ Poor
Outlets present: ☑ Yes ☐ No GFCI protected: ☐ Yes ☑ No *Operates*: ☑ Yes ☐ No
Open ground/reverse polarity within 6' of water: ☐ Yes ☑ No
Potential safety hazards present: ☐ Yes ☑ No **(See Remarks page)**
Heat source present: ☑ Yes ☐ No **(See Remarks page)**
Exhaust fan: ☑ Yes ☐ No *Operates*: ☑ Yes ☐ No ☑ Noisy

General Comments

Sink stopper is not working, recommend repair as needed. Some mold noted on window trim, recommend cleaning With detergent solution. Fan is working but noisy. Some stains noted on tiles, wall paper and base of shower enclosure.Door is delaminated, recommend repair or replacement as needed.

Bath: First floor bath –off bedrooms

Sinks Faucet leaks: ☐ Yes ☑ No Pipes leak: ☐ Yes ☑ No
Tubs Faucet leaks: ☐ Yes ☑ No Pipes leak: ☐ Yes ☑ No
Showers Faucet leaks: ☐ Yes ☑ No Pipes leak: ☐ Yes ☑ No
Toilet: Bowl loose ☐ Yes ☑ No *Operates*: ☑ Yes ☐ No ☐ Cracked bowl ☐ Toilet leaks
Whirlpool: ☐ Yes ☑ No *Operates*: ☐ Yes ☐ No
Shower/Tub area: ☑ Ceramic/Plastic ☐ Fiberglass ☐ Masonite ☐ Other
Condition: ☑ Satisfactory ☐ Marginal ☐ Poor ☐ Rotted floors
Caulk/Grouting needed: ☑ Yes ☐ No Where: small areas in tile of tub/shower enclosure
Drainage: ☐ Satisfactory ☐ Marginal ☑ Poor
Water flow: ☑ Satisfactory ☐ Marginal ☐ Poor
Moisture stains present: ☐ Yes ☐ Walls ☐ Ceilings ☑ No
Window/doors: ☐ Satisfactory ☑ Marginal ☐ Poor
Outlets present: ☑ Yes ☐ No GFCI protected: ☐ Yes ☑ No *Operates*: ☐ Yes ☑ No
Open ground/reverse polarity within 6' of water: ☐ Yes ☑ No
Potential safety hazards present: ☐ Yes ☑ No **(See Remarks page)**
Heat source present: ☑ Yes ☐ No
Exhaust fan: ☐ Yes ☑ No *Operates*: ☐ Yes ☐ No ☐ Noisy

General Comments

Tub is draining extremely slow, recommend repair as needed. Sink stopper is not working, recommend repair as needed. Outlet on light fixture is not working-(no power), recommend repair or replacement as needed . Some stains On vanity, base of tub, tile flooring and door noted. Window is sticking, recommend repair as needed. Toilet is working, however appears to have been installed on an angle (cosmetic defect only). Recommend adding exhaust fan Vented to outside air to aide moisture control.

BATHROOM REMARKS

Stall Shower

The metal shower pan in a stall shower has a potential or probable life of 10-20 years depending on quality of the pan installed. Although a visible inspection is made to determine whether a shower pan is currently leaking, it cannot be stated with certainty that no defect is present or that one may not soon develop. Shower pan leaks often do not show except when the shower is in actual use.

Ceramic Tile

Bathroom tile installed in a mortar bed is excellent. It is still necessary to keep the joint between the tile and the tub/shower caulked or sealed to prevent water spillage from leaking through and damaging the ceilings below.

Ceramic tile is often installed in mastic. It is important to keep the tile caulked or water will seep behind the tile and cause deterioration in the wallboard. Special attention should be paid to the area around faucets and other tile penetrations.

Exhaust Fans

Bathrooms with a shower should have exhaust fans where possible. This helps to remove excess moisture from the room, preventing damage to the ceiling and walls and wood finishes. The exhaust fan should not be vented into the attic. The proper way to vent the fans is to the outside. Running the vent pipe horizontally and venting into a gable end or soffit is preferred. Running the vent pipe vertically through the roof may cause condensation to run down the vent pipe, rusting the fan and damaging the wallboard. Insulating the vent pipe in the attic will help to reduce this problem.

SLOW DRAINS on sinks, tubs, and showers are usually due to build up of hair and soap scum. Most sink pop-ups can be easily removed for cleaning. Some tubs have a spring attached to the closing lever that acts as a catch for hair. It may require removing a couple of screws to disassemble. If you cannot mechanically remove the obstruction, be kind to your pipes. Don't use a caustic cleaner. There are several bacteria drain cleaners available. They are available at hardware stores in areas where septic tanks are used. These drain cleaners take a little longer to work, but are safe for you and your pipes.

Safety Hazards

Typical safety hazards found in bathrooms are open grounds or reverse polarity by water. Replacing these outlets with G.F.C.I.'s are recommended. **(See Electrical section)**

Whirlpool Tubs

This relates to interior tubs hooked up to interior plumbing. Where possible, the motor will be operated to see that the jets are working. Hot tubs and spas are not inspected.

LIVING ROOM

Location: First floor

Walls & Ceiling: ☐ Satisfactory ☑ Marginal ☐ Poor ☑ Typical Cracks ☐ Holes
Moisture stains: ☐ Yes ☑ No
Flooring: ☐ Satisfactory ☑ Marginal ☐ Poor ☐ Squeaks ☑ Unlevel
Ceiling fan: ☑ N/A ☐ Satisfactory ☐ Marginal ☐ Poor
Electrical: Switches: ☑ Yes ☐ No Outlets: ☑ Yes ☐ No *Operates*: ☑ Yes ☐ No
Open ground/reverse polarity: ☐ Yes ☐ **Safety Hazard** ☑ No ☐ Covers missing
Heat source present: ☑ Yes ☐ Not visible Holes: ☐ Doors ☐ Walls ☐ Ceilings
Doors & Windows: ☑ Sat. ☐ Marg. ☐ Poor ☐ Cracked glass ☐ Evidence of leaking insulated glass

General Comments:

Ceiling has some stains and long fine cracks across room, recommend repair as needed. Floor is unlevel, possibly due To some settling of slab foundation or expansion and contraction of concrete due to heated flooring.There is a gap between baseboard moulding and floor, recommend repositioning moulding onto floor and monitoring in the future.

DINING ROOM

Location: First floor

Walls & Ceiling: ☐ Satisfactory ☑ Marginal ☐ Poor ☑ Typical Cracks ☐ Holes
Moisture stains: ☐ Yes ☑ No
Flooring: ☐ Satisfactory ☑ Marginal ☐ Poor ☐ Squeaks ☑ Unlevel
Ceiling fan: ☑ N/A ☐ Satisfactory ☐ Marginal ☐ Poor
Electrical: Switches: ☑ Yes ☐ No Outlets: ☑ Yes ☐ No *Operates*: ☑ Yes ☐ No
Open ground/reverse polarity: ☐ Yes ☐ **Safety Hazard** ☑ No ☐ Covers missing
Heat source present: ☑ Yes ☐ Not visible Holes: ☐ Doors ☐ Walls ☐ Ceilings
Doors & Windows: ☑ Sat. ☐ Marg. ☐ Poor ☐ Cracked glass ☐ Evidence of leaking insulated glass

General Comments:

Floor is unlevel

FAMILY ROOM

Location: First floor

Walls & Ceiling: ☐ Satisfactory ☑ Marginal ☐ Poor ☑ Typical Cracks ☐ Holes
Moisture stains: ☐ Yes ☑ No
Flooring: ☑ Satisfactory ☐ Marginal ☐ Poor ☐ Squeaks ☐ Slopes
Ceiling fan: ☑ N/A ☐ Satisfactory ☐ Marginal ☐ Poor
Electrical: Switches: ☑ Yes ☐ No Outlets: ☑ Yes ☐ No *Operates*: ☑ Yes ☐ No
Open ground/reverse polarity: ☐ Yes ☐ **Safety Hazard** ☑ No ☐ Covers missing
Heat source present: ☑ Yes ☐ Not visible Holes: ☐ Doors ☑ Walls ☐ Ceilings
Doors & Windows: ☐ Sat. ☑ Marg. ☐ Poor ☐ Cracked glass ☐ Evidence of leaking insulated glass

General Comments:

Recessed and track lighting fixtures are missing some bulbs, add as needed. Wall and ceiling has some stains and chipping paint, recommend repair as needed.Wall panel has some small holes and water damage (cracks) in one corner due to leaking rubber roof, recommend repair as needed. A few window sills have excessive flaking paint, Recommend adding 1/8 inch weep holes under storms on top of sills to allow rain water to drain to the outside as necessary.

BEDROOM

Location: First floor –front middle

Walls & Ceiling: ☐ Satisfactory ☑ Marginal ☐ Poor ☑ Typical Cracks ☐ Holes
Moisture stains; ☐ Yes ☑ No
Flooring: ☑ Satisfactory ☐ Marginal ☐ Poor ☐ Squeaks ☐ Slopes
Ceiling fan: ☐ N/A ☐ Satisfactory ☑ Marginal ☐ Poor
Electrical: Switches: ☑ Yes ☐ No Outlets: ☑ Yes ☐ No *Operates*: ☑ Yes ☐ No
Open ground/reverse polarity: ☐ Yes ☐ **Safety Hazard** ☑ No ☐ Covers missing
Heat source present: ☑ Yes ☐ Not visible Holes: ☐ Doors ☐ Walls ☐ Ceilings
Doors & Windows: ☐ Sat. ☑ Marg. ☐ Poor ☐ Cracked glass ☐ Evidence of leaking insulated glass

General Comments:

Door is delaminated, recommend repair or replacement as needed. Fan light fixture has gap near ceiling and some Wrong bulbs being used, recommend replacing bulbs with proper bulbs and reattaching fixture to eliminate gap as Needed.

BEDROOM

Location: First floor –front left

Walls & Ceiling: ☐ Satisfactory ☑ Marginal ☐ Poor ☑ Typical Cracks ☐ Holes
Moisture stains: ☐ Yes ☑ No
Flooring: ☑ Satisfactory ☐ Marginal ☐ Poor ☐ Squeaks ☐ Slopes
Ceiling fan: ☑ N/A ☐ Satisfactory ☐ Marginal ☐ Poor
Electrical: Switches: ☑ Yes ☐ No Outlets: ☑ Yes ☐ No *Operates*: ☑ Yes ☐ No
Open ground/reverse polarity: ☐ Yes ☐ **Safety Hazard** ☑ No ☐ Covers missing
Heat source present: ☑ Yes ☐ Not visible Holes; ☐ Doors ☐ Walls ☐ Ceilings
Doors & Windows: ☐ Sat. ☑ Marg. ☐ Poor ☐ Cracked glass ☐ Evidence of leaking insulated glass

General Comments:

Large thin crack noted on ceiling, recommend repair as needed. Light fixture has exposed wiring with fixture resting on wires, recommend reattaching light fixture and enclosing wires in fixture as necessary.Awning window crank is Not working, recommend repair or replacement of crank(hardware) as needed.

BEDROOM

Location: First floor –rear left

Walls & Ceiling: ☑ Satisfactory ☐ Marginal ☐ Poor ☐ Typical Cracks ☐ Holes
Moisture stains: ☐ Yes ☑ No
Flooring: ☑ Satisfactory ☐ Marginal ☐ Poor ☐ Squeaks ☐ Slopes
Ceiling fan: ☐ N/A ☐ Satisfactory ☑ Marginal ☐ Poor
Electrical: Switches: ☑ Yes ☐ No Outlets: ☑ Yes ☐ No *Operates*: ☑ Yes ☐ No
Open ground/reverse polarity: ☐ Yes ☐ **Safety Hazard** ☑ No ☐ Covers missing
Heat source present: ☑ Yes ☐ Not visible Holes: ☐ Doors ☐ Walls ☐ Ceilings
Doors & Windows: ☐ Sat. ☑ Marg. ☐ Poor ☐ Cracked glass ☐ Evidence of leaking insulated glass

General Comments:

Fan light fixture has wrong bulbs being used and is wobbling, recommend replacing bulbs with proper bulbs for fixture and securing fan as necessary. Awning window crank is not working, recommend repair or replacement of crank(hardware) as needed.

MASTER BEDROOM

Location: First floor

Walls & Ceiling:	☑ Satisfactory	☐ Marginal	☐ Poor	☐ Typical Cracks	☐ Holes
	Moisture stains:	☐ Yes	☑ No		
Flooring:	☑ Satisfactory	☐ Marginal	☐ Poor	☐ Squeaks	☐ Slopes
Ceiling fan:	☑ N/A	☐ Satisfactory	☐ Marginal	☐ Poor	
Electrical:	Switches: ☑ Yes ☐ No	Outlets: ☑ Yes ☐ No	*Operates*: ☑ Yes ☐ No		
	Open ground/reverse polarity:	☐ Yes	☐ **Safety Hazard**	☑ No	☐ Covers missing
Heat source present:	☐ Yes ☑ No	Holes:	☐ Doors	☐ Walls	☐ Ceilings
Doors & Windows:	☐ Sat. ☑ Marg.	☐ Poor	☐ Cracked glass	☐ Evidence of leaking insulated glass	

General Comments:

There is no heat source present in this room, recommend adding heat source as necessary. Small tears in screen noted, Recommend repair as needed. There is unfinished joint compound present at wall and ceiling intersection of one wall, Recommend sanding compound and finishing with paint as needed.

ROOMS (INTERIOR) REMARKS

Door Stops

All swinging doors should be checked for door stops. Broken or missing door stops can result in door knobs breaking through drywall or plaster.

Closet Guides

Sliding closet doors should be checked to see that closet guides are in place. Missing or broken closet guides can cause scratches and damage to doors.

Cold Air Returns

Bedrooms that do not have cold air returns in them should have a 3/4" gap under the doors to allow cold air to be drawn into the hall return.

AN INSPECTION VERSUS A WARRANTY

A home inspection is just what the name indicates, an inspection of a home...usually a home that is being purchased. The purpose of the inspection is to determine the condition of the various systems and structures of the home. While an inspection performed by a competent inspection firm will determine the condition of the major components of the home, no inspection will pick up every minute latent defect. The inspector's ability to find all defects is limited by access to various parts of the property, lack of information about the property and many other factors. A good inspector will do his or her level best to determine the condition of the home and to report it accurately. The report that is issued is an opinion as to the condition of the home. This opinion is arrived at by the best technical methods available to the home inspection industry. It is still only an opinion.

A warranty is a policy sold to the buyer that warrants that specific items in the home are in sound condition and will remain in sound condition for a specified period of time. Typically, the warranty company never inspects the home. The warranty company uses actuarial tables to determine the expected life of the warranted items and charges the customer a fee for the warranty that will hopefully cover any projected loss and make a profit for the warranty seller. It is essentially an insurance policy.

The service that we have provided you is an inspection. We make no warranty of this property. If you desire warranty coverage, please see your real estate agent for details about any warranty plan to which their firm may have access.

WINDOWS / FIREPLACES / ATTIC

Interior Windows/Glass

General condition: ☐ Satisfactory ☑ Marginal ☐ Poor ☐ Painted shut
☑ Hardware not working ☐ Glazing compound needed ☐ Cracked glass ☐ Broken counter-balance mech.
☐ Surface deterioration: **(See Remarks page)** ☑ Representative number of windows operated
Evidence of leaking insulated glass: ☐ Yes ☑ No ☐ Not determinable ☐ N/A
Safety glazing: ☑ N/A ☐ Safety issue Where:
Security bars present: ☐ Yes ☑ No ☐ Not tested ☐ Test release mechanism before moving in

Fireplace ☑ None Location(s):

☐ Gas ☐ Wood ☐ **Woodburner stove (See Remarks page)**
☐ Masonry insert ☐ Metal insert ☐ Metal ☐ Electric
☐ Blower built-in *Operates:* ☐ Yes ☐ No ☐ *Damper operates* ☐ *Damper missing*
☐ Open joints or cracks in firebrick should be sealed ☐ Pre-fabricated panels damaged/worn
Hearth: Satisfactory: ☐ Yes ☐ No Mantle: ☐ Satisfactory ☐ Loose
☐ **Recommend having flue cleaned and re-examined** ☐ Ventless

Stairs - Not Applicable ☐ Satisfactory ☐ Marginal ☐ Poor ☐ None

Handrail: ☐ Satisfactory ☐ Marginal ☐ Poor ☐ **Safety Hazard**
Risers/Treads: ☐ Satisfactory ☐ Marginal ☐ Poor ☐ Risers/treads uneven

Smoke/CO Detectors **(See Remarks page)**

Smoke detector: ☑ Yes ☐ No *Operates:* ☐ Yes ☐ No ☑ Not tested CO detector: ☐ Yes ☑ No

Attic

Access: ☐ Stairs ☑ Pulldown ☐ Scuttlehole ☐ Knee wall ☐ **No access**
Inspected from: ☐ Access panel ☑ In the attic ☐ Other
Location: ☑ Bedroom hall ☐ Bedroom closet ☐ Garage ☐ Other
Flooring: ☐ Complete ☑ Partial ☐ None
Insulation: Type: Fiberglass ☑ Batts ☐ Loose Average inches: 1-3, 6 on addition
Installed in: ☑ Floor ☐ Rafters ☐ Walls ☐ Not Visible
Vent fans: ☑ Present ☑ Not working ☐ Thermostat controlled ☐ **Safety Hazard**
Ventilation: ☐ Appears adequate ☑ Recommend additional venting
Roof structure: ☑ Wood rafters/joists ☐ Metal rafters/joists ☑ Collar ties
Roof sheathing: ☐ Plywood ☐ OSB ☑ 1x wood ☐ Other
☐ Rotted ☑ Stained-1area ☐ Delaminated ☑ Satisfactory ☐ Marginal ☐ Poor
Fans exhausted to: Attic: ☑ Yes ☐ No Outside: ☐ Yes ☑ No ☐ Not visible ☐ N/A
(See Remarks page)
Chimney vent pipe: ☑ Satisfactory ☐ Needs repairs ☐ Not visible
Structural problems observed: ☐ Yes ☑ No ☐ See comments below
Vapor barriers: ☐ Not visible ☑ Improperly installed **(See Remarks page)**

General Comments

Smoke detectors were not tested at the time of inspection, recommend a minumum of one smoke detector and carbon monoxide detector per floor and to change batteries every 6 months as needed.Gable fan did not appear to be working at the time of inspection, recommend repair or replacement as needed. Recommend increasing the size of gable vents to allow for more cross flow of air and adding ridge vent and soffit vents when reroofing in the future. Exposed electrical wiring noted in attic, recommend enclosing wire in junction box as necessary. Recessed lighting has insulation touching fixtures, these fixtures can get very hot, recommend pulling insulation back 4-5 inches from fixtures as needed. There is a gap in the sheetrock in the attic (missing in one area creating a Fire Egress /Hazard), recommend filling in gap in ceiling behind refrigerator with sheetrock as necessary. Bathroom fan vent pipe connection to aluminum vent pipe in attic has come unfasted and louver does not appear to be opening properly, recommend reattaching pipe connection and checking to make sure louver is opening to allow for proper discharging of moisture to the outside as necessary. Some moisture stains and mold exist on sheathing in attic in one area below rubber roof, however sheathing is functionally okay, recommend sealing valleys and any holes in rubber roofing where water can penetrate or replacing roofing as needed. Original attic has only a couple inches of insulation with the vapor barrier facing the wrong way, recommend removing insulation and installing new insulation with the vapor barrier facing the warm side of home(down).

WINDOWS / FIREPLACES / ATTIC REMARKS

Window Frames and Sills

Window frames and sills often are found to have surface deterioration due to condensation that has run off the window and damaged the varnish. Usually this can be repaired with a solvent style refinisher and fine steel wool. This is sometimes a sign of excess humidity in the house.

See comments regarding caulking doors and windows above (Chimneys/Gutters/Siding).

Fireplaces

It is important that a fireplace be cleaned on a routine basis to prevent the buildup of creosote in the flue, which can cause a chimney fire.

Masonry fireplace chimneys are normally required to have a terra cotta flue liner or 8 inches of masonry surrounding each flue in order to be considered safe and to conform with most building codes.

During visual inspections, it is not uncommon to be unable to detect the absence of a flue liner either because of stoppage at the firebox, a defective damper or lack of access from the roof.

Woodburners

Once installed, it can be difficult to determine proper clearances for woodburning stoves. Manufacturer specifications, which are not usually available to the inspector, determine the proper installation. We recommend you ask the owner for paperwork verifying that it was installed by a professional contractor.

Ventilation

Ventilation is recommended at the rate of one square foot of vent area to 300 square feet of attic floor space, this being divided between soffit and rooftop. Power vents should ideally have both a humidistat and a thermostat, since ventilation is needed to remove winter moisture as well as summer heat. Evidence of condensation, such as blackened roof sheathing, frost on nail heads, etc. is an indication that ventilation may have been or is blocked or inadequate.

Insulation

The recommended insulation in the attic area is R-38, approximately 12". If insulation is added, it is important that the ventilation is proper.

Smoke Detectors

Smoke detectors should be tested monthly. At least one detector should be on each level.

Vapor Barriers

The vapor barrier should be on the warm side of the surface. Most older homes were built without vapor barriers. If the vapor barrier is towards the cold side of the surface, it should be sliced or removed. Most vapor barriers in the attic are covered by insulation and therefore, not visible.

Safety Glazing

Safety glazing requirements vary depending on the age of the home. Every attempt is made to identify areas where the lack of safety glazing presents an immediate safety hazard, such as a shower door. In some older homes it is difficult to determine if safety glazing is present, since the glass is not marked. Therefore, no representation is made that safety glazing exists in all appropriate areas.

Insulated Glass

The broken seals are not always detectable due to dirty windows, covered windows, etc. In most cases, leaking glass seals take some time before they are evident.

BASEMENT

(See Remarks page)

Stairs

Condition:		☐ Satisfactory	☑ Marginal	☐ Poor	☐ **Safety Hazard**
Handrail:	☐ Yes	☑ No Condition:	☐ Satisfactory	☐ Marginal	☐ Poor
Headway over stairs:		☑ Satisfactory	☐ Marginal	☐ Poor	
Under carriage:		☑ Satisfactory	☐ Marginal	☐ Poor	☐ Not visible

Foundation Walls

	☑ Concrete block	☐ Poured concrete	☐ Brick	☐ Fieldstone	☐ Other
Horizontal cracks:	☐ North	☐ South	☐ East	☐ West	☑ None
Step cracks:	☑ North	☐ South	☐ East	☐ West	☐ None
Vertical cracks:	☑ North	☐ South	☐ East	☐ West	☐ None
Covered walls:	☐ North	☐ South	☐ East	☐ West	☑ None
Movement apparent:	☐ North	☐ South	☐ East	☐ West	☑ None
Condition:	☑ Satisfactory	☐ Marginal	☐ **Have evaluated**		☐ **Monitor**

*** **Note:** See below for basement diagram

Condition reported above reflects visible portion only

Floor **(See vapor barrier remarks)**

	☑ Concrete	☐ Dirt/Gravel	☐ Not visible	☐ Other
Condition:	☑ Satisfactory	☐ Marginal	☐ Poor	☐ Typical/excessive cracks

Seismic Bolts

☑ N/A ☐ None visible ☐ Appear satisfactory ☐ **Recommend evaluation**

Basement Drainage

Indication of moisture:	☐ Yes		☑ No	☐ Fresh	☐ Old stains
Sump Pump:	☐ Yes	☑ No	☐ Working	☐ Not working	☐ Not tested
Floor drain(s) present:	☐ Yes	☑ No	☐ Not tested	☐ Efflorescence present	

Drain Tile (See Remarks page) ☐ Palmer valve present ☑ Not Visible **(See Remarks page)**

Girders (1), Columns (2) ☐ N/A

	☑ Steel-2	☑ Wood -1	☐ Block	☐ Concrete	☐ Not visible
Condition:	☑ Satisfactory -1	☐ Marginal	☐ Poor	☑ Stained/rusted-2	

Joists /Trusses

☑ Joist ☐ Trusses	☐ I-Joist	☐ Steel	☑ Wood	☐ Concrete	☐ Not visible
	☐ 2x6	☑ 2x8	☐ 2x10	☐ 2x12	

Sub Floor

☐ Indication of moisture stains/rotting

** Areas around shower stalls, etc., as viewed from basement or crawl space

General Comments

Foundation showed only typical minor shrinkage cracks. Floor appeared to be in overall satisfactory condition. No active seepage visible at the time of the inspection. There is a concrete wall built around basement bilge doors that has to be stepped over to enter the basement, **Be Careful** entering basement .

North

Step/ Vert

West East

South

BASEMENT REMARKS

Basement

Any basement that has cracks or leaks is technically considered to have failed. Most block basements have step cracks in various areas. If little or no movement has occurred, and the step cracks are uniform, this is considered acceptable. Horizontal cracks in the third or fourth block down indicate the block has moved due to outside pressure. They can be attributed to many factors, such as improper grading, improperly functioning gutter and downspout system, etc. Normally, if little or no movement has taken place and proper grading and downspouts exist, this is considered acceptable. If the wall containing the stress crack(s) has moved considerably, this will require some method of reinforcement. Basements that have been freshly painted or tuckpointed should be monitored for movement. This will be indicated by cracks reopening. If cracks reappear, reinforcement may be necessary. Reinforcing a basement wall can become expensive.

Foundation (Covered Walls)

Although an effort has been made to note any major inflections or weaknesses, it is difficult at best to detect these areas when walls are finished off, or basement storage makes areas inaccessible. ***No representation is made as to the condition of these walls.***

Monitor indicates that the walls have stress cracks, but little movement has occurred. In our opinion, the cracks should be filled with mortar and the walls monitored for further movement and cracking. If additional movement or cracking occurs, re-inforcement may be necessary.

Have Evaluated — We recommend that the walls be re-evaluated by a structural engineer or basement repair company and estimates be obtained if work is required.

Vapor Barrier

Floors that are dirt or gravel should be covered with a vapor barrier.

Moisture Present

Basement dampness is frequently noted in houses and in most cases the stains, moisture or efflorescence present is a symptom denoting that a problem exists outside the home. Usual causes are improper downspout extensions or leaking gutters and/or low or improper grade (including concrete surfaces) at the perimeter of the house. A proper slope away from the house is one inch per foot for four to six feet.

Expensive solutions to basement dampness are frequently offered, and it is possible to spend thousands of dollars on solutions such as pumping out water that has already entered or pumping of chemical preparations into the ground around the house, when all that may be necessary are a few common sense solutions at the exterior perimeter. However, this is not intended to be an exhaustive list of causes and solutions to the presence of moisture. ***No representation is made to future moisture that may appear.***

Palmer Valve

Many older homes have a valve in the floor drain. This drain needs to remain operational.

Drain Tile

We offer no opinion about the existence or condition of the drain tile, as it cannot be visibly inspected.

Basement Electrical Outlets

We recommend that you have an outlet within 6' of each appliance. The appliance you plan to install may be different than what exists, therefore the inspection includes testing a representative number of receptacles that exist. It is also recommended to have ground fault circuit interrupts for any outlet in the unfinished part of the basement and crawl spaces.

CRAWL SPACE / SLAB ON GRADE

Slab On Grade
☑ N/A ☐ Not visible Signs of settlement: ☐ Yes ☐ No
☐ Anchor bolts not visible ☐ No anchor bolts ☐ **No Access**

Crawl Space
☐ Full ☐ Combination basement/crawl space

Access to Crawl Space
☐ Exterior ☐ Interior hatch door ☐ Via basement ☐ **No Access**
Inspected from: ☐ Access panel ☐ In the crawl space

Foundation Walls
☐ Concrete block ☐ Poured concrete ☐ Stone ☐ Wood
☐ Brick ☐ Piers & columns ☐ Other
☐ Cracks ☐ Movement ☐ **Have evaluated** ☐ Monitor

Floor
☐ Dirt ☐ Concrete ☐ Gravel ☐ Other
☐ Typical cracks ☐ Large cracks noted

Seismic Bolts
☐ N/A ☐ None visible ☐ Appear satisfactory ☐ **Recommend evaluation**

Drainage
☐ Outside drain ☐ Sump pump Tested: ☐ Yes ☐ No ☐ None apparent
Evidence of moisture damage: ☐ Yes ☐ No

Ventilation
☐ Wall vents ☐ Power vents ☐ None apparent
Tested: ☐ Yes ☐ No

Girders (1), Columns (2)
☐ N/A
☐ Steel ☐ Wood ☐ Block ☐ Concrete ☐ Not visible
Condition: ☐ Satisfactory ☐ Marginal ☐ Poor ☐ Rusted ☐ Cracks

Joists
☐ Joists ☐ Trusses ☐ I-Joist
☐ 2x8 ☐ 2x8 ☐ 2x10 ☐ 2x12

Sub Floor
☐ Not visible ☐ Wood ☐ Concrete ☐ Other

Moisture Stains
☐ Walls ☐ Sub floor ☐ Other

Insulation
☐ None ☐ Walls ☐ Ceiling ☐ Other

Vapor Barrier
☐ Yes ☐ No **(See Remarks page)**
☐ Kraft face ☐ Plastic ☐ Other ☐ Not visible

Basement/Crawl Space Walls
Diagram indicates where wall not visible
and type of covering:
P = Paneling C = Crack(s)
D = Drywall M = Monitor
S = Storage E = Evaluate

North
West East
South

General Comments

CRAWL SPACE / SLAB ON GRADE REMARKS

Crawl Spaces

Crawl spaces are shallow spaces between the first level floor joist and the ground. Access to this area may be from the inside, outside, or not accessible at all. Ductwork, plumbing and electrical may be installed in the space in which access may be necessary. The floor of the crawl space may be covered with concrete, gravel, or may be the original soil. A vapor barrier may be a sheet of plastic or tar paper and installed over or under this material. The vapor barrier will deter the moisture from the earth from escaping into the crawl space and causing a musty smell. Ventilation is also important to control excess moisture buildup. Vents may be located on the outside of the house and are normally kept open in the summer and closed for the winter (where freezing may occur).

The basement/crawl space diagram indicates areas that are covered and not part of a visual inspection. Every attempt is made to determine if paneling is warped, moisture stains are bleeding through, etc. Storage that blocks the visibility of a wall is not removed to examine that area. Therefore, it is important that on your walk-through before closing, you closely examine these areas.

Closed crawl spaces that have vents to the outside should have insulation under the floor above the crawl space.

Have Evaluated

We recommend that the walls be re-evaluated by a structural engineer or basement repair company and estimates be obtained if work is required.

Monitor

Monitor indicates that the walls have stress cracks, but little movement has occurred. In our opinion, the cracks should be filled with mortar and the walls monitored for further movement and cracking. If additional movement or cracking occurs, reinforcement may be necessary.

PLUMBING

Water Service — Shut off location: Unknown

Water entry piping: ☐ Not visible ☐ Copper/Galv. ☐ Plastic/PB ☑ Unknown
Water lines: ☑ Copper ☐ Galvanized ☐ Plastic ☐ **Polybutylene** ☐ Unknown
Lead *(other than solder joints)*: ☐ Yes ☑ No ☐ Service entry ☐ Unknown
Water flow: ☑ Satisfactory ☐ Poor Cross connection: ☐ Yes ☑ No
Water pressure: ☑ Satisfactory ☐ Poor ☐ Above 80 psi **(Needs evaluation)**
Pipes: ☐ Corroded ☐ Leaking ☐ Valves broken/missing ☐ Dissimilar metal
Drain/waste/vent pipe: ☐ Copper ☑ Cast iron ☐ Plastic ☐ Other
Condition: ☐ Satisfactory ☑ Marginal-rusted ☐ Poor ☐ Not visible
Waste discharge: ☐ Satisfactory ☑ Slow drain-1 tub

Gas Lines — ☐ Not visible ☐ Shutoff missing
☑ Copper ☐ Brass ☑ Black iron ☐ Stainless steel ☐ CSST

Well Pump — ☑ N/A **(See Remarks page)**
☐ Submersible ☐ In basement ☐ Well house ☐ Well pit ☐ Shared well
Pressure gauge operates: ☐ Yes ☐ No ☐ Unknown

Sanitary Pump — ☑ N/A
Sealed crock: ☐ Yes ☐ No Check valve: ☐ Yes ☐ No Vented: ☐ Yes ☐ No

Water Heater
Brand name: Bradford White ***Serial #:*** PH9710579 ***Model #:*** M4I0S6LN10
☑ Gas ☐ Electric ☐ Oil ☐ Other Approx. age: 8 yr(s)
Capacity: 40 gallons Seismic restraints needed: ☑ N/A ☐ Yes ☐ No
Relief valve: ☑ Yes ☐ No **Extension proper:** ☑ Yes ☐ No ☐ Missing
Vent pipe: ☐ N/A ☑ Satisfactory ☑ Proper pitch ☐ Rusted ☐ **Safety Hazard**

Water Softener — **(Unit not evaluated)**
☐ Yes ☑ No Plumbing hooked up: ☐ Yes ☐ No

General Comments

Hose faucet was not tested. Turn off valve on the inside of the house and open the outside faucet to allow drainage and to prevent freezing when winterizing. Rust noted on cast iron drain and waste pipes. Did not locate the main water Shutoff at the time of inspection, recommend checking with homeowner as to its location and noting for future reference. Iron gas line feeding gas hot water heater is dangling with no bracing support, recommend adding brace To flooring to support gas line as necessary.Recommend adding dehumidifier to basement to aide moisture control.

PLUMBING REMARKS

Wells

Examination of wells is not included in this visual inspection. It is recommended that you have well water checked for purity by the local health authorities and, if possible, a check on the flow of the well in periods of drought. A well pit should have a locked cover on it to prevent anyone from falling into the pit.

Septic Systems

The check of septic systems is not included in our visual inspection. You should have the local health authorities or other qualified experts check the condition of a septic system.

In order for the septic system to be checked, the house must have been occupied within the last 30 days.

Water Pipes

Galvanized water pipes rust from the inside out and may have to be replaced within 20 to 30 years. This is usually done in two stages: horizontal piping in the basement first, and vertical pipes throughout the house later as needed.

Copper pipes usually have more life expectancy and may last as long as 60 years before needing to be replaced.

Polybutylene pipes are grey pipes that have a history of failure and should be examined by a licensed plumber.

Hose Bibs

During the winter months it is necessary to make sure the outside faucets are winterized. This can be done by means of a valve located in the basement. Leave the outside faucets open to allow any water standing in the pipes to drain, preventing them from freezing. Hose bibs cannot be tested when winterized.

Water Heater

The life expectancy of a water heater is 5-10 years. Water heaters generally need not be replaced unless they leak. It is a good maintenance practice to drain 5-10 gallons from the heater several times a year. ***Missing relief valves or improper extension present a safety hazard.***

Water Softeners

During a visual inspection, it is not possible to determine if water is being properly softened.

Plumbing

The temperature/pressure valve should be tested several times a year by lifting the valve's handle. Caution: very hot water will be discharged. If no water comes out, the valve is defective and must be replaced.

Shut-Off Valves

Most shut-off valves have not been operated for long periods of time. We recommend operating each shut-off valve to: toilet bowl, water heater, under sinks, main shut-off, hose faucets, and all others. We recommend you have a plumber do this, as some of the valves may need to be repacked or replaced. Once the valves are in proper operating order, we recommend opening and closing these valves several times a year.

Polybutylene Piping

This type of piping has a history of problems and should be examined by a licensed plumber and repaired or replaced as necessary.

MECHANICAL DEVICES MAY OPERATE AT ONE MOMENT AND LATER MALFUNCTION; THEREFORE, LIABILITY IS SPECIFICALLY LIMITED TO THOSE SITUATIONS WHERE IT CAN BE CONCLUSIVELY SHOWN THAT THE MECHANICAL DEVICE INSPECTED WAS INOPERABLE OR IN THE IMMEDIATE NEED OF REPAIR OR NOT PERFORMING THE FUNCTION FOR WHICH IS IT WAS INTENDED AT THE TIME OF INSPECTION.

HEATING SYSTEM

Fuel Shutoff for Building	Main fuel shutoff location: Outside at the gas meter				
Boiler System	☐ N/A				
	Brand name: Peerless		***Approximate age:*** 13+ year(s)		
	Model #: 1USA-WC		***Serial #:*** MMW111498-0989		
Energy source:	☑ Gas	☐ LP	☐ Oil	☐ Electric	
Distribution:	☑ Hot water	☑ Baseboard	☑ Floor	☐ Radiator	
Circulator:	☑ Pump	☐ Gravity	☑ Multiple zones		
Controls:	Temp/pressure gauge exist:	☑ Yes ☐ No	*Operating:*	☑ Yes	☐ No
Relief valve:	☑ Yes ☐ No ☐ Missing	Extension proper:	☑ Yes	☐ No	
Operated:	When turned on by thermostat:	☑ Fired	☐ Did not fire		
Operation:	Satisfactory: ☑ Yes ☐ No	☐ **Recommend HVAC technician examine**	☐ Before closing		
Others	☐ N/A				
	☐ Electric baseboard	☐ Radiant ceiling cable	☐ Gas space heater		
	☐ Woodburning stove	**(See Remarks page)**			

General Comments

Boiler appeared to be in normal working order at the time of the inspection.

HEATING SYSTEM REMARKS

HEATING AND AIR CONDITIONING units have limited lives. Normal lives are:

GAS-FIRED HOT AIR......................15-25 years
OIL-FIRED HOT AIR.......................20-30 years
CAST IRON BOILER........................30-50 years
(Hot water or steam) or more
STEEL BOILER..............................30-40 years
(Hot water or steam) or more
COPPER BOILER............................10-20 years
(Hot water or steam)
CIRCULATING PUMP (Hot water).......10-15 years
AIR CONDITIONING COMPRESSOR...8-12 years
HEAT PUMP..................................8-12 years

Gas-fired hot air units that are close to or beyond their normal lives have the potential of becoming a source of carbon monoxide in the home. You may want to have such a unit checked every year or so to assure yourself that it is still intact. Of course, a unit of such an age is a good candidate for replacement with one of the new, high efficiency furnaces. The fuel savings alone can be very attractive.

Boilers and their systems may require annual attention. If you are not familiar with your system, have a heating contractor come out in the fall to show you how to do the necessary things. ***Caution: do not add water to a hot boiler!***

Forced air systems should have filters changed every 30 to 60 days of the heating and cooling season. This is especially true if you have central air conditioning. A dirty air system can lead to premature failure of your compressor - a $1,500 machine.

Oil-fired furnaces and boilers should be serviced by a professional each year. Most experts agree you will pay for the service cost in fuel saved by having a properly tuned burner.

Read the instructions for maintaining the humidifier on your furnace. A malfunctioning humidifier can rust out a furnace rather quickly. It is recommended that the humidifier be serviced at the same time as the furnace, and be cleaned regularly. ***During a visual inspection it is not possible to determine if the humidifier is working.***

Have HVAC Technician Examine - A condition was found that suggests a heating contractor should do a further analysis. We suggest doing this before closing.

Heat exchangers cannot be examined nor their condition determined without being disassembled. Since this is not possible during a visual, non-technically exhaustive inspection, you may want to obtain a service contract on the unit or contact a furnace technician regarding a more thorough examination.

Testing pilot safety switch requires blowing out the pilot light. Checking safety limit controls requires disconnecting blower motor or using other means beyond the scope of this inspection. If furnace has not been serviced in last 12 months, you may want to have a furnace technician examine.

CO Test - This is not part of a non-technical inspection. If a test was performed, the type of tester is indicated on page 27.

Combustible Gas Test (Potential Safety Hazard) - If a combustible gas detector was used during the inspection of the furnace and evidence of possible combustible gases was noted, we caution you that our test instrument is sensitive to many gases and not a foolproof test. None-the-less, this presents the possibility that a hazard exists and could indicate that the heat exchanger is, or will soon be, defective.

COOLING SYSTEM

System Components

Energy source: ☑ Electric ☐ Gas ☐ Other Approximate age: ??? year(s)
Central air: ☐ Air cooled ☐ Water cooled ☐ Evaporative cooler ☐ Heat pump
Operated: ☐ Yes ☐ No ☐ Not operated due to outside temperature
Temperature differential: Unit 1: ??? °F Unit 2: ??? °F **(See Remarks page)**
Operation: Satisfactory: ☐ Yes ☐ No ☐ **Recommend HVAC technician examine** ☐ Before closing
Refrigerant lines: ☐ Leak ☐ Damaged ☐ Insulation missing ☐ Satisfactory
Through wall unit(s): ☐ N/A *Operated*: ☐ Yes ☑ No ☐ Satisfactory ☐ Needs service

General Comments

Through wall A/C unit not tested

ELECTRICAL

Main Panel Location: Dining Room

Amps: 100 Volts: 240 ☑ Breakers ☐ Fuses
Appears grounded: ☑ Yes ☐ No GFCI present: ☐ Yes ☑ No *Operates*: ☐ Yes ☐ No
Main Wire: ☐ Copper ☑ Aluminum ☐ Copper clad aluminum ☐ Not visible
Branch Wire: ☑ Copper ☐ **Aluminum** ☐ Copper clad aluminum ☐ Not visible
☐ Romex ☑ BX cable ☐ Conduit ☐ Knob & tube
☐ Multiple tapping ☐ Branch wires undersized ☐ **Federal Pacific panel (see Remarks)**
☐ Arc fault present *Operates*: ☐ Yes ☐ No ☑ N/A **(see Remarks)**
☐ Panel not accessible ☐ Not evaluated Reason:

Sub Panel(s) ☐ None apparent

Location 1: Basement Location 2: Location 3:
☐ Panel not accessible ☐ Not evaluated Reason:
Branch Wiring: ☑ Copper ☐ **Aluminum** ☐ Copper clad aluminum
Neutral/ground separated: ☑ Yes ☐ No ☐ Have electrician separate
Neutral isolated: ☑ Yes ☐ No ☐ Have electrician isolate
☐ Multiple tapping ☐ Branch wires undersized ☐ **Safety Hazard**

Electrical Fixtures

A representative number of installed lighting fixtures, switches, and receptacles located inside the house, garage, and exterior walls were tested and found to be:

☑ Satisfactory ☐ Marginal ☐ Poor
☐ Open grounds ☐ Reverse polarity ☐ GFCIs not operating ☐ Ungrounded 3-prong outlets
☐ **Solid conductor aluminum branch wiring circuits** **(See Remarks page)**
☐ **Recommend a licensed electrician evaluate the service**

General Comments:

Recommend replacing outlets in kitchen, bathrooms, basement and anywhere within 6 feet of water with GFCI receptacles as needed.

COOLING SYSTEM / ELECTRICAL REMARKS

Electrical

Every effort has been made to evaluate the size of the service. Three wires going into the home indicate 240 volts. The total amps is sometimes difficult to determine. We highly recommend that ground fault circuit interrupters (G.F.C.I.) be connected to all outlets around water. This device automatically opens the circuit when it senses a current leak to ground. This device can be purchased in most hardware stores. G.F.C.I.'s are recommended by all outlets located near water, outside outlets, or garage outlets. Pool outlets should also be protected with a G.F.C.I.

The G.F.C.I. senses the flow of electricity through a circuit. If more current is flowing through the black ("hot") wire than the white ("neutral") wire, there is a current leakage. The G.F.C.I., which can sense a ground leak of as little as .005 amps, will shut off the current in 1/40 of a second, which is fast enough to prevent injury.

If you do have G.F.C.I.'s, it is recommended that you test (and reset) them monthly. When you push the test button, the reset button should pop out, shutting off the circuit. If it doesn't, the breaker is not working properly. If you don't test them once a month, the breakers have a tendency to stick, and may not protect you when needed.

Knob and tube wiring found in older homes should be checked by an electrician to insure that the wire cover is in good condition. Under no circumstances should this wire be covered with insulation. Recess light fixtures should have a baffle around them so that they are not covered with insulation. The newer recessed fixtures will shut off if they overheat.

Federal Pacific electrical panels may be unsafe. See www.google.com and search for "Federal Pacific" for additional and up-to-date information.

Aluminum wiring in general lighting circuits has a history of overheating, with the potential of a fire. If this type of wiring exists, a licensed electrical contractor should examine the whole system.

Arc Faults

In some areas, arc faults are required in new homes, starting in 2002. These control outlets in the bedrooms.

Reverse Polarity

A common problem that surfaces in many homes is reverse polarity. This is a potentially hazardous situation in which the hot and neutral wires of a circuit are reversed at the outlet, thereby allowing the appliance to incorrectly be connected. This is an inexpensive item to correct.

Each receptacle has a brass and silver screw. The black wire should be wired to the brass screw and the white wire should go to the silver screw. When these wires are switched, this is called "reverse polarity". Turning off the power and switching these wires will correct the problem.

Main service wiring for housing is typically 240 volts. The minimum capacity for newer homes is 100 amps, though many older homes still have 60 amp service. Larger homes or all electric homes will likely have a 200 amp service.

Main service wiring may be protected by one or more circuit breakers or fuses. While most areas allow up to six main turnoffs, expanding from these panels is generally not allowed.

Cooling

Testing A/C System and Heat Pump - The circuit breakers to A/C should be on for a minimum of 24 hours and the outside temperature at least 60 degrees for the past 24 hours or an A/C system cannot be operated without possible damage to the compressor. Check the instructions in your A/C manual or on the outside compressor before starting up in the summer. Heat pump can only be tested in the mode it's running in. Outside temperature should be at least 65° for the past 24 hours to run in cooling mode.

Temperature differential, between 14°-22°, is usually acceptable. If out of this range, have an HVAC contractor examine it. It is not always feasible to do a differential test due to high humidity, low outside temperature, etc.

SUMMARY*

ITEMS NOT OPERATING

Lack of heat source in one room(master bedroom)

MAJOR CONCERNS

Item(s) that have failed or have potential of failing soon.

Lack of heat source in one room and aged rubber single ply membrane roof.

POTENTIAL SAFETY HAZARDS

Exposed electrical wiring in attic. Gap in sheetrock between attic and kitchen.

DEFERRED COST ITEMS

Items that have reached or are reaching their normal life expectancy or show indications that they may require repair or replacement anytime during the next five (5) years.

Hot water heater and aged rubber single ply membrane roof.

* Items listed in this report may inadvertently have been left off the Summary Sheet. Customer should read the entire report, including the Remarks.

DEFINITIONS

SATISFACTORY (Sat.) - Indicates the component is functionally consistent with its original purpose but may show signs of normal wear and tear and deterioration.

MARGINAL (Marg.) - Indicates the component will probably require repair or replacement anytime within five years.

POOR - Indicates the component will need repair or replacement now or in the very near future.

MAJOR CONCERNS - A system or component that is considered significantly deficient or is unsafe.

SAFETY HAZARD - Denotes a condition that is unsafe and in need of prompt attention.

COSTS OF REMODELING OR REPAIR

The prices quoted below include a range of prices based on a typical metropolitan area. Individual prices from contractors can vary substantially from these ranges. We advise that several bids be obtained on any work exceeding several hundred dollars. DO NOT RELY ON THESE PRICES... GET FURTHER ESTIMATES.

ITEM	UNIT	ESTIMATED PRICE	
Masonry fireplace	Each	$3,000 -	$6,000
Install prefab fireplace	Each	2,000 -	4,000
Insulate attic	Square foot	.75 -	1.25
Install attic ventilating fan	Each	200 -	300
Install new drywall over plaster	Square foot	1.75 -	2.75
Install new warm air furnace	Each	2,000 -	3,000
Replace central air conditioning electric 3T, on existing ductwork	Each	1,400 -	2,000
Install humidifier	Each	300 -	500
Install electrostatic air cleaner	Each	800 -	1,500
Increase elec. svc. to 60-100 amps	Each	600 -	1,200
Run separate elec. line for dryer	Each	125 -	200
Run separate elec. line for A/C	Each	135 -	200
Install hardwired smoke detector	Each	100 -	180
Install new disposal	Each	250 -	400
Install new dishwasher	Each	500 -	750
Install new hot water boiler	Each	2,000 -	4,000
Install new 30-40 gal water heater	Each	350 -	650
Install new 30 gal. water heater	Each	300 -	500
Dig and install new well	Each	get estimate	
Install new septic system	Each	get estimate	
Regrade around exterior	Each	500 -	900
Install new sump pump and pit	Each	400 -	600
Build new redwood or pressure-treated deck	Square foot	20 -	30
Install storm windows	Each	60 -	150
Install wood replacement windows	Each	400 -	800
Install aluminum or vinyl replacement windows	Each	300 -	800
Install new gutters and downspouts	Linear foot	3.50 -	5.00
Install asphalt shingle over existing roofing	Square foot	1.20 -	1.70
Tear off existing roof and install new asphalt shingle roof	Square foot	2.50 -	4.00
Instl 1-ply membrane rubberized roof	Square foot	get estimate	
Instl new 4-ply built-up tar & gravel	Square foot	get estimate	
Remove asbestos from pipes in bsmt (with probable minimum)	Linear foot	get estimate	
Concrete drive or patio	Square foot	3.00 -	4.00
with removal of old	Square foot	2.25 -	3.00
Clean chimney flue	Each	100 -	200
Add flue liner for gas fuel		900 -	1,200
Add flue liner for oil or wood		2,800 -	3,500

Deferred Costs - It is impossible to determine how long these items will last before needing replacement. The report addresses most of these items from a "condition" standpoint.

PREVENTIVE MAINTENANCE TIPS

I. FOUNDATION & MASONRY: ***Basements, Exterior Walls***: To prevent seepage and condensation problems.
a. Check basement for dampness & leakage after wet weather.
b. Check chimneys, deteriorated chimney caps, loose and missing mortar.
c. Maintain grading sloped away from foundation walls.

II. ROOFS & GUTTERS: To prevent roof leaks, condensation, seepage and decay problems.
a. Check for damaged, loose or missing shingles, blisters.
b. Clean gutters, leaders, strainers, window wells, drains. Be sure downspouts direct water away from foundation. Cut back tree limbs.
c. Check flashings around roof stacks, vents, skylights, chimneys, as sources of leakage. Check vents, louvers and chimneys for birds nests, squirrels, insects.
d. Check fascias and soffits for paint flaking, leakage & decay.

III. EXTERIOR WALLS: To prevent paint failure, decay and moisture penetration problems.
a. Check painted surface for paint flaking or paint failure. Cut back shrubs.
b. Check exterior masonry walls for cracks, looseness, missing or broken mortar.

IV. DOORS AND WINDOWS: To prevent air and weather penetration problems.
a. Check caulking for decay around doors, windows, corner boards, joints. Recaulk and weatherstrip as needed. Check glazing, putty around windows.

V. ELECTRICAL: For safe electrical performance, mark & label each circuit.
a. Trip circuit breakers every six months and ground fault circuit interrupters (G.F.C.I.) monthly.
b. Check condition of lamp cords, extension cords & plugs. Replace at first sign of wear & damage.
c. Check exposed wiring & cable for wear or damage.
d. If you experience slight tingling shock from handling or touching any appliance, disconnect the appliance & have it repaired. If lights flicker or dim, or if appliances go on and off unnecessarily, call a licensed electrician.

VI. PLUMBING: For preventive maintenance.
a. Drain exterior water lines, hose bibs, sprinklers, pool equipment in the fall.
b. Draw off sediment in water heaters monthly or per manufacturer's instructions.
c. Have septic tank cleaned every 2 years.

VII. HEATING & COOLING: For comfort, efficiency, energy conservation and safety.
a. Change or clean furnace filters, air condition filters, electronic filters as needed.
b. Clean and service humidifier. Check periodically and annually.
c. Have oil burning equipment serviced annually.

VIII. INTERIOR: General house maintenance.
a. Check bathroom tile joints, tub grouting & caulking. Be sure all tile joints in bathrooms are kept well sealed with tile grout to prevent damage to walls, floors & ceilings below.
b. Close crawl vents in winter and open in summer.
c. Check underside of roof for water stains, leaks, dampness & condensation, particularly in attics and around chimneys.

IX. Know the location of:
• Main water shutoff valve. • Main electrical disconnect or breaker.
• Main emergency shutoff switch for the heating system.

LESSON #20: APPRAISING/APPRAISALS

What is an appraisal? Review of the *Dictionary of Real Estate Appraisal* offers definitions of appraisal and evaluation. When one studies and expresses his or her opinion based upon professional and work related experience, it is an appraisal. It is a process of estimating market value, insurance values, or some other defined value of a parcel of real estate which is identified either with a legal description or a property address as of a certain point in time, either the past, the present, or the future.

It is a supportable opinion of value.

Methods of Reporting.

An appraisal can be either oral or written. Most appraisals are in a written format. They are done to state and federal guidelines and regulations. One of the most recent guiding regulations is called USPAP. These are the 'Uniform Standards of Professional Appraisal Practice.' They are followed as federal guidelines.

Sometimes an individual may encounter what is called a Market Value Analysis. These are reports that are formulated by Real Estate Agents and REALTORS® to give a range of possible sale prices. Many of these market value analyses can be very accurate and helpful. However, they are not held to the state and federal guidelines as appraisals are. Often they are not accepted by the court systems or by lenders, banks and mortgage companies, or insurance companies.

Valuation Methods for Residential Appraisals

There are three recognized valuation methods in the residential appraisal industry.

The first method is called the **cost approach to value**. This approach is an estimation of what it costs to rebuild a house or buildings on a property. This is then compared to physical depreciation or functional depreciation or external depreciation. The experience and research by the appraiser applies what is acceptable in that real estate market. This can be on a mathematical basis, or it can be based on judgment and experience. After the land and buildings are estimated, there are estimates of the land or lot value and the site improvements. Sometimes the appraiser is asked to do a separate appraisal of land and/or lot values. This gets into a detailed process of checking the features of one property versus several other recently sold properties, and coming up with a valuation, after adjustments, based upon front footage, lot size, acreage, or on square footage of the lot.

The combination of the depreciated cost of the house/buildings, lot and site improvements, give a cost approach value.

The second widely used method is called the **sales comparison analysis**. What is done is listing and analyzing the features of the subject property. Many times there are from 16 to 30 areas of comparison. Then comparing them to at least three recently sold comparable properties. Judgment and experience in the local real estate market is essential to make proper comparisons.

Obviously the most accurate analysis is on matching Chevrolet-type properties to Chevrolet-type properties, not comparing them to Cadillac or Yugo-type properties. Enclosed is a sample appraisal report that uses the grid type demonstration so that adjustments can be made either in a positive fashion or a negative fashion. If the compared property (comparable) needs to be brought up to the subject property, a positive or plus adjustment is given. If it has a superior feature such as being larger than the subject property, it is given a negative adjustment. The dollar adjustments are totaled and applied to the sales price, giving a range of at least three values for three comparables used. Then it is dependant on the appraiser's judgment and experience to establish a value by the sales comparison approach, and give his or her reasoning behind that valuation.

(A quick value check is to compare the subject value/S.F. to the sales price/S.F. of the comparables. The subject value should be similar to or fall within the range of the comparables.)

The third recommended and recognized valuation method is called the **income approach**. This is based upon being able to accurately establish a market rent. The market rent is something that is very difficult to research because it is based upon a rental property with similar features like the subject. The next step is establishing a multiplier called a gross rent multiplier, which is established after considerable research. The market rent is multiplied times the multiplier to give the valuation. In some real estate markets, this information is available. In the real world, being able to research and verify this data is very difficult and rare. This method is not often used because of the lack of good, current, credible information.

So most appraisal reports you will see will be using the cost approach and the sales comparison approach. Then the appraiser indicates which approach, or if both approaches, are most applicable to the valuation. Where the income approach information is available, that could be the most accurate indicator. An appraiser is obligated to comment if that approach was or was not used, and if it is appropriate for that appraisal.

Length of Validity

Appraisal reports are completed as of a definite date. This is to be specified on the report. In situations involving mortgages and home loans, many banks and mortgage companies will accept appraisals done from 6-12 months prior to their business transaction. It can vary from bank to bank on what they accept. An appraiser can update the report or reestablish the value in a supplemental report. There are certain procedures to do that. Some banks/mortgage companies will accept an updated report. Some will not, demanding that a new report be completed with new data and new sales.

Functions/Types of Appraisals

Here are seven common types of appraisals.

1. **Sales/refinance/proposed construction**. These appraisal reports are most common when home buying, home refinancing, or when a home is to be built or a manufactured home is moved to a vacant lot to be permanently attached to the real estate. These are often completed on a pre-printed form which are usually to government regulations, with check-the-box or fill-in-the-blank type forms. They use and/or recognize all three approaches to value.

2. **Divorce appraisal.** This type can be very similar to a sales type of appraisal, and using the same type of form. Again, it is done to a specific date. Some types of divorce appraisals have a dual function or dual appraisal values. This is because the appraiser is asked to appraise the house or property as of two different valuation dates. This can be done as of the present date, and also the date of marriage. The reason for this is because if one of the couple was living in and owned the house prior to the marriage, there is a need to establish the value at that time. Then there is a need to establish the value at a later date. The attorneys or the court systems can determine how much the property has increased in value during the marriage, to make a settlement. Suppose the house was worth $100,000 at the date of marriage. Then after several years there was a divorce involved. When the couple separated, or at the specific date of the appraisal, it was worth $150,000. The house had appreciated $50,000 during the course of the marriage, and there would then be some determination of how that would be split. This may differ from state to state, but this has been my experience in the State of Michigan. Obviously you're going to need an appraiser who can handle this more difficult type of valuation. It is more difficult to go back in time, estimate the cost approach, and also to have the records and materials to compare what properties were selling for and bring up comparables at dates that may have been 10 or 15 years prior to the present date.
3. **Estate appraisal.** This type is often used to settle the demands for court purposes or for the heirs to settle the worth and division of real estate. Usually the value is established at the date of death. The form used can be similar to a sales type of appraisal.
4. **Insurance appraisal.** This type can be used at the time of disaster, such as a fire, windstorm, tornado, or other calamity that makes the house a total loss. If you would like to see more details and discussion, I refer you to the chapter about Assessor Cards. In an insurance appraisal,

there is an estimate of what it would cost to rebuild the house, less depreciation, and less the cost of the lot and site improvements. This is because the land and site improvements are usually not destroyed in a catastrophe. The insurance policy does not insure the lot, because it is still salvageable. The key to checking about insurance appraisals is to see if the appraiser has sufficient current knowledge and experience in the cost of rebuilding homes. Sometimes the book values and cost services that are available are not accurate to the local area. Those are questions to be asked if the appraiser actually deals with local builders in formulating the costs.

Sometimes insurance appraisals are developed to properly estimate the cost of rebuilding the structure prior to obtaining insurance.

5. **Relocation appraisals**. These are used by management companies, when an employee is transferred out of state or out of country. If the employees are not able to sell their home, the employer may be obligated to buy that house. Sometimes there are two or three appraisals completed, and consideration of both or all three valuations are taken in which to buy out the employee's house. These appraisals take different types of formats. Commonly they do not include the cost approach. They do include the sales comparison approach, often with provisions for forecasting what is going on in the local market. This involves research by the appraiser to see if prices are actually decreasing, and if sellers are giving concessions to finalize the sale of their houses.

Also included in relocation appraisals are comparisons of three or more similar listed properties that are for sale. Then the features of the subject are compared to the features of those competing properties, and judgments are made. One of the big differences in this type of appraisal is the ability to understand trends, and have a basis on which to project future trends by the appraiser.

6. **Foreclosure appraisals**. These are often engaged by banks or mortgage companies. Estimating the cost of repairs after taking back a home in the foreclosure process is critical. Sometimes the value is asked to be identified both prior to and after the foreclosure.
7. Another type of appraisal is for **tax purposes**. These may be used to appeal state property taxes through the state and local boards of appeal.

Report Formats

Reports can be in a narrative fashion explaining the various topics that are needed to solve that appraisal problem. They can be anywhere from one to many pages in length. The narrative type of appraisal reports are more common in tax appeals and government actions involving easements, and the taking of property by eminent domain.

The most common type of appraisals are pre-printed, government approved forms which are almost like multiple-choice tests. They consist of checking boxes or filling in blank lines on the report form. There are several types of forms available. Included is an example of an appraisal report form. The first page involves the address and a legal description, so we will know the property location. Then we get a description of the type of neighborhood, location, property values, marketing times, prices and ages of properties in that area. The next section is the actual lot or land involved, its size and the utilities. Next involves a description of the actual house, indicating the number of stories, its design, its age, the type of windows, the exterior, and the type of construction. The following section involves listing the room count on each level by types, such as living room, dining room, kitchen, bedrooms, baths. Some forms even give other options. Then we come down with a room count, and the square footage of the gross living area. Often at the bottom of these forms are comments, so the appraiser can give more detail about good and bad features of the home.

Page 2 involves a very simplistic cost approach which gives an estimation of lot value, the dwelling cost, basement cost and garage cost, less depreciation, and coming up with a sum total valuation by the cost approach. In the right-hand portion of the page is a calculation of the gross living area, showing the math and calculations.

The sales comparison approach is next. In this example there are 13 rows of comparison. The subject and its features are listed in the first column, and then it is compared to three comparable sales and dollar amount adjustments, either positive or negative, based upon how they compare. There is the comment section giving some additional detail. Next involves valuation arrived at by the sales comparison approach. There is also a space for the income approach.

Next are comments that have a bearing on the report, and how the appraiser reconciled the values used in coming at a final valuation, and the date of report.

Many times there are additional pages to the report. One of these pages can be a drawing of the house, lot, and a location of the house on a particular street or in a particular city. Another addendum can be a set of guidelines or limiting conditions that can define market value and the appropriate use of the report, and the conditions by which the appraiser did the appraisal.

The comparable photo page is another supplemental page, which includes photos of the comparables used.

A location map shows where the comparables are located in relation to the subject property.

Some appraisers will attach a comment page, going into more detail of the analysis used and how the comparisons of the subject versus the comparables used in completing the appraisal.

In most home buying situations, an appraisal will be on a printed form with various supplemental pages attached.

APPRAISAL REPORT

ADDRESS: 1245 Maple St. Grand Blanc, MI. 48439

LEGAL DESCRIPTION: Lot 39 Maplewood Subdivision

APPRAISER: Richard C. Smith

LOCATION: ☒ Urban ☐ Suburban ☐ Rural

PROPERTY VALUES: ☒ Increasing ☐ Stable ☐ Declining

MARKETING TIMES: ☐ Under 3 mos. ☒ 3- 6 mos. ☐ Over 6 mos.

PRICES: $100,000 to $175,000

AGE: New to 80 yrs.

LOT: 85' x 100'

UTILITIES: ☒ Electric ☒ Gas ☒ Water ☒ Sewer

NO. STORIES: One

EXTERIOR Brick

CRAWLSPACE: Yes

DESIGN: Ranch

ROOF: Comp. Shingle

EXISTING: Yes

WINDOW TYPE: Casement

BASEMENT: Yes

AGE: 45 yrs.

MANUFACTURED HOME: No

ROOMS	LIVING	DINING	KITCHEN	BEDROOMS	BATHS	S.F.
Basement						1067
Level 1	1	Area	1	2	1.5	1297
Level 2						

ROOM COUNT: 4 **Rooms** 2 **Bedrooms** 1.5 **Baths**

COMMENTS: Remodeling: heating system, roof, plumbing, exterior doors, ceiling fans, garbage disposal, garage door opener. Whole house fan, basement hobby room and storage room. 2 fireplaces, ample closets and storage. Above average condition.

APPRAISAL REPORT

COST APPROACH

						Lot Value	$	25,000
Dwelling	1297	s.f.	@	$	113.51	=		147,222
Basement	1067	s.f.	@	$	32.81	=		35,008
Garage	440	s.f.	@	$	27.18	=		11,959
							$	194,189

DEPRECIATION

PHYSICAL	FUNCTIONAL	EXTERNAL	
87,385	2,000		-89,385
			104,803
		SITE IMPROVEMENTS	17,500
			$ 147,303

VALUE BY COST APPROACH

GROSS LIVING AREA

See attached sheet
Functional for shop
and fireplace

SALES COMPARISON

	SUBJECT	SALE 1		SALE 2		SALE 3	
	1245 Maple	11803 Stuart		328 Rust Park		11738 Scram	
SALES PRICE:		$140,900		$140,200		$145,000	
SAELS PRICE/S.F.:	$110.64/s.f.	$119.91/s.f.		$107.85/s.f.		$139.96/s.f.	
SITE:	85 x 100	60x120	+2500	98 x 250	-5000	60 x 398	-5000
DESIGN (STYLE):	1 story	1 story		1 story		2 story	+2000
AGE:	45	54	+2100	56	+ 2800	74	+8000
CONDITION:	Avg/Good	Good	-2500	Avg/Good		Avg/Good	
SQ.FT:	1297	1175	+4800	1300	+1100	1036	+9000
BATHS:	1.5	1	+500	1.5		1	+500
BASEMENT:	Yes	Yes		Slab	+5000	Yes	
FINISHED:	Hobby Room	Finish	-3500		+500		+500
GARAGE:	G-1/shop	G-2	-2500	G-2	-2500	G-2	-2500
OTHER:	C. Por, Pat	C. Por	+200	En.Por	-1800	C. Por	+200
OTHER:	2FP	FP,DW	+800	FP, DW	+800	DW	+2300
ADJUSTMENTS:			+2400		+900		+15000
ADJUSTED SALES PRICES:			$143,200		$141,300		$160,000

Most credence placed on #1's value.

VALUE BY SALES APPROACH $143,500

VALUE BY INCOME APPROACH N/A

COMMENTS: Income Approach not applicable, lack of data.

RECONCILIATION: Cost Approach and Sales Approach were reviewed. Most credence placed on the sales Approach Value

APPRAISER: Richard C. Smith **DATE of APPRAISAL**: August 1, 2004

COMMENTS: Market Conditions in the Subject Neighborhood

The subject neighborhood is part of the local School District. Statistics are kept by the Local Multiple Listing Service on a district-wide basis. The subject neighborhood reflects the market conditions of the district. Per the local MLS second quarter 2004 report for this district: the average marketing time was 97 days. The sales price to listing price ration was 96%. The average sold price as $170,000. There were 241 sales. Slowing market has resulted in longer marketing times. Exposure and seasonal marketing times should coincide. Financing methods are 90% conventional mortgages, 10% down payment, 5% FHA financing, 3% of the sales prices as concessions to assist with closing costs. Last year's report reflects the average marketing time was 70 days. There are an unusually high number of houses for sale on the subject's street (8).

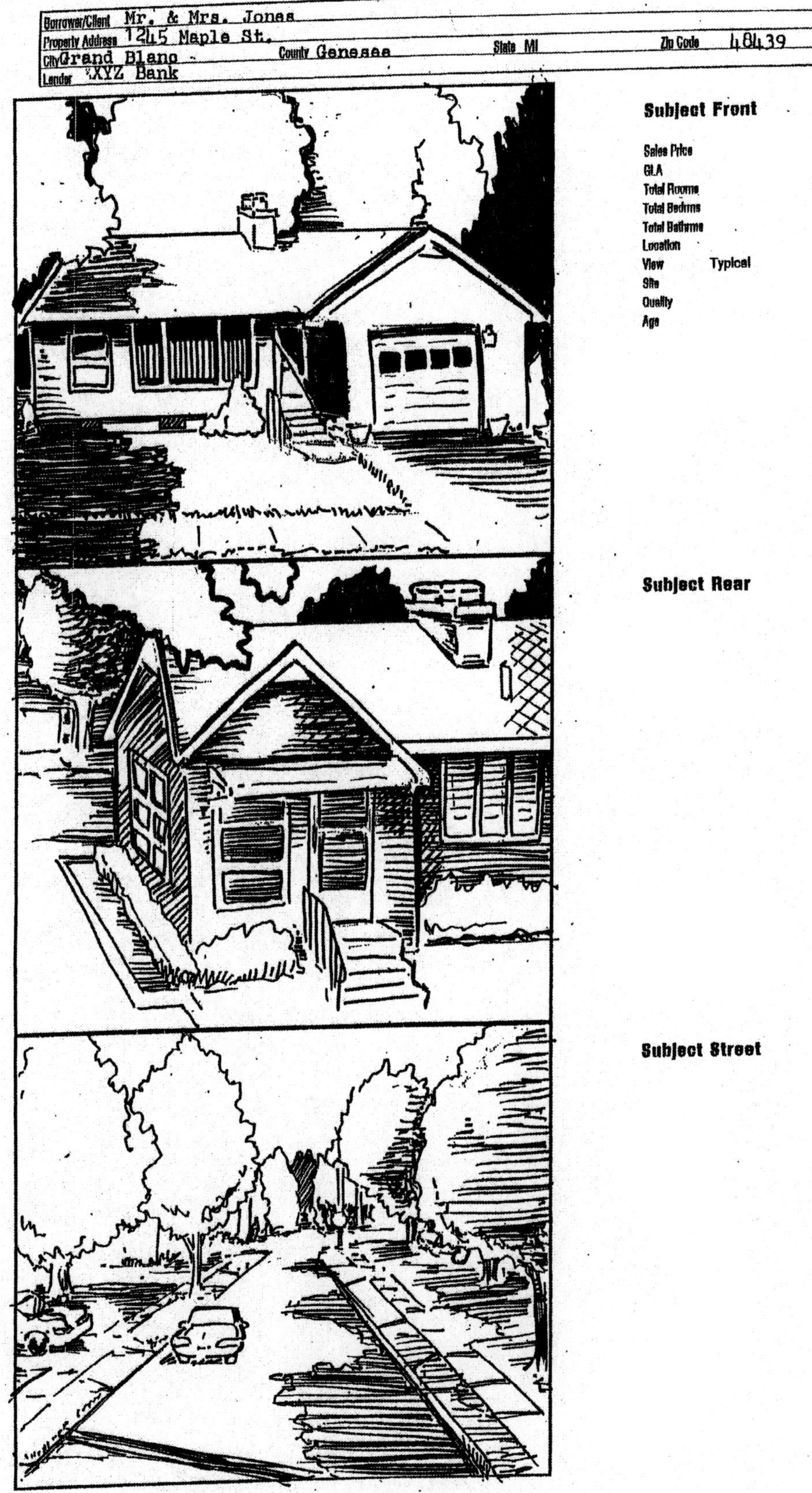

Subject Photo Page

Borrower/Client	Mr. & Mrs. Jones
Property Address	1245 Maple St.
City	Grand Blanc
County	Genesee
State	MI
Zip Code	48439
Lender	XYZ Bank

Subject Front

Sales Price
GLA
Total Rooms
Total Bedrms
Total Bathrms
Location
View Typical
Site
Quality
Age

Subject Rear

Subject Street

SKETCH/AREA TABLE ADDENDUM

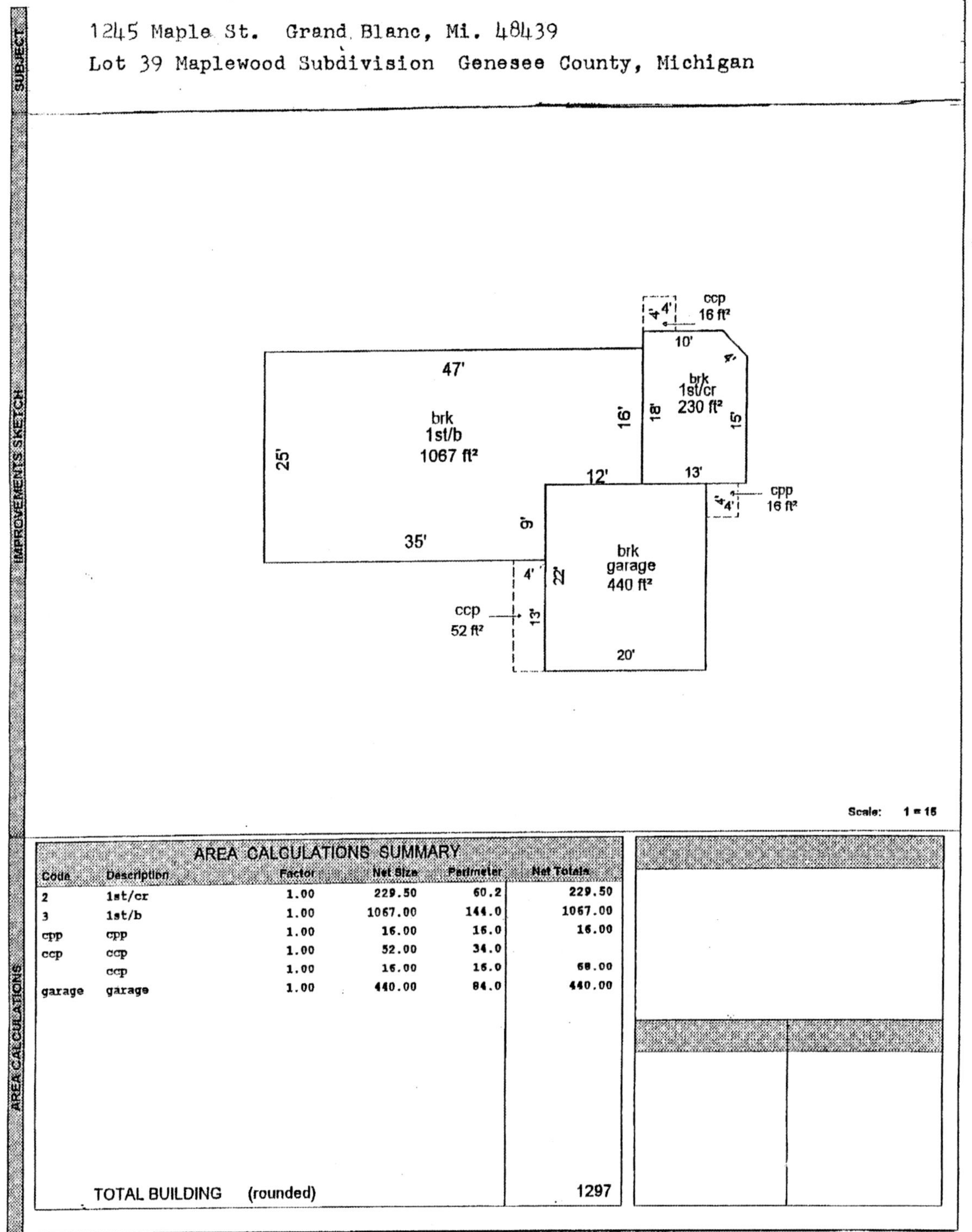

SUBJECT

1245 Maple St. Grand Blanc, Mi. 48439
Lot 39 Maplewood Subdivision Genesee County, Michigan

IMPROVEMENTS SKETCH

Scale: 1 = 16

AREA CALCULATIONS

AREA CALCULATIONS SUMMARY

Code	Description	Factor	Net Size	Perimeter	Net Totals
2	1st/cr	1.00	229.50	60.2	229.50
3	1st/b	1.00	1067.00	144.0	1067.00
cpp	cpp	1.00	16.00	16.0	16.00
ccp	ccp	1.00	52.00	34.0	
	ccp	1.00	16.00	16.0	68.00
garage	garage	1.00	440.00	84.0	440.00
TOTAL BUILDING	(rounded)				1297

Comparable Photo Page

Borrower/Client Mr. & Mrs. Jones
Property Address 1245 Maple St.
City Grand Blanc County Genesee State MI Zip Code 48439
Lender XYZ Bank

Comparable 1

11803 Stuart

Proximity	.5 Block South
Sale Price	140,900
GLA	1,175
Total Rooms	6
Total Bedrms	3
Total Bathrms	1
Location	Urban
View	Typical
Site	60 x 120
Quality	Alm/Avg
Age	54

Comparable 2

328 Rust Park

Proximity	.6 Mile North
Sale Price	140,200
GLA	1,300
Total Rooms	6
Total Bedrms	3
Total Bathrms	1.5
Location	Urban
View	Typical
Site	98 x 253
Quality	Alm/BV/Av-Gd
Age	56

Comparable 3

11736 Schram

Proximity	.7 Mile Southwest
Sale Price	145,000
GLA	1,036
Total Rooms	6
Total Bedrms	3
Total Bathrms	1
Location	Urban
View	Typical
Site	66 x 396
Quality	Alm/Avg
Age	74 / 65 EF

This addendum is designed to simplify the reporting of comments most often required by banks, mortgage companies and clients.

COMMENTS

Every effort has been made to conform to FNMA and FHLMC Guidelines; and, in most cases, an even stricter interpretation found common to most investors in the secondary market.

The appraiser has chosen what are believed to be the best comparable sales available from the market search. Adjustments in the "Market Data Approach" are based on market extraction, not cost figures. Occasionally it is necessary to use comparable sales that occurred over 6 months prior to the appraisal date, have individual adjustments exceeding 25% of the comparable's sale price that have net adjustments more than 15% of the comparables' sale price and that are located more than 10 blocks from the subject, etc.

Not every subject property can be compared to "ideal" comparable sales, the best sales are chosen from the market search which meet investor underwriting standards but also guidelines established by FNMA, Appraisal Institute and National Association of Independent Fee Appraisers. This appraisal complies with (FIRREA) and USPAP).

In Michigan, all apprasiers are required to be licensed.

Measurements are per the standards of the Appraisal Institute and Marshall Swift.

Every effort is made to verify information with local government records. Where records/data are not available, we are forced to rely upon other sources.

1. Please be advised that in the market approach grid, the middle adjustment line is for the baths and bedrooms. the bottom adjustment line is for the square feet.

2. All comparable sales are closed to the best of the appraiser's knowledge. Verification is with buyer, seller, Realtor, Agent, or MLS.

2a. All sales dates used are the closing date, not contract dates.

3. I am unable to verify the insulation "R" factor. The presence of UREA-FORMALDEHYDE FOAM INSULATION could not be determined. If UFFI is present, the appraised market value may be adversely affected or voided. Any information about insulation stated on the appraisal was provided by inspection, owner or agent, and is assumed to be accurate for appraisal purposes only.

8. It is noted comparable sales No.(s) 2 are located more than 10 blocks from the subject but is/are considered the best available.

9. Subject is located in a small urban area. Comparable sales in the immediate neighborhood are lacking. We were required to select sales at a greater distance than normal. Those selected are the most comparable sales revealed.

12. It is noted the price per living area number for sales No.(s) 1, 3 varies by more than $10. per S.F. compared to the subject and the sales chosen are considered the best available.

15a. No items of personal property were considered in value: such as, but not limited to, portable dishwashers, window air conditioners, above ground pools and satellite antenna dishes.

30. It is not known if Radon gas is present. If it is present, the market value of the subject property may be adversely affected or voided. No warranty is made with this appraisal, as special tests are required to detect Radon gas.

32. We assume all appliances, electrical, heating, cooling and plumbing systems are functional.

34. It should be noted that subject was built prior to 1978 and may have lead based paint.

35. It is unknown if hazardous material exist on and/or below this property such as: petroleum products, Urea-Formaldehyde or any other environmental hazards. The value estimated is predicated upon the assumption none exist. If you assume that any hazardous material may exist, you may wish to engage the services of an expert in that field. The appraiser is not an engineer, contractor and/or a legal expert and is not licensed in any of these fields of expertise. I do not assume any responsibility for any unknown or unseen condition or latent defect.

36. Property not sold within past 12 months.

Any party who uses or relies upon any information in this report, without the preparer's written consent, does so at their own risk.

Please Note: If a name change conversion is requested on the appraisal there may be a minimal charge for this service.

Replacement Cost Calculated from Marshall-Swift Cost Book, local multipliers were used.

Opinion of Market Value is predicated upon an occupancy permit provided by the local unit of government and a survey.

This appraisal is not a home inspection or gurarantee of condition.

This report, including conclusions about the property value is intended for the sole use of the client. Any further distribution of this report is unintended and the appraiser assumes no obligation, liability, or accountability to any part other than the client.

n Michigan, Appraisers are required to be Licensed/Certified and are regulated by Michigan Department of Labor and Economic Growth, PO Box 30016, Lansing, MI 48909.

If court testimony or depositions is/are required, our fee is $500.00 (per day) or any part thereof. Pretrial conferences are at our hourly rate of $50.00 (per hour). Standby testimony is $100.00 (per day) or any part thereof.

In Michigan, all appraisers are required to be licensed.

(Rev 3-03)

ADDITONAL COMMENTS:

There was a limited supply of recently sold comparables for the appraisal. Subject has an overabundance of 3 fireplaces for homes in this size and value range. The main detracting feature is having only 2 bedrooms as most comparables have 3 bedrooms. This could narrow the market especially for families with children.

COMP # 1 - Nearby, smaller lot, aluminum construction, older, remodeling per MSL includes updated kitchen, 3 bedrooms, smaller house, finished basement with bath, 2 car garage. Good value indicator.

COMP # 2 - Originally listed at $146,900. Price was reduced to $142,000 after 18 days. Seller concessions. Larger lot. Aluminum-brick construction, older house, 3 bedrooms, smaller house, slab (no basement), 2 car garage, enclosed porch, shed. Sets low end of value range.

COMP # 3 - Seller concessions, larger lot, inferior 2 story style, aluminum construction, older house, 3 bedrooms, smaller house, 2 car garage, no fireplace, shed. Sets high end of value range.

Most credence placed on # 1's value.

Location Map

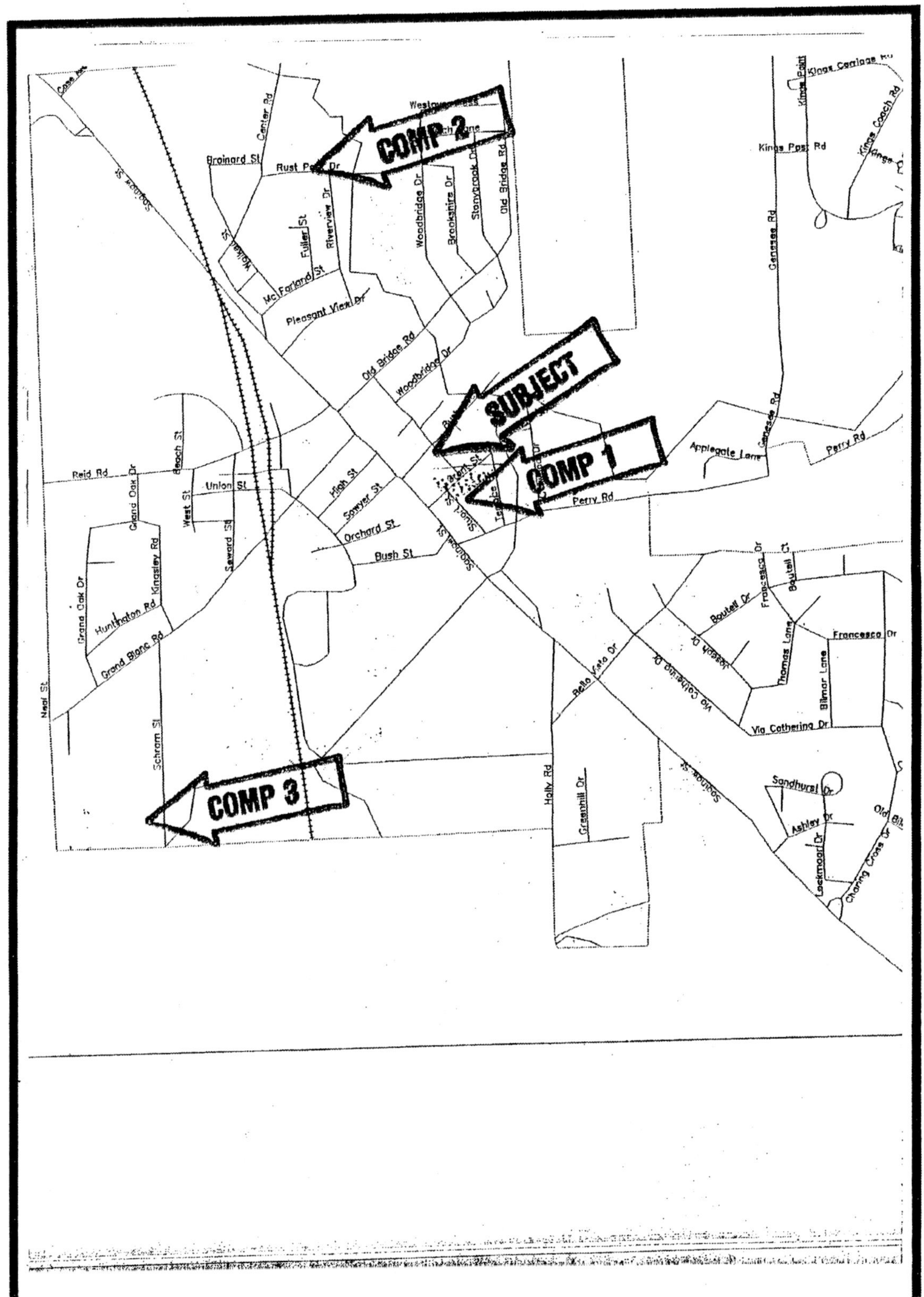

Double-checking on Appraisals/Appraisers

A relocation management company needed to hire two appraisers: Appraiser A and Appraiser B. The assignment was to appraise a transferee's suburban 7-year-old home. Mrs. Transferee is a full-time real estate agent specializing in that market. The home was listed with a real estate company for $240,000.

There are only 60 homes in this small rural subdivision. Several similar competing subdivisions are within 1-3 miles.

The transferee was allowed to pick one appraiser. The management company provided an approved list of appraisers, from which Mr. & Mrs. Transferee could interview and choose an appraiser.

Mrs. Transferee called Appraiser A asking, "Are you familiar with and have you done appraisals in our subdivision? Our house has many extra customized features, making it one of the best in the subdivision."

"Yes," replied Appraiser A.

Mrs. Transferee asked, "Do you use only comparables from our small subdivision, as sales are limited and slow? Or do you use comparables from outside our subdivision?"

"From a recent appraisal in your subdivision (with limited sales)," replied Appraiser A, "I was forced to consider comparables from within the subdivision and from other nearby ***similar*** *competing subdivisions to match the subject home's features and value. The reason is that I'm obligated to look/home-shop through the eyes of educated homebuyers. They would also consider other subdivisions."*

Mrs. Transferee learned Appraiser A's philosophy/training/attitude and was satisfied. She requested A do an appraisal via the management company.

Appraiser A and Mrs. Transferee were not acquainted, nor were they business associates.

When A did the inspection phase, Mrs. Transferee provided three comparables supporting the listed price of $240,000. One comparable was from within the subdivision selling for $235,000 ***18 months ago****. It was too old to be used in the appraisal. Her information is allowable, but A is obligated to reveal this to the management company.*

Appraiser A used different nearby comparables. He had already researched two of her comparables.

A's appraisal value was $220,000. (This is known only to A and the management company.) He used sales from nearby subdivisions, after finding no ***recently*** *sold* ***suitable*** *sales from the subdivision.*

Two weeks later, the management company faxed a memo to A. There was a wide difference of value ranges between A's appraisal and B's appraisal (no value was revealed). They requested A to review comparables #1, #2, and #3 from B's appraisal. B used ***only*** *sales from* ***within*** *the subdivision. However, A felt these sales/comparables were not good comparisons.*

Appraiser A realized that Mrs. Transferee's extra customized features costs (such as a specially installed cedar wood deck versus standard wood decks, custom stair railings) would not be fully rewarded in the marketplace. (Functional obsolescence.)

Appraiser A verified B's #1, #2 and #3 comparables, and ran comparisons. He reported his disagreements.

It appeared that B's appraisal was $200,000.

Appraiser A knew that the subdivision's assessment (assessor's estimated market values) were very accurate. This is due to new to 7-year-old homes with ***recent*** *deeds of lot sales, and recently built* *homes' sale prices reflecting builders' costs. Home sale price records reflected the differences of $175,000 homes versus $250,000 homes, which are entered into the assessor's database.*

As a crosscheck, A compared the assessor's estimated market value of B's #1, #2, and #3 (all from within the subdivision) versus their recent sale prices. #1: $193,000/sold for $199,000; #2: $170,200/sold for $200,950; and #3: $189,000/sold for $190,000. So the assessor had accuracy rates of 97%, 85% and 99 %.

The assessor's estimated market value of Mrs. Transferee's property was $217,400.

As you recall, A's appraisal was $220,000.

In my opinion of the four value opinions, A's appraisal and the assessor's are most accurate.

The lesson learned is this: Check if the appraiser has experience in the area and what is his/her philosophy/methodology/training in using **suitable** comparisons wherever the source. (They can be from within the subdivision or from **similar** competing subdivisions reflecting the current market and buyer's attitudes/requirements.)

Pick your experienced/well-trained appraiser wisely. Don't be "high-balled" or "low-balled."

How to Pick an Appraiser

Included are some suggestions that I have developed when clients or individuals have asked how to pick or hire an appraiser in a different city or state.

1. Is he or she licensed? Will they provide a copy of the license?

2. How long have they been licensed? Are there different types of licenses in the area where they practice their business? In some areas there are regular residential appraisal licenses, some licenses for commercial property appraisers, and some licenses for trainees. What type of license do they hold?
3. How long have they been a resident of the area where the property is located? How long have they been appraising properties in that area?
4. Does that person have any similar job experience or licenses? Do they have training as a home inspector, or do they have a builder's license? Do they have a real estate license?
5. Do they carry insurance? Not only is it important to have errors and omissions insurance for some serious defect in the appraisal, but does that appraiser carry any type of health and accident insurance, or workman's comp insurance? How about bonding insurance? *I have been attacked by the neighbor's dog while I was on the homeowner's premises, and fortunately escaped without serious injury. The dog was tied up and hidden without any knowledge of the homeowner, but he very possibly could have been subject to a lawsuit. If the appraiser has no other means to recover his or her medical bills, guess who's going to get sued.* (Bonding includes criminal exposure, or the stealing of property from within a house.)
6. What types of residential appraisals do you do?
    1. Sales:
        A. For sale by owner.
        B. Sales after the purchase agreement, such as for a mortgage.
    2. Proposed construction from plans and specs (from blueprints and specification sheets).
    3. Divorce appraisals.

4. Estates.

5. Relocation appraisals.

6. Foreclosure appraisals.

7. Tax appraisals/government taking by eminent domain.

8. Insurance.

7. Do you have any additional training leading to present or past professional degrees or designations?

    1. What are the designations?

    2. Describe the training involved.

8. Do you have any court testimony experience or deposition experience?

It would not be wise to get a cheapy divorce or estate appraisal, and later have the appraiser testify or have to give a deposition to attorneys, making less than a believable presentation of the appraisal. *(Paying the fee of an expert is usually cheapest in the long run. I have actually testified in a case where the opposing appraiser turned to the judge in the beginning of the questioning and said, "Your Honor, I am not a licensed appraiser even though I have done this appraisal." Believe me, that did not go over very well.)*

9. Can he or she give references such as names of past customers, and their names and/or phone numbers?

10. Personal endorsements and references are the best. Ask bankers, attorneys, REALTORS®, or other friends who had appraisals done. Their recommendations can be like gold.

11. Telephone book classified advertising sections can be extremely helpful to get credentials and experience, but much of this information can be inflated.
12. Looking over directories from state or national appraiser organizations can be a good guide. Ask the appraiser if he or she has ever been listed in any of these directories, or is presently listed.
13. Many states have registers of closed rural landfills. They are rated according to Environmental Protection Agency potential hazards. Does/has the appraiser studied or have a register when doing rural appraisals?

Sometimes people trying to make a killing in real estate-- shoot themselves in the foot!

LESSON #21: NEGOTIATING

As a refresher in composing this chapter, I reviewed several references. Three dictionaries and one how-to book were consulted: *The Dictionary of Real Estate Appraisal; The American Heritage Dictionary; Webster's Dictionary;* and *You Can Negotiate Anything.* From those sources a definition for negotiating was formulated. Plus drawing upon numerous years of negotiations, experience skills and techniques learned from attorneys, adjusters, and real estate practitioners.

Negotiating is the process of bargaining/conferring with another person(s) to reach an agreement to exchange the ownership of real estate (a home or land) for financial benefit.

The three main elements involved in the negotiating process are:

1. **Knowledge**
2. **Deadlines**
3. **Financial ability**

I do not claim to have negotiated thousands of home sales. However, listening to many stories over the years of individuals and their home buying and home selling stories has been a continuing education.

The purpose is to give you a good basis to do some thinking, investigating, and analyzing to proceed in reaching your goals.

Knowledge

Obviously knowledge can be gained from the experience of other people, from studying home-buying books such as this one, or instruction. It is easier on one's wallet and one's sanity to learn from the mistakes of others. That is the objective of this manual.

Deadlines

Deadlines deal with the time period of an activity. There is a beginning, an action, and an end. It may or may not accomplish the goals and objectives of either party. Deadlines create motivated sellers. It is the 'Why' of, "Why are you selling the house?"

Some of the elements of a deadline are:

Death: In an estate sale there is often pressure from the heirs and the court system to resolve the selling of homes or land because of the tremendous holding costs involved. One can sit down or calculate the holding costs involved: real estate taxes, insurance, maintenance, utilities such as heating, electrical charges, snow removal, homeowners association dues, lawn and swimming pool care, to get an idea of these (home-owning) holding costs. These can be a very large negotiating figure.

Divorce: There are financial pressures to sell a home due to dual house payments or apartment rents, along with the holding costs we just mentioned.

Job transfers: Knowing when an individual has to report to a new job in a new city or a new state becomes very important. The selling individual may make concessions, compromises in regards to closing costs, repair costs, or even just take a discounted price in order to avoid dual ownership as the deadline approaches.

Retirement: Sometimes retirees are anxious to leave and sell their home in order to move to more favorable climates, or to be closer to family and friends. Knowing when they actually will be retiring and when they plan to make their move is extremely important.

Downsizing: As their families leave home through school, marriage, or pursuing careers, people find that they no longer need or can live in the home. They wish to go to a smaller home, condo, or apartment. Knowing that the children or family will be moving out opens up negotiations with the owner.

Building a new home: Knowing when that home may be completed gives you a deadline.

Business failure/job layoff: By being aware of the local scene, watching the newspapers, you can get an idea of deadlines for people who are being laid off and companies that are closing. Obviously that is a pressure to sell.

Health issues/accidents/illness: Unfortunately those things do happen in this world, and it forces people to change their living arrangements. Houses go on the market because of these unfortunate circumstances, and there may be a great financial pressure to sell the house.

Fluid with the Truth: Is this the first time the property has been on the market? Has the price ever been reduced? Research of listing history often finds the home has been listed with more than one real estate agent. It could have been listed six months ago for $150,000 for a 3-month listing. After no interest/inquiries, it was listed with a second company for $125,000, which tells prospective buyers it has only been on the market from the beginning of his/her listing period. It could even be more extreme than this example, with numerous prices and numerous real estate agents over months or years!

It makes one wonder why it has been on the market so long … overpriced, oddball style, overbuilt for the neighborhood, structural problems, adverse influences from outside the property, future change in land use?

Knowing these issues is a great advantage of understanding the length of time involved in the negotiations. You can present offers, hold, improve, or withdraw offers. How does the person get to know these things? Walking around the neighborhood, either alone or as a couple, sometimes finds neighbors working in their yard, and conversations begin. A garage sale, FSBO (For Sale by Owner) house, or cars for sale are great openings for a visit.

Should you canvass the neighborhood, be diplomatic. Smile, be agreeable, compliment the neighbors on their lawn, shed, flowers, garden, car or dog, remodeling, etc. A good listener with the right questions can gain a tremendous amount of information. Simple questions like asking if the individuals are moving out of this area, or if they're building a new home, can get a conversation started.

Good, friendly neighbors have it in their own best interest to encourage good, friendly potential new neighbors to come to the neighborhood. During your visiting you may find the reason why the house is on the market.

Speaking of dogs, keep a dog biscuit in your pocket when going to homes. Nasty dogs become friendly. Sometimes they sit, beg, smell my pocket. A UPS deliveryman taught me that.

Don't surprise the dog ... he may be asleep, or deaf. Often, I whistle low when walking to the house, plus looking for dog toys, kennels, dog houses, tie-out chains. Call me spooky, but a trip to the ER is not entertainment to me.

The dog-biscuit-in-the-pocket and low-whistle tricks could save you hundreds of dollars avoiding the ER.

Sometimes the seller is represented by a real estate agent who may tell you the reason why they are moving, and the deadline.

It pays to be a good listener and ask the right questions. A very motivated seller with a very short negotiating time and an impending deadline has a lot more motivation to be reasonable. They can become less demanding and open to offers, counter-offers, and negotiation. People with months and even years can hold fast to their prices and positions without really needing to concede.

Financial Ability

Financial ability, or the capacity to act or perform effectively, is very powerful. In order to do this one can get pre-approved/pre-qualified letters for bank financing. Or, if they are able to make this a cash deal, they can always get a letter from their banker verifying that they have the funds with which to complete the deal. As the old saying goes, "Money talks and b_lls__t walks."

Throughout this manual we have illustrated and attempted to enlighten you on many areas involving the repair or areas of negotiation in picking that home or land. Knowing that many readers jump from chapter to chapter and don't always completely read through a manual, please pardon me if I repeat some of the information in this chapter.

"TIMBER!"
Tree too close to shed.

Here is a partial listing of negotiable items:

1. Worn out roofs -- cost to replace.
2. Exterior painting. Often in 25- to 30-year-old houses with upper stories, such as in split levels or two stories, with aluminum siding on the upper areas and brick or masonry on the lower areas, bleaching and chalking of the paint flows onto the brick. The cost of cleaning the brick and painting the upper area could be considerable.
3. Trees that are adjacent to the house and outbuildings can propose hazards and may cost several hundred dollars to remove.
4. Basement leaks.
5. Major structural problems with walls, roofs, and floors.
6. Electrical problems, and the inadequacy of the electrical system to service the home.
7. Plumbing problems.
8. Outbuildings in need of demolition. (Sometimes in rural areas fire departments will burn those buildings down as training exercises, which could save a considerable amount.)
9. Septic and/or sewer problems.
10. Well and city water problems.
11. Drainage problems that may require the digging of a retention pond, or bringing in fill dirt to create positive drainage.
12. Encroachments by neighbor's building, or dumping items on the property, with clean-up costs.
13. Asking for carpeting or decorating allowances if those are in bad condition or not suitable to your taste.

14. Understanding local conditions and quarantines. I know of a family in California who bought a very lovely home. He was a commander of a naval air base. Then they found out a blight was affecting palm trees in the area, and they were forced to cut down all the trees per city ordinance. Someone new to the area would not have been aware of that expense, or the way it affects the amenities of the property.
15. Swimming pools. Many times pools that are 20 years of age can face serious maintenance situations, or the possibility of being filled in. Knowing that cost, and bringing it up in your negotiations, is obviously beneficial.
16. Rural lots with heavy woods and no city sewer can be a big problem. Tree roots do clog the drain field and can be an expensive problem. Find out what it would cost to clear the lot, or search for a more suitable lot. (I've heard of lot clearing costs up to $12,500!)
17. Timing. Sometimes there are off-season cycles in the market, especially after the school year has begun and most people have moved and gotten their kids enrolled in school
18. Homes with skylights. Locally, many builders refuse to install them because there are maintenance problems sooner or later. Look around the skylights to see if there is any discoloration or leakage, and include that in your negotiation for repairs.
19. Get an understanding of what the local regulations and state laws are regarding land divisions. *An individual bought an old farmhouse with 5 acres, with road frontages on two sides of the corner lot. He did not understand the land restrictions and the Michigan Platt Act, which prevented him from selling lots. In this example, discuss in your negotiations that the land cannot be split off, and the property's highest and best use is as the farmhouse with the acreage.*
20. With gas hot water heating systems, there are extra costs in the event you choose to upgrade for central air conditioning, which needs additional ductwork.

21. The lack of egress or safety windows to comply with building codes for basement bedrooms or finished areas.
22. Panic or security bars: They must be operable to meet with most codes, or they must be repaired or removed.
23. The including of personal property with a sale, such as a satellite dish, refrigerator, stove, or other personal furnishings.
24. Asking for seller concessions to help with the closing costs. If you are involved in a buyer's market with very slow sales, sometimes this can run to 3 to 6 percent of the sales price, depending on the common financing method in your area.
25. Rent. The amount the seller will pay, prior to you occupying the house.

Many of these items involve repair issues. A local REALTOR® suggested that three repair estimates be obtained. The repairs were to be completed by the seller, or be reduced from the sales price at the closing. If a person is handy in doing repairs, the buyer may wish to do those themselves and save money.

In situations where there is no obvious immediate need for repairs, a home warranty policy could be agreed upon. Some of these can be purchased from your local insurance agent, or if you are involved with a buyer representative, they may have a source. (These can run one, two, or three years, with different options as to how much a service call might cost. I have seen quotes of $375 up to more than $750.)

Whole books have been written on the art of negotiation, and I would recommend, if you are really into that, to make a study. Or have a buyer's representative handle negotiations for you.

We've really beaten up the issues of repair costs and adverse influences from outside the property affecting value. If those are not issues, let's go directly at the asking sales price.

How was it set? Was it by a **recent** market value analysis? Or by a **recent** appraisal? Or from a government assessment estimate?

Ask to see a copy of the analysis or appraisal. Are the comparables suitable, recent, from similar competing neighborhoods?

Does the appraiser (do your homework with a REALTOR® or banker friend) have a reputation as liberal, conservative, or realistic?

Sometimes FSBO (For Sale by Owner) homes have unrealistic approaches to value. *About 10 years ago I appraised a pending rural home sale for a local bank. The price seemed unrealistic. During my inspection, I asked the owner how the sales price was determined. He said, "I took the price I paid 40 years ago, added each year's real estate taxes, plus the value of the riding lawn mower!" I made no reply, but shared the story with the bank. The appraised current market value versus his over-optimistic method were worlds apart.*

Be diplomatic. A little charm goes a long way. Disarming phrases such as, "Is that right?" or "Sounds pretty optimistic", can soften the blow.

If you choose to get your own appraisal or hire a professional for research, ask for the ratio of local sales prices to listing prices. If most sales end up to be 95% of the listing prices, you only have a 5% negotiating range. Ask what the common financing methods are: conventional mortgages with 10% down payments, FHA with 3% concessions by sellers, or land contracts with 10% down payments, or cash. Offering better financing may get a lower sales price.

Understand local trends. *Many local auto-related company employees recently were being transferred to a city in Texas from Michigan. Large numbers left the local market slow, which was already stagnant. Sales concessions and lowered prices resulted. In Texas, the market became hotter with ready, willing, and able buyers. Transferees looking at a house on a Saturday, which had no offers, returned for a second look on Monday to find it sold!*

Ask your appraiser or professional to research sales on the same street or subdivision during the last five years. You will get the low values to high values range, plus market trends. The same can be determined in checking recent listings. Don't buy a house outside the usual value ranges.

HAVE AN EXIT POLICY. If you're buying a home with a partner (either as a domicile or investment), plan ahead. If the relationship should change (accident, death, divorce), it's easier to dissolve the ownership with a written agreement. Inflated appraisals, lack of direction/agreement can create major headaches. I've seen it happen.

Quickie Lot Valuation method: From an actual case. An older neighbor's husband passed away suddenly. She was left with a home on one side of the street and a large separate vacant parcel across the street. It had its own address and government real estate parcel number. So we have two separate properties. The lady wished to sell and move. An appraisal on the house solved that valuation. But no one wanted to pay for a second appraisal for the other property. The land had sewer, natural gas, and electric in this suburban subdivision. Lot measurements were approximately 258 feet frontage by 500 feet deep. Going to the local government office (in this case the township assessor) one could learn the lot size regulations. It could require 75 front footage with the lot depth meeting regulations. Or it could be on a square footage or acreage basis. So three lots could be developed (the highest and best use), per local regulations. Next, lot prices could be obtained from developers, lots for sale by owners, or from land sales *studies from the local government assessor's office. If this research concluded that $30,000 lot prices were typical, we then multiply by the three lots allowed. The estimated value of this second property could be $90,000 less the costs for surveying, title work, and other development fees, etc ($1,000-$5,000). Knowing the value will guide your offer and negotiations. (This is especially accurate as the estimated cash value per the tax assessor for this property was outdated ... it was $19,000!)*

In closing this chapter, allow me to share a few more real world stories of negotiation, both good and bad.

About three years ago I did an appraisal for a bank on rural acreage. The owners were in the process of building this house. They related buying the acreage three years earlier, prior to attempting to build. The sales price had been dramatically reduced because the percolation test for the required septic system would not pass. The area was very wet. The buyers were very knowledgeable of the area, and knew a lot about soils and how to cure some of these problems. During a period of very dry weather (a near drought) they dug a large pond about 250 feet away from their future home site. The pond was about 10 feet deep and 100 feet in diameter. They spread the excavated soil around the building site. The main advantage of the pond was that it provided a place for the above and below ground moisture to drain into. They did not hit a spring or have to drill another well, but in a very short period of time the pond was filled naturally. Then percolation tests were completed prior to building the house, and they passed by the local Health Department. (The pond was dug near the bottom of the rear downward slope of the lot.)

They gained a very nice pond and a large building site for 30-50 percent below the asking price, because it did not percolate in the earlier tests.

I know of a REALTOR® who was interested in building a home on some acreage in a rural area. She was familiar with the area and got an engineering study of the sub-soils, in addition to studying local reference books. (Many county governments have manuals showing the different type of soils throughout a county, and maps and colored pictures as a reference, available through a local Soil Conservation District.) This study enabled her to determine where there was a buildable site versus wasteland, because there was a peat bog and peat moss under some of the surface. She was able to negotiate a lower sales price because of the limited building site area.

Sometimes when a house burns down in a city, the house is not rebuilt and the lot is left vacant. If an individual offered a basic land amount, he or she would be saving perhaps $5,000 to $7,000 or more for all the underground work that is already in place. The sewer connection and public water line would be underground and very likely not affected. A concrete driveway may not be affected by the fire, an underground gas line connection may not be damaged. So in essence, the individual is buying an improved lot that would not require them to pay these additional hookup fees.

A local builder bought an old farmhouse on a large lot with road frontage wide enough to accommodate two houses (size-wise and local regulation-wise). The house was at the east end, while a small, ugly, cattail-filled swale/pond the size of a house was on the west end. Its only crop was mosquitoes!

He paid the market price of the farmhouse, on a large lot.

*Knowing the local regulations, soil conditions, and construction methods, he split the property into two lots. The farmhouse was on the east lot. He dug a basement on the west lot, completely removing the shallow swale before building a new house. He sold the farmhouse for a small profit. But he got a $30,000 lot for **free** when he built and sold the new house on the west lot.*

Allow me to relate a story of what not to do.

Several years ago I was hired to appraise a small farm with an old farmhouse and dilapidated farm buildings in a very high-demand market. Acreage in that area was rapidly increasing in value. The use was not for farming, but to be split into 5- and 10-acre parcels for residential purposes.

The seller was an older widow with serious terminal health challenges and no nearby family or friends to assist her. The one thing she did correctly was have an independent appraisal of the property. A nearby doctor who owned some land approached her about buying the farm, even before she put it up for sale. This lady was very lonely and very talkative. Not only did she reveal that she had bought another home in a nearby city and was pressed to conclude the sale there, but she also related to the doctor the intimate details of her illness. The doctor, knowing the ***deadline*** *and the time frame involved, did not speed up his negotiations. Unfortunately, his knowledge of her illness and her deadline to sell the property to conclude the new home situation, put her in a very bad situation.*

Sometimes we hurt ourselves in revealing too much information in the negotiating process, both as buyers and sellers.

My dad grew up in the "bootheel" country of Missouri in the early 1900s. Rural lifestyles of farming, fishing, hunting, and trapping were almost inbred into those hard-working souls.

Two of his best friends were brothers living nearby. The older brother, nicknamed "Wink," grew up to be a "crack" pistol shot. The brothers worked whatever odd jobs they could to survive the 1930s depression.

In the late summers they worked as hired farmhands harvesting wheat in the Dakotas and other western states. Camping/living was in their car. Wink's marksmanship supplemented the groceries with wild cottontail rabbit and tasty pheasant.

Wink married and settled down in a rural area of Michigan. Vicious stray dogs often reeked havoc near his home. Animal control/dog catchers didn't exist, and the police didn't respond to such matters.

One day a stray, unlicensed mongrel dog entered Wink's back yard. Tired of "city people" dropping off their dogs in the country, where they eventually ran wild, Wink had

enough. Grabbing his .22 caliber pistol from inside of the house, he raced to the back yard. On the way, he promptly shot himself in the foot! (The police did respond to that -- at the hospital ER.) We read about it in the newspaper before getting the graphic details from "the horse's mouth."

Even crack shots can blunder and shoot themselves in the foot.

A successful businessman bought fixer-upper houses as a sideline career. After remodeling and selling them he was doing fairly well. With seven or eight successes, he felt pretty cocky in knowing values, remodeling costs, the markets, timing and negotiating with ***deadlines****. He especially liked to buy houses for sale with bridge loans (where couples take out a loan when selling their home while a new house is being built. Delays, cost over runs, the present home not selling, can strain the "marital bliss.") (See Glossary for bridge loans.) (Seek counseling for marital bliss.) As* ***deadlines*** *approach, sellers often are forced to "bail out" with reduced sale prices. (He usually waited ten months into a bridge loan before making an offer as the financial pressures mounted for the owners of the un-sold house.)*

Mr. Businessman was infatuated by a lakefront home fitting the above scenario. Everybody knows that lakefront properties, especially on prestigious "Golden Lake" sell like hotcakes. He had never bought or sold lakefront property before, but could almost count those $1,000 bills of profit. Mr. Businessman bought the house. "I took a $50,000 bath ... the only house I ever lost money on."

He took the inflated appraisal at face value.

The lakefront home was located at the corner entrance of a subdivision, backed up to a high-traffic county road. All the bedrooms backed up to the noisy high-traffic street. The waterfront was a small shoreline at the end of a small canal. The gross living area (square footage) included part of the walkout basement (below grade). No detrimental locational adjustment was considered in the appraisal. Comparables with major lake frontages were used lacking proper adjustments.

He never considered that each waterfront property is a unique case valuation study in itself.

Mr. Businessman lived in a false fantasy world ... fixing up the house. Then reality hit when he tried to sell it! Oops! (Actually that was not the language used.) Why he did not sue the appraiser was never revealed.

If only Mr. Businessman had done his smart home buying homework: checking assessor cards, determining the competency/reputation of the appraiser, evaluating (driving by the comparables or having an impartial appraiser review the appraisal). (In this market, waterfront properties and old farmhouses are the most difficult to appraise.) Or quite frankly admitting that he was out of his area of expertise ... a $50,000 blow to his wallet and an insult to his sanity could have been avoided. He could have gone on to a better deal.

Even “crack shots” can sometimes blunder and shoot themselves in the foot.

Have options. Consider other homes as backups. Don’t be heartbroken or overpay on one house, should negotiations “Go South.”

LESSON #22: APPRAISER SMITTY'S CHECKLIST

1. Private wells: Check with local well drillers for salt water maps. See if this is in a salty water area.
2. **Get a reliable local city and/or county map as you go home shopping**. See if there are any rivers or streams listed. Flood insurance might be a factor in buying this property or building a home.
3. Private well: Get a well test to check if the water volume is adequate, so you don't need to install a new well in the near future. *You might also consider that what may be adequate for a household of two people may not be adequate for a household of six or eight people.*
4. Don't buy a house that could be adjacent to a landfill, abandoned filling stations, or other external environment hazards such as a chicken farm, slaughterhouse, or shooting range.
5. Does this house sit on a high-traffic street? Check the volume at different times of the day and different days of the week, as it may vary according to shift changes from factories, hospitals, schools, or other employers.
6. Is the lot located at a subdivision entrance or a corner lot, with a stop sign where cars are constantly stopping, starting, squealing their brakes, and hitting their accelerator?

7. Don't buy a property that is overbuilt for the neighborhood, even though the price may be attractive. It may take a very long marketing time to sell that house, and it may have to be marketed over a very large area of two or three counties to make a sale.

8. Don't buy a house in a declining neighborhood, where your chances are very slim of recovering your original purchase price. This can be checked out by driving around, or reviewing an assessor card from a local government agency.

9. Look at the lay of the land. Is the lot where the house is or, a future house may be, below the road level so that it acts as a catch basin? This could be subject to chronic flooding from surface water, with resulting wet basements and extra expenses.

10. Consider that the house may be next door to a higher property or lot, so all of the rain runoff from that lot or area or a shopping center with its paved parking lot may flow and channeled over onto you, with constant maintenance and repairs.

11. Private roads: Ask if there is a private road maintenance agreement, and who is responsible amongst the neighbors to pay for what, and what the dollar amounts are. Don't be the person who has to chip in or hire a tractor or contractor to make the repairs so the private road is passable.

12. Does the property have a joint driveway with neighbors who do not share the driveway?

13. Muddy and impassable roads: When you buy the house everything may be fine, but at certain seasons of the year, especially in the spring or even the fall, the roads may be impassable. Check this out.

14. Is there a common wall of a garage or a common fence that you share with a neighbor? If so, whose responsibility is it to maintain and repair it?

15. Is there a common well that is shared by the two properties? If so, who is responsible for the common well and its costs, should it need to be replaced?
16. Is the driveway large enough to handle all the cars in the family, or do you have to be constantly jockeying them in and out?
17. Buying a bargain-priced building lot that needs fill dirt trucked in can be more expense than buying a finished lot that is ready to build on.
18. Vacant, unheated/unoccupied houses: How long was it vacant? Check with local utility company records to discover when the electricity and gas were turned off.
19. Vacant houses/unused heating, plumbing, and air conditioning systems may require extra dollars for repairs, and for being reactivated. This is a specialty area that should be checked out with the appropriate contractors.
20. Have varmints or critters moved into the vacant house? Skunks and woodchucks love to dig dens under wood decks. Have a sharp eye to check that out, or have a varmint control/exterminator check it out.
21. Vacant houses and property: Have the neighbors taken over part of the driveway or parking area, or stored cars or building materials or other personal property on the property as it sat vacant?
22. Did the previous owners or tenants sabotage the property before they left? Ask the owners, and find out the extent of damages or repairs made. Or walk around the neighborhood and ask the neighbors. They may know more and be more willing to tell you about these things than the owners will.
23. In the wintertime, or when windows are open, you may not be able to detect that pets have urinated or defecated in the house, and saturated carpet or wood flooring. Only when the

heat is started and windows are closed, might you become aware of this. Be on guard. Many homebuyers are allergic to cats, dogs, etc.

24. Basements and inspections: Recent painting and paneling in a basement may be done to cover up leaks or other problems. Ask why. Be very concerned about that.
25. Plumbing: Is it all one material, or is it a mixture of copper pipes and galvanized pipes that can lead to chemical actions between those two materials, and the failure of the systems and replacement with expensive repairs?
26. Electrical service: Is it adequate for the size of the house and the various features that it has now? Will it be adequate if you add on a second garage/pole barn/central air conditioner/jet tub?
27. Go to builders' shows and become aware of the various types of high-efficiency furnaces, as there are differences between 70, 80, and 90 percent rated furnaces. Know what you're buying.
28. Is the heating system a radiator/boiler/hot water heat? If so, to add central air conditioning you will have to run extra ductwork to provide central air conditioning.
29. Check the age of well pumps and sump-pumps.
30. If the house has a basement bedroom and you need to use it for a family member, and there is no escape proof or egress approved windows, be aware that it could cost $500 to $1,000 or more to install one to meet the building codes, and for safety purposes.
31. Look and shine a flashlight in the areas underneath the toilets and drains to see if the floors are deteriorating, or any of the structural members are in bad shape.
32. Look for rusty sheet-metal covers of furnaces or furnaces set up on concrete blocks, which could give you a hint to basement leaks and/or flooding.

33. Ask about unfinished home repairs. Is it because of a lack of time or lack of money, or is it because they can't figure out the problem? This is often the case with outside excavations, such as trenches that go out to the sewer line or to the septic line. Perhaps there has been an ongoing problem they haven't been able to figure out.
34. Spend a lot of time inspecting the kitchen and bath, because they are the most expensive areas in the home. Open the cabinets, and look in and underneath the sink.
35. Be aware that old houses are not square. Measure all four sides of a room that you may be planning to remodel, as fitting drywall or paneling or ceiling tile could be a real problem.
36. Check in older homes to see if the floors are level.
37. Check out ceiling water stains. Often this comes from roof leaks such as ice damming, or rain.
38. Does the bathroom have a pocket door? Does it work?
39. Is there a patio sliding door? Is there a screen for the patio sliding door?
40. How old is the toilet? Have there been any recent repairs?
41. Inspect the bathroom floor for curling, loose linoleum, tiles, or carpet at or near the base of the toilet.
42. Has the lavatory or the bathtub overflowed, damaging the floors? They may feel spongy as you walk across them, or press against them with your hands. Have there been any repairs, and how extensive were they? How much did they cost?
43. Does the bathroom floor appear to be water-soaked when you look at it from underneath, or feel of it, or walk across it?
44. Flush the toilets and turn on the faucets for water pressure. Is it adequate?
45. Sit on the toilet. Does it give or wobble?

46. When you turn the plumbing off or on, is there a shuddering or water hammer in the plumbing system?
47. Do the faucets leak? Is there a water stain in the lavatory basin from ongoing water leaking?
48. Are the sinks, lavatories, and/or bathtubs slow to drain out when they are filled? Fill them with water and drain them.
49. Check the shower, the tub head diverter lever, and the tub plug mechanism to see if it functions properly.
50. Check for hairline cracks in the toilet, especially in seasonal dwellings such as cabins or cottages, as many times there is improper or inadequate draining of the pipes, or the use of improper antifreeze.
51. Look underneath the sinks and around the toilets. Are there shut-off valves so that the water can be turned off? How about for the outside faucet?
52. Windows: Open and close them: crank them, raise them and lower them. Many times the newer windows are put in the most used or front portion of the house, and the older windows, which may be broken or not functioning, are behind draperies and blinds. Look behind them in every room.
53. Where are the screens or storm windows for these windows?
54. If the house has replacement windows, are there warranties that go with them? Where are the warranties?
55. Access to the garage: Is there an outside service door, or do you have to go through the house to get outside, or vice versa? Sometimes there is no access from the house directly to the garage, or there is no access to the outside without putting up the overhead door. See if there are these two additional entrances. They make your life a lot easier.

56. Does the garage overhead door operator work?

57. Where are the remote controls?

58. Measure the garage. Does it appear to be an older style, or something in which your car does not fit? Keep in mind that many cars are at least 6½ feet wide by about 16 feet long. Measure your car and the garage to see if it will fit.

59. Are there any homeowners association or deed restrictions that would prevent you from parking a car, motor home, or boat outside?

60. If there is an attic or storage above the garage, is there a safe pull-down ladder?

61. Do the garage doors functions properly, opening and closing?

62. Appliances/machines: Test them.

    1. Dishwasher
    2. Water heater
    3. Garbage disposal
    4. Jet tub
    5. Ceiling fans
    6. Whole house fans

63. Are there adequate phone jacks and cable TV jacks in the house?

64. How do you get access to the attic? Sometimes people don't know.

65. What is the quality of the interior carpentry? Sometimes there are gaps where the moldings do not come together, which could indicate poor installation or even green, uncured lumber.

66. Is there personal property or boxes stored in some areas, like over a floor or in one area of the basement where you can't really inspect the floor to see if there may be a rotted out floor, or if there are cracks in the concrete?

67. Roofs: Look at all sides. One side may be older than the other, or it may be a different color because it was replaced due to a wind storm, hail storm, or fire.
68. Are there roof vents or vents up underneath the eaves, for air circulation? They lengthen the roofing material life.
69. Does the roof have double thick shingles so that it would require stripping to the roof board when the roof is replaced?
70. Are there any worn out holes, or worn out places in the valleys of the roof?
71. Does the chimney need a roof cricket or saddle?
72. Was an addition put onto the house? Look inside to see if there has been water penetration and leaks from snow or rain because of where the siding is, and where the roofs do not match up.
73. Roofs with a very steep pitch last much longer than roofs with a very slight pitch where ice, water and snow can build up and leak down through and shorten the life span.
74. Are the gutters and downspouts in place, or is there a very large overhang around the edges of the house? Are the gutters the proper size for the large roof area?
75. Are the gutters level to catch water that then acts as a pond, or do they drain?
76. Gutters: Are there missing downspouts or bottom diverters?
77. Look around the foundations. Is there undermining or water that seems to be draining in towards the house rather than away from it?
78. What's the condition of the roof? Do any of the shingles appear to have bare spots or curling? Are there missing shingles? What is the life expectancy of the roof?
79. Driveways and sidewalks and surface walks and steps: Are they cracking, sinking, shifting, or tilting?

80. Crawl spaces: Do they have vents for ventilation and have you been able to look underneath them, or has your home inspector looked underneath them?
81. Have your home inspector take photos with a flash to see if there are any structural problems or less than acceptable methods of repair, such as plumbing, wiring, carpentry, foundations in the crawl spaces. Or do it yourself.
82. Is the house on a slab? If so, is it being undermined by water?
83. Are the overhangs and soffit areas in good condition, or do they need repairs?
84. Are there window wells around the basement? Are they draining properly, or do they have transparent covers or caps?
85. Is there freshly brought in dirt, or landscaping? Could this be hiding a problem to the foundation?
86. Look at the house from the front, rear, and sides from a distance. Does it look okay? Does anything look weird?
87. Is the lawn unusually soft or spongy, compared to other yards? Maybe it is collecting surface water and drainage from other homes.
88. Does the property have positive drainage? Does the rain water or surface water flow out and away from the house?
89. Is there a need to dig out a retention pond or swale or hole for the surface water to go into, because it does not go down into the surface because of a hard pan or clay?
90. Septic system: Is there black sludge seeping to the surface?
91. Septic systems: Check with local septic cleaning services and find out what the normal cleaning period is in that area. If the normal cleaning period for a house of that size with that number of family members is every 10 years, then ask the homeowner or their representative

when was the last it was cleaned. Then find out when it was cleaned before that. **If it appears that the septic system is being cleaned quite often, such as every six months or every year or every two years, it could indicate that the septic drain field is failing. The cost of replacement could run $2,000-$5,000,** depending upon the area of the country that you are in.

92. Small sheds, outbuildings, and barns: Are they more of a liability that would be very expensive to tear down and haul the debris to a landfill? Or are they really an asset?

93. Are the chimneys and vent pipes the adequate length and height above the house?

94. How does the house appear to you? In other words, what is the "curb appeal?" Does it look like something that you would be proud to be in, and would be very easy to move if a resale is needed?

95. Is this a split-level home with constant stair climbing up and down? The better quality 2-story homes have a first floor bedroom and bath for easier living for the main occupants.

96. Is the house on a slab? People who live in slab-type houses have more fatigue, back problems, and leg problems than those who live in houses with crawl spaces or basements.

97. What is the ratio of bedrooms to baths? Are there enough bathrooms to serve all the people who live in the house?

98. What is the location of the bathrooms? Is it on the second floor, or in a poor location so everybody has to go tromping through the house to get to it?

99. Is the heating system experimental or exotic, so it is difficult to find service or parts?

100. Does the house have electric heat, which could result in very expensive utility bills?

101. Is it an earth-berm house, or exotic design that could be very difficult to sell in the future?

102. Old farmhouses: Often the heating and cooling systems are adequate for the first floor, but not for the second floor. Check this out.

103. Are there solar panels to the house in a region of the country that has a lot of cloudy weather, such as the New England states or the Great Lakes, where you will not get the huge benefits of the solar panels?

Are there energy-saving features that could be helpful to enjoyment of the house, and for utility bills?

105. Have the owners added any insulation? How much?

106. Review the energy bills.

107. Did the builder win any awards for his energy features? Was there an energy audit by the local utility company?

108. Understand marketing/timing and supply and demand of the housing market in your area. Research the local cost of living compared to the area you may have come from. Is it higher or lower?

109. What is the typical marketing time for that area? Are there any unusual seasons when houses do or don't sell?

110. What is the typical sales price, compared to the listing price? It might give you an idea if you can negotiate.

111. What are the customary financing methods used?

112. Are most of the sales by real estate companies or private owners? It may indicate whether you are in a very hot or very cold home market.

113. Are there any special assessments, ongoing or in the future? Check the local unit of government.

114. If you are planning to build, check with building material suppliers, lumber yards, and home centers, to get an idea of what the turn-around time of sub-contractors are, and for a possible list of sub-contractors.

115. Are there any smoke detectors?

116. Is radon gas testing needed in the area?

117. Is lead-based paint testing needed? Houses built before 1978 often have lead-based paint in them.

118. Are there ground fault interrupter electrical outlets in the bathrooms, kitchens, laundry area, the outside electrical outlets, and other electrical outlets near water?

119. Are there adequate handrails on the stairs, and are the stairs properly lighted?

120. Is there a water discharge pipe and pressure relief valve with the water heater, so it does not blow up or discharge, injuring someone at shoulder or head level?

121. Are there proper escape-size windows for basement living areas?

122. Is U.F.F.I. insulation a factor?

123. Are there asbestos-wrapped pipes or heating systems in the house? This is often found where houses have been converted from old-style furnaces to modern furnaces.

124. If you are building, perhaps it would be wise to hire an independent inspector to monitor the construction of the home as it progresses.

125. How safe is the wood stove?

126. Does the chimney and/or the wood stove and fireplace have any history of chimney fires? When was the last time they were cleaned? What type of wood is burned in the system? Softwoods leave a flammable residue or pitch in chimneys, which can cause chimney fires.

127. Are there features of the house that do not conform with similar houses or to houses in the neighborhood, such as having a oversized deck which is not typical for the area, or an oversized swimming pool or pole barn? *In a recent appraisal I noted a 4-car garage where all the other houses in the neighborhood had 2-car garages. The house was on the same size lot and similar in size to others in the neighborhood.*

128. Are there outside in-ground pools in an area of the country that has very short, unpredictable summer seasons, where they cannot actually be used very often?

129. What is the age of the pool? As pools age to 15-25 years, sometimes the major components and parts of the pool need such extensive repairs that it is not feasible to repair them, and you are left with the option of either filling in or demolishing the pool.

130. Are there any anticipated changes in nearby zoning or of adjacent properties that could effect the resale of this house? Check local newspapers, relatives, and friends, they may be aware of what's going on in the area. Or stroll around and talk with some of the neighbors. If you see many "For Sale" signs in the neighborhood, something unusual is going on.

131. Is the dishwasher adequate for the present occupants but may not for a larger family? *I know of a case where an older couple who dined out a lot had a dishwasher that served their needs. The house was sold to a large family with teenagers who were constantly cooking and using the dishwasher. The dishwasher failed.*

132. Was there a fuel oil heating system? Often these are converted to propane or natural gas, and there are underground storage tanks for the fuel oil. They can be very costly to clean up and/or remove.

133. Is this a 20- to 25-year-old house where major replacement items are needed such as roof, furnace, well, and/or air conditioner or other major components?

134. Is this a 10-year-old house that may need septic tank cleaning? When was it last done? Dishwasher replacement may be needed, and the water heater may need to be replaced.

135. Is there a garage conversion to a living area? Often the heating and cooling systems are not adequate.

136. Home inspectors: Have them photograph or video the attic, roof, crawl spaces, and problem areas. This could be a good negotiating tool to show the need for repairs.

137. Home inspectors: Get independent references and call them.

138. Home inspectors: Get a certificate of their malpractice insurance with the insurer's name, address, policy number, and policy dates. Call, write, or fax to verify the policy is in force.

139. From the owner get a list of the following locations of:

    1. The sewer tap-in,
    2. or the septic tank and drain field location, and its clean-out access (FHA sale requirement).
    3. Drain clean-outs.
    4. The well or public water line (FHA sale requirement for well location).

140. Get the instruction manuals of:

    1. garbage disposal
    2. dishwasher
    3. well pump
    4. built-in stove/range
    5. microwave
    6. any other appliances

141. Get warranty information for:

    1. furnace

2. air conditioner

3. roof

4. well

5. sump-pump

6. replacement windows

7. other mechanical components

142. Get the name, addresses and telephone numbers of:

1. furnace and/or air conditioning company

2. electrician

3. plumber

4. roofer

5. well driller and/or well pump installer

6. septic tank man

143. Do a final walk-through before closing.

144. Get a copy of the local assessor card to review for value trends, previous sales prices and history, permits, remodeling, the age of the house, the dimensions of the house, lot sizes.

145. With new built houses, check records. (Building permit dates versus certificate of occupancy dates. Talk with neighbors.) *Sometimes houses are half-built and left open to the weather due to lack of money to finish, builder bankruptcy, divorces, zoning disputes, etc. Who would want a damp, water-soaked house (covered over by siding, shingles, drywall, carpet) which could be breeding grounds for mold or deterioration of the building materials? I've seen some houses that take 5-7 years to build when the local custom/routine is 6 months.*

REFERENCE MATERIALS AND OTHER BOOKS

Dictionary of Real Estate Appraisal

The American Heritage Dictionary

Webster's Dictionary and Thesaurus

You Can Negotiate Anything - Herb Cohen

How to Estimate Building Losses and Construction Costs - Paul I. Thomas

Mortgage Terms - Mortgage Guaranty Insurance Corporation

How to Win Friends and Influence People - Dale Carnegie

Modern Carpentry - Willis Wagner

Evidence in Procedure for Boundary Location - Curtis L. Brown and Winfield Eldridge

BOCA Code Books

Great Lakes Realty Systems, Inc. Continuing Education Manual

100 Q&A about Buying a New Home

U.S. Dept. of Housing and Urban Development, 19209 P. Chennault Way, Box 8, Gaithersburg, MD 20879-1786

Buying Your Home: Settlement Costs and Helpful Information

U.S. Department of Housing and Urban Development (HUD), 451 7th Street, SW, Washington, DC 20410

Web site: http://www.hud.gov

Fannie Mae Foundation, P.O. Box 1810, Aurora, IL 60507-9806

Web site: www.fanniemaefoundation.org

1. *Opening the Door to a Home of Your Own* (Free)
2. *Knowing and Understanding Your Credit*
3. *Choosing the Mortgage That's Right for You*
4. *Borrowing Basics: What You Don't Know Can Hurt You*

MOLD:

Testing For Mold - Minnesota Department of Health

A Brief Guide to Mold, Moisture and Your Home

EPA

Web site: www.epa.gov/iaq/molds

U.S. Environmental Protection Agency's (EPA) Indoor Air Quality

Web sites: www.epa.gov/iaq

www.epa.gov/iaq/pubs/moldresources.html

Questions and Answers on Stachybotrus chartarum and other molds

Centers for Disease Control and Prevention (CDC), National Center for Environmental Health

Web site: http://www.cdc.gov/nceh/asthma/factsheets/molds/default.htm

Minnesota Department of Health

Web sites: www.health.state.mn.us -- www.health.state.mn.us/divs/eh/aialr/lair/moldweb.html

California Department of Health Services, Environmental Health Investigations Branch

Web sites: www.dhs.ca.gov

http://www.dhs.ca.gov/deodc/ehib/EHIB2/topics/mold.html

Consumer Information on Home Purchasing and Related Topics

U.S. Department of Housing and Urban Development (HUD), 451 7th Street, SW, Washington, DC 20410

Web site: http://www.hud.gov

For information about FHA-Insured home mortgage loans on one-to-four family dwellings call: 1-800-CALL FHA (800-225-5342)

For information about buying a HUD home call: 1-800-767-4HUD (800-767-4483)

For consumer counseling referrals call: 1-888-HOME4US (1-888-466-3487)

For Information regarding housing discrimination issues contact: 1-800-669-9777

Web site: http://www.hud.gov/fhe/fheo.htm

For information about RESPA contact: Office of Consumer and Regulatory Affairs (see above HUD address)

Web site: http://www.hud.gov/fha/res/respa_hm.html

Other Agencies:

For information about programs and pamphlets offered by the Department of Veterans Affairs, contact your nearest VA Regional Office.

Web site: http://www.va.gov/vas/loan

For information about rural housing loan programs contact: Department of Agriculture Rural Development/Rural Housing Services, Stop 0783, Washington, DC 20250.

Web site: http://www.rurdev.usda.gov

For information about the Truth in Lending Act and the Equal Credit Opportunity Act contact: Federal Reserve Board, 20th Street and Constitution Avenue, NW, Washington, DC 20551.

Web site: http://www.bog.frb.fed.us

Septic System References/Michigan State University Extension Service

On-site Domestic Sewage Disposal Handbook, MWPS-24, Midwest Plan Services

Request from Department of Agricultural Engineering, Michigan State University ($6)

Septic Tank Systems: A Homeowner's Guide

Michigan Environmental Health Association

Web site: www.meha.net.

So ... Now You Own a Septic System

Groundwater Protection and Your Septic System

These and several additional on-site waste disposal publications, National Small Flows Clearinghouse

Web site: www.nsfc.wvu.edu.

Onsite Works! An Introduction to Decentralized Wastewater Treatment Systems

Housing Education and Research Center (HERC) at Michigan State University

Web site: www.canr.msu.edu/cm/herc/onsite/index.html.

Several bulletins on septic systems are available in Michigan State University Extension's WQ (water quality) bulletin series. Contact your local MSUE office, or the MSU Bulletin Office, 10-B Agriculture Hall, MSU, East Lansing, MI 48824-1039.

Web site: www.msue.msu.edu/waterqual/wq-mats.html.

These bulletins include:

Home "A" Systems (WQ-51)

Managing Shorelines to Protect Water Quality (WQ-52)

What to Do if Your Septic System Fails (WQ-14)

Buying or Selling a Home? What to Find out about Your Water and Septic Systems (WQ-

How to Conserve Water in Your Home and Yard (WQ-16)

Managing Your Septic System (WQ-39)

The following titles are also available, from the Consumer Information Catalog/U.S. General Services Administration, P.O. Box 100, Pueblo, CO 81002

Web site: www.pueblo.gsa.gov

Buying Your Home: Settlement Costs and Helpful Information

Consumer Handbook on Adjustable Rate Mortgages

A Consumer's Guide to Mortgage Lock-ins

A Consumer's Guide to Mortgage Refinancing

Energy Efficient Mortgage Home Owner Guide

Guide to Single Family Mortgage Insurance

How to Buy a Home with a Low Down Payment

How to Buy a Manufactured (Mobile) Home

The HUD Home Buying Guide

Selling a Home

Twelve Ways to Lower Your Homeowners Insurance Costs

Never Say Never (Flood Insurance Guide)

How to Recognize Hazardous Defects in Trees

Selecting a New Water Heater

Repairing Your Flooded Home

Addresses and websites often change. There is no guarantee of accuracy of these addresses and websites.

GLOSSARY

Acre: An area of 43,560 square feet; i.e. lot with 100 feet front footage X 435.6 feet deep = 1 acre.

All-Weather Road: A functionally serviceable road usable in all seasons of the year for normal traffic usage.

Amenities: The real and intangible qualities of a property; i.e. sandy beaches, sunrise/sunset views, golf course views, large yard, etc.

Appraisal: A supportable written estimate of market value performed by a duly trained, experienced and licensed individual whose report is accepted by lenders, federal mortgage markets, insurance companies, and the court systems.

Appraisal Forms: Most bank-financed sales involve government forms. Be sure the appraisal is performed on a bank-acceptable report form. There are some abbreviated/quickie-type forms which banks will not accept. Ask your appraiser up front to specify that it will be on a bank acceptable report form.

Arbitration: A method to resolve disputes without the use of the court systems. Used often in contracts for home buying, home building with contractors, and home inspections. Arbitration is agreed upon within and **before** signing the contract for purchase or services, **before** a dispute arises between the parties. It is cheaper and quicker than the court systems, where the legal costs can make it impractical to dispute claims less than $10,000. Legal cases are usually settled in a compromised manner, often taking 2-4 years. Via the court system, the common result is that neither party is made "whole," but each incurs huge legal costs. *At a recent seminar, the American Arbitration Association reported that over 90 percent of their home buying disputes involved defective, leaking basements.* It is a practical recourse for the "little guy" against "big business" and the "legal" systems.

You might consider having your attorney or buyer representative insert this provision into your contract. If it is already there, now you understand it.

There are companies that handle disputes where contracts have arbitration agreements. One of these is the American Arbitration Association, a worldwide company headquartered in New York City. Having attended their seminars, I feel comfortable in recommending them. They have a regional office at 27777 Franklin Road, Suite 1150, Southfield, MI 48034. Phone: (248) 352-5500. Web site: www.adr.org.

Attached is their 4-page booklet, an excellent source for the Home Buyer/Home Seller Dispute Resolution System, outlining Who, What, Why, How, and Costs of the procedures. "Reprinted by permission of American Arbitration Association. © 2004."

American Arbitration Association
Dispute Resolution Services Worldwide

QUESTIONS AND ANSWERS ABOUT THE HOME BUYER/HOME SELLER DISPUTE RESOLUTION SYSTEM

INTRODUCTION

Each year in Michigan tens of thousands of real estate transactions take place. Occasionally disputes develop over these business transactions. The Home Buyer/Home Seller Dispute Resolution System responds to the need for an efficient, voluntary arbitration procedure to resolve these disputes privately, promptly and economically. The American Arbitration Association and the Michigan Association of Realtors have developed these arbitration procedures to meet consumer and real estate agents' needs in resolving disputes.

WHAT IS THE AMERICAN ARBITRATION ASSOCIATION?

The American Arbitration Association (AAA) is a not-for-profit, public service organization which offers a broad range of dispute resolution services through offices located in major cities throughout the United States. In addition, through its headquarters in New York City, the AAA provides education and training, specialized publications, and research on all forms of dispute settlement. The office located in Southfield, Michigan serves the entire state of Michigan.

WHAT IS ARBITRATION AND THE DRS?

Arbitration is the submission of a dispute to one or more impartial persons for a final and binding decision. It is an informal process for persons with a dispute to present their case to a neutral third party who will decide the matter for them.

The Dispute Resolution System, or DRS, is a voluntary alternative to litigation and refers to the arbitration procedure used to resolve home buyer/home seller and realtor disputes.

WHO MAY USE ARBITRATION?

Any party who initialed the arbitration clause may participate, or any party who stipulates to the arbitration process may participate.

WHO BENEFITS?

Everyone who voluntarily agrees to use the DRS will benefit. Their disputes will be resolved fairly, economically, quickly and privately.

WHAT KINDS OF DISPUTES MAY BE SUBMITTED?

All types of disputes relating to the physical condition of the property may be submitted, including defects in the home such as water leaks, furnace problems, plumbing, electrical, etc. Other disputes include fraud, misrepresentation and deposit refunds.

HOW LONG DO I HAVE TO FILE?

The rules do not specify a time period within which to file these claims. The law concerning the statute of limitations varies depending on the nature of the claim. Michigan law governs.

HOW LONG DOES THE PROCESS TAKE?

It is estimated the process will be resolved within three months from time of filing to resolution.

WHAT IS THE ROLE OF THE AAA AND WHAT DOES THE CASE ADMINISTRATOR DO?

The AAA functions as the administrator of the arbitration process. The Case Administrator arranges for the appointment of the arbitrator, the scheduling of the hearing, and handles all communications between the parties and the arbitrator except at the actual hearing. The Case Administrator also ensures that all parties receive a copy of the arbitrator's award. The Case Administrator is available during regular business hours to answer general and procedural questions concerning the arbitration process.

THE AAA, AS AN ADMINISTRATIVE AGENCY, DOES NOT EVALUATE THE VALIDITY OF CLAIMS SUBMITTED FOR ARBITRATION.

WHO IS THE ARBITRATOR?

The arbitrator is the impartial decision-maker whose authority comes from the Home Buyer/Home Seller Arbitration Rules, the Michigan Arbitration Law and the arbitration agreement. The arbitrator is not an employee of the AAA. The arbitrator will have experience in a field related to real estate or specific to the nature of the dispute.

HOW MANY ARBITRATORS WILL THERE BE?

One arbitrator will be appointed to hear the case. The arbitrator is compensated $150 for his or her services. This fee is included in the filing fee.

DO I NEED AN ATTORNEY?

No. Although you may choose to be represented by an attorney, it is not a requirement.

HOW DO I INITIATE THE PROCESS?

The arbitration process begins when a party files a Demand for Arbitration with the American Arbitration Association, enclosing a copy of the Purchase Agreement (inclusive of the agreement to arbitrate) as indicated in the rules.

WHERE WILL THE HEARING BE HELD?

Almost all case hearings are scheduled at the property in question. In rare instances, the hearing may be scheduled at another location as decided by the arbitrator or agreed upon by the parties.

WHAT SHOULD I BRING TO THE HEARING?

The parties should assemble all of the documents and papers necessary to proving their claims, including a copy of the Purchase Agreement, Seller's Statement of Condition, and any estimates. Parties should thoroughly familiarize themselves with the Home Buyer/Home Seller Arbitration Rules. Making a summary or checklist of points to be proved is very useful. This allows the parties to present their cases in an orderly and concise fashion and helps the arbitrator understand his or her position.

HOW IS THE HEARING CONDUCTED?

An arbitration hearing is informal. Any hearing will be conducted according to Michigan law and will meet all basic requirements of due process. Each party is given a full opportunity to present his/her case. Witnesses may also be called by any party to give testimony. These witnesses may be cross-examined by the other side. The arbitrator will usually give a brief introductory statement in which he/she will instruct the parties on how the hearing will be conducted. All persons who will be testifying may be sworn in. Each party will be given time to tell his/her side of the story and ask questions of the other persons there.

The arbitrator can ask as many questions as he/she thinks are necessary to clarify the issues. After all parties have finished their presentations, each is offered the chance to make a closing statement. These statements serve to summarize their positions and to conclude the hearing.

Once everyone has testified and the parties have given the arbitrator all the evidence they want to submit, the arbitrator will close the hearings. After the arbitrator has closed the hearings, no new or different evidence will be accepted by the arbitrator.

WHAT IS A PARTY'S ROLE AT THE HEARING?

The arbitrator usually requests that each party give a brief description of his or her position and make a short statement about how he/she intends to prove the case.

After the opening statements, each party has an opportunity to tell his/her side of the story to the arbitrator. The home buyer will be permitted to show each claimed defect in the house to the arbitrator and to the respondent. This is the advantage of conducting the hearing on site.

The arbitrator can ask as many questions as he or she thinks are necessary to clarify the issues. After both parties have finished their presentations, each is offered the chance to make a closing statement. These statements serve to summarize the positions of the parties and to conclude the hearing.

WHEN WILL I GET THE ARBITRATOR'S DECISION?

The arbitrator will not make an award at the time of the hearing. After hearing all the evidence, the arbitrator will close the hearing. The arbitrator has 10 days to make his/her decision. The Rules and the Law require the arbitrator to make his/her award in writing. Neither the rules nor the law require the arbitrator to provide reasons for the decision. The arbitrator, however, may provide his/her findings in summary form.

All parties will receive the arbitrator's written decision (award) by mail. The award is final and binding. The award will contain a decision on each claim presented by the parties.

HOW AND WHEN DOES THE AWARD GET PAID?

The award payment is made directly to the person to be paid, as stated in the award. Since the parties have agreed to use arbitration to resolve their dispute, they have agreed to abide by the arbitrator's decision. Once you receive the award, contact the other party, by phone or by mail, to arrange for payment.

IS THE AWARD LEGALLY BINDING ON BOTH PARTIES?

Yes. The award is binding upon the parties to the arbitration and can be enforced by the courts.

TO WHOM SHOULD A PARTY TURN IF THERE ARE PROBLEMS IN ENFORCING THE FINAL AWARD?

The AAA's function ends when it transmits the arbitrator's award to the parties. Subsequent inquiries regarding compliance should be made to the other party.

If the losing party refuses to comply with the terms of the award, the winning party may take the award to court and have a judgment filed against the losing party.

MAY I APPEAL THE DECISION IN MY CASE?

An arbitrator's award is final and binding. There is no appeal process to an award through the American Arbitration Association. There are limited appeal rights through the court system which are outlined in the Michigan arbitration Law.

ADMINISTRATIVE FEE SCHEDULE

Amount of Claim	Fee
$1 to $10,000	$500
$10,001 to $20,000	$750
$20,001 and up	$1,100

The filing party is responsible for paying the administrative fee at the time of the request for arbitration is submitted. This fee may be allocated in the final arbitral award, either on the arbitrator's own motion, or at the specific request of the filing party. The allocation of fees may be in any amount based on the arbitrator's determination of what is fair and appropriate.

Mileage and out-of-pocket expenses of the arbitrator shall be borne by the parties equally.

Postponement Fee: $75 is payable by a party causing a postponement of any scheduled hearing.

Refund Schedule: There are no refunds of administrative fees.

AMERICAN ARBITRATION ASSOCIATION
Suite 1150
27777 Franklin Road
Southfield, Michigan 48034-8208

Telephone (248) 352-5500 **Fax** (248) 352-3147

Office Hours: 8:30 a.m. until 5:00 p.m.

Assistant Vice President: Janice Holdinski
District Vice President: Eileen Vernon

Arsenic: See home inspector interview.

Asbestos: A building material used in ceiling tiles and insulation (often wrapped in old style furnace arms) known now to be a health hazard.

ASHI: American Society of Home Inspectors.

Assessed Value: See Assessor Card chapter.

Assessor: A government official to value real estate for property taxes.

Assessor Cards (also known as Field Sheets/REALTORS® Field Sheets): See Assessor Card chapter.

Balloon: A sum due on a mortgage on a specific date.

Bi-level house (split-level): See drawing.

BOCA Code Book/Building Codes: There are several building codes around the country. Check your local building department to see which one (if any) they use to pattern their regulations. Public libraries in metropolitan areas usually carry a copy. The BOCA Code Book offers definitions, diagrams, and explanations for everything construction-related, from footings to retaining walls to anchoring devices. Make copies (if permissible), and study them. Very likely you will know more about the regulations than the building inspector who may have been bull "dozing" the public for years. Probably no one questioned them or showed them definitions or drawings from the book. Believe me, it works on controversial issues.

Borough: In Alaska, a state land division similar to a county.

Breakers (circuit breakers): A mechanical switch inside the electric service panel to turn electricity on/off to a circuit.

Bridge Loan: A short-term loan used when individuals begin building a new home and are in the process of selling their existing home. (Usually an appraisal is performed on their existing home and a separate appraisal is performed on the proposed new-built home.)

BI-LEVEL (split level) with upward and downward stairs to upper and lower living areas

Carbon Monoxide: An odorless, tasteless, potentially poisonous gas often produced by cars and defective furnaces.

Ceiling Height (BOCA Code): The standard is 7 feet 6 inches, except in hallways, baths, kitchens, and basements.

Census Tract: A U.S. Government identification number of a geographical area, often by township/part of a township/city/part of a city.

Chimney Flue Liner: Vertical members inside a chimney, usually terra cotta or metal tubular, to allow the exhaust of smoke or gases.

Chimney Spark Arrester: Device on top of a chimney to keep sparks from flying out of fireplaces, and to keep varmints from coming in.

Chipping Paint: Modern paints are water- or oil-based. Prior to 1978, lead was a paint component. Paint chips in older homes have been eaten by toddlers, resulting in serious health problems.

Closing: Usually a meeting of buyers, sellers, closing agent(s), and other interested parties where the financial obligations are prorated; i.e., taxes, insurance, etc., and formally agreed upon, and title to the property is passed.

Cloud on title: An impairment to restrict a deed from being passed, such as a mechanic's lien for unpaid repairs or construction of a house.

Comparable: See Appraiser chapter.

Condemnation: Taking of real estate by the government for government use after payment; i.e. buying homes for a new highway.

Condominium: A form of home ownership in clustered attached, semi-attached, or detached homes in a multi-family zoned area with jointly owned common areas; i.e. swimming pools, tennis courts, parks, governed by ownership rules subject to maintenance fees for lawn mowing, snow removal, etc.

Cost Approach to Value: See Appraisal chapter.

Cost of Living Index: Government study of the basic life necessities, and how those prices compared to a base year.

County: A geographical area of a state with its local government; i.e. Michigan has 83 counties.

Cracking (horizontal): A major foundation problem with inward bowing, caused by outside pressure via improper back-filling, drainage problems, defective materials/workmanship. See attached illustration.

Cracking (Step cracking): Foundation cracking in a stair-step pattern, often correctable without major problems. See attached illustration.

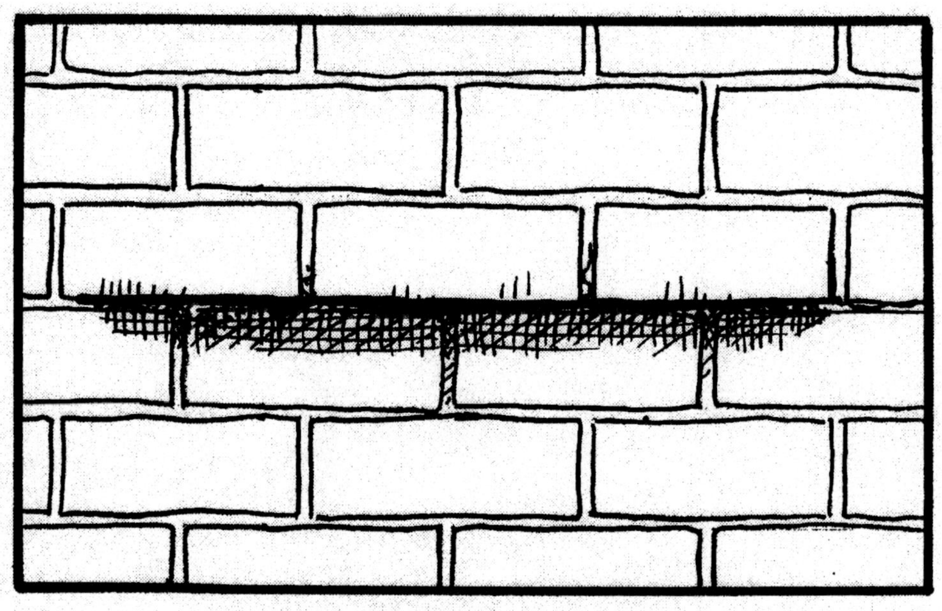

Horizontal Crack

Side view (cut away of wall)

Step Crack

Crawl Space: An area below the first floor of a house, from several inches to several feet in height. Usually with concrete walls (cement blocks or poured concrete) or on pillars, over a dirt base, with ventilation openings, depending on local customs and construction methods.

Cricket/Saddle: See roof chapter.

Cupola: A small structure on top of a building, for ventilation and to let out heat, on old farm-houses, usually small (3 x3 feet square and 3-4 feet in height). I've seen some with a stairway and floor with room for a chair, allowing a scenic view.

Curbs, Gutters: Concrete or asphalt structures along asphalt paved or concrete streets, serving to direct rainwater to underground storm drains.

Deed: A written document transferring ownership of real estate from a seller (owner) to a buyer.

Deed Restriction: A **legal** restriction on real estate placed with the passing of ownership; i.e. an estate selling acreage to a city for use only as a park, not for residential subdivision. *Illegal restrictions have been superseded by Federal and State Fair Housing Laws; i.e. a restriction allowing someone of a religious belief to own a cabin retreat, but forbidding them to sleep overnight there (actual case about 50 years ago).*

Deed, Quit Claim: Streamlined method of passing a real estate interest without guarantee that anyone else has interests in the property.

Deed, Warranty: A common method of passing title with the guarantee that the seller has ownership to sell, then indicating that no other parties have interests in the property.

Departure in Appraising: Written condition in an appraisal stating deviation from normal/recognized methods in performing the appraisal.

Depreciation: Decrease in value from many causes:

Physical -- wearing out from natural causes; i.e. with a 100-year life cycle, 1 percent per year depreciation is calculated.

Functional -- from obsolescence, super adequacy, or inadequacy; i.e. oversize wood deck compared to market acceptance, 1-car garage where 2-car garages are normal.

External -- factors outside the property affecting value; i.e. an active landfill across the street detracting the property's appeal.

District: Can be a neighborhood or combination of many neighborhoods, often within a school district or government area.

Diverter: A tubular device at the bottom of the downspout, to carry water out/away from the house.

DOM (Days on Market): How long it takes to sell the house, where a REALTOR® or real estate agent is involved from the listing date to the sale date.

Double Tapping: Inside an electric service box, more than one wire is connected to a circuit breaker.

Down Payment: The sum paid by the buyer. The down payment and mortgage amount total up to the sales price.

Downspouts: Tubular devices to carry rainwater down from the eaves/troughs/gutters.

Earnest Money: A deposit given to bind a sale with the submission of a purchase agreement, i.e. often $500, $1,000 or more.

Earth-Berm House: Earthen embankments surrounding a house so that only the roof is exposed, with variations.

Easement: A right in real estate that allows use, but not ownership, of a part of a property.

Eaves/troughs/gutters: Vessels installed along the roof edges to catch/collect rainwater.

Effective Age: An age resulting from the condition and usefulness of a property. For example: A house has 1,500 square feet. The 1,000 square foot portion is 50 years old. A 500-square foot addition is 10 years old. The effective age is calculated:

1,000

1,500 X 50 years = 33.33 years

500

1,500 X 10 years = 3.33 years

Effective Age = 36.66 years (adding 33.33 years and 3.33 years)

Electric Service Panel: A metal box serving to distribute electricity to various circuits, and as an enclosed safety device.

Eminent Domain: The right of the government to take private land for public projects.

Encroachments: Unlawful trespass onto another's property; i.e. fence built over the property line.

Encumbrance: A lien or encumbrance attached to real estate, which passes with title.

Engineered septic system: A very expensive system, usually with an elevated (compared to normal depths) holding tank and extra large drain field, often costing two or three times more than a normal system. Check your local health department regulations. Often needed for areas with percolation problems.

Enhancing/Detracting Influences: See External Depreciation.

Equity: The homeowner's interest in the property.

Excess Land: Lot size or land beyond the normal need to support/compliment; i.e. residential lot with 100 front footage X 1,000 feet deep, versus the normal lot size of 100 front footage X 250 feet deep.

Exposure Time: The predicted **future** time length it will take to sell a house(s) in a district or neighborhood. Most commonly used in relocation appraisals. See Appraising chapter.

Fee Simple: The highest degree of property ownership, which includes all rights; i.e. mineral rights, rental rights, right to sell, right to occupy, etc.

FHA Approved: Newly developed condos or single-family residential units meeting FHA standards and financing. (Good idea to ask about this up front, before a sale falls through years later.)

FHA Conditions: FHA Guidelines specify that the house and property meet certain conditions for health, safety, and to function properly. If these are not present or need updating, the appraiser lists them on a V.C. Sheet with the estimated cost of repairs for "generally" the seller to do. Examples:

Provide handrail on basement stairs -- $100.

Provide water heater discharge pipe to 6 inches above the floor -- $50.

Provide GFCI (ground fault circuit interrupter outlets) at the bathroom sink to prevent electrocution -- $60.

Repair front step (a trip hazard) -- $50.

Provide railing around wood deck which is above the ground -- $300.

Total Conditions -- $560.

After these repairs are made, a FHA compliance inspector/appraiser will re-inspect the house/property and report on the completion.

Flood: A federal government-declared disaster area, enabling eligibility for flood insurance.

Flood Map: Often with one to 12 panels for a township or city, showing major creeks, lakes and rivers, with flood zones. These are identified by panel number and dates; i.e. Panel 260255-0001 B, July 2, 1980

Flood Plains: See Flood Insurance chapter.

Floor Trusses/I-Beams/H-Beams: Horizontal framing members carrying the house framework; i.e. I and H beams (have an end view resembling the letters I and H); steel girders; trusses (have top and bottom horizontal members supported by diagonal members).

Fluoroscope: A medical device to examine internal structures by use of X-rays.

Forced Warm Air Furnace: Fueled by natural gas, liquid propane (LP), or fuel oil, sending heated air through ductwork into rooms via registers.

Foreclosure: The legal process by which a borrower's interest/rights are eliminated, allowing the lender to take possession/ownership of the property.

Fuses: Circular or tubular devices in older style electrical boxes, to facilitate electrical distribution inside an electrical box.

Gross Living Area: The sum finished residential area **above** grade, based upon exterior measurements of the house.

Gross Rent Multiplier: See Appraisal chapter.

Ground Fault Interrupter Electrical Outlets: Reset style electrical outlets placed within 5-6 feet (depending upon which building code is used as a reference) of any potential wet area. Designed to trip/interrupt the electrical circuit a fraction of a second before a person is shocked.

Heat Exchanger: The part of the furnace where the flames are located. The burners burn up inside the heat exchanger, and the gases from that combustion go directly outside. The outside of the heat exchanger is where the heat is picked up with a fan to blow into the house.

Highest and Best Use: The highest value of a property subject to four tests:

1. Is it a legal use (zoning)?
2. Is it physically feasible (will the lot support the size of the house)?
3. Is it financially feasible?
4. Will it bring the maximum return?

H.O.A. Dues (Homeowner Association Dues): Fees assessed or voluntary, often used for upkeep; i.e. planting flowers at the subdivision entrance.

Hot Water Heat/Boilers: Heated water or steam distributed through the home via piping, noted as a steady heat source without on/off bursts of heat from a forced warm air system. Usually more expensive to install than a forced warm air system.

HUD: Department of Housing and Urban Development. Federal Housing Administration (FHA) is an agency within HUD.

Humidifier: Device to add water content into the heated air of a forced warm heating furnace.

Income Approach: See Appraisal chapter.

In-house Offer: A listing receiving an offer from within a real estate company prior to being publicized on the MLS (Multiple Listing Service).

Jet Tub: Generic name for a bathtub, often oversized, with powerful streams of water injected for therapeutic/relaxation proposes.

KISS Method: Keep It Simple, Stupid. See SWAG Method.

Knob and Tube Wiring: Outdated wiring style, circa early 1900s, with wires attached to ceramic knobs on ceiling joists and other structural members.

Land Contract: For the sale of real estate, a formal written legal agreement between a buyer and seller, with a down payment and a series of regular payments until the sales price is paid off. A deed is passed after fulfillment of this contract.

Lead Based Paint: See Chipping Paint.

Legal Description: The identity of real estate by its name per lot, subdivision, state or by metes and bounds; i.e. Lot 123 Maplewood Subdivision, City of Grand Blanc, Genesee County, Michigan.

Lender: A bank or mortgage company.

Levees: Manmade earthen dams to protect against/hold back river water or lakes from flooding.

Life Cycle: Neighborhoods have lives: growth, stability, decline, and revitalization.

Limited Service Agreement: A REALTOR® only inserts a listed property into the Multi-Listing Service; no other services are performed.

Manufactured Housing/Modular Homes: Often the terms are used interchangeably by builders, appraisers, assessors, lenders and inspectors.

Some styles can be easily identified by visual inspection of the style, some can't. Most manufactured homes use structural steel beams as their base, with platform-style construction built above.

Modular homes can be difficult to distinguish from stick-built homes. They are built with similar style floor joists (2" x 8", 2" x 10") and quality windows, siding, and roofing, and their exterior styles and roof pitches can be similar.

The title process can differ. A manufactured home may have a title like a vehicle.

Modular homes are factory-built, constructed to comply with local, regional, or state building codes.

Manufactured homes are factory-built housing (either single section or multi-section homes) built to comply with the HUD code. Manufactured homes have metal identification tags with serial numbers on opposite sides of the exterior; i.e. #123456A (for part A) and #123456B (for part B).

The range of quality varies greatly, some having better quality components (windows, doors, cabinets, etc.) than conventionally built stick homes. Also, the manufactured home may have interior labels with retailer's name, manufacturer's name, HUD serial number, year manufactured, number of sections, number of stories, and certification label number.

These often are found inside a utility room cabinet, kitchen cabinet or bedroom closet.

See the Assessor Card chapter for additional help.

Now that you know the difference, you can identify them properly.

Market Rent: The amount of fair market rent for a home, compared to other homes with similar features: square footage, room count, amenities, functionality. As this is very difficult to find, a simple approach is to use the monthly house payment plus 10 %/investment return as a substitute in negotiations.

Market Value: The most probable price in cash with the following:

1. Reasonable exposure time in a competitive market with all components to a fair sale (arm lengths transaction).
2. Educated buyers and sellers.
3. Each acting in their own self-interest.
4. Without outside pressures.

(Definitions vary, but the major components are constant.)

Market Value Analysis: A report performed by a REALTOR® or real estate salesperson, comparing the subject property (your house) to other sold or listed homes in the area, to estimate a listing or sales price. These reports are not accepted for financing purposes by lenders.

Market Value Per Assessment (Michigan): Assessed Value X 2 = Cash Value; i.e. $50,000 X 2 = $100,000

Marketing Time: Historical facts of how long it took in the past to sell houses in that neighborhood or district. *(Want to separate the novice appraisers from the senior appraisers? Ask them the difference between exposure time and marketing time.)*

Marshal-Swift Cost Handbook: A leading national authority on building costs, categorized by state and major metropolitan areas.

Mechanic's Lien: A lien placed on real estate by a builder, subcontractor, or repairman after doing services on property (i.e. a home) to insure payment for those services. The deed cannot be passed with these liens (the house can't be sold). People building their homes get Waiver of Lien Certificates signed by subcontractors, after satisfactory completion of services and payment by the owner.

Mechanical Room/Area: Where the heating plant (furnace, boiler, geo-thermal unit) and water system are located, often in a basement room.

Metes and Bounds Legal Description: The identity of real estate by mathematical terms and section number in a township, county and state, referenced by Township and Range parameters of a map; i.e. N½ of E½ of Section 12, T5N,R6E Mundy Township, Genesee County, Michigan.

T (township) denotes north and south. R (range) denotes east and west markers along the map edges. Thus, T5N, R6E denotes Township 5 North, Range 6 East.

MLS: Multiple Listing Service, usually operated by a local REALTOR® Association, gathering listings and sales of homes, vacant land, and commercial properties.

MLS Set-Up Sheet: Information submitted by a REALTOR® or real estate salesperson via computer, or written on a 8½ x 11-inch sheet. This sheet contains: address, city, listing price, sold price, days on market, directions, home style, age, room count, lot size, tax ID number, legal description, updates, sales history, garages, school district, comments, financing method if sold, photo, and other pertinent data. Usually in active or sold categories. Can also be in expired or withdrawn categories.

Mold: An organism often associated with wet areas, adversely affecting some people's health. Suggest local health department references listed in the reference section.

Mortgage, Adjustable Rate: A loan with fluctuating interest rates, and the chance for changing monthly payments over the term of the loan.

Mortgage Applicant: The borrower who applies for a mortgage.

Mortgage Broker: An individual representing the borrower and lender, responsible for bringing the parties together.

Mortgage Collateral: The real estate pledged as security for a loan.

Mortgage Construction Loan: A short-term loan for new home construction.

Mortgage, Conventional: A mortgage issued by a bank/mortgage company without needed government-funded loan approval.

Mortgage, Earnest Money Deposit: Money given to "seal a deal" prior to the payment of the balance of the sales price (partial consideration in the contract).

Mortgage, Fixed Rate: A loan with a fixed interest rate, and a fixed monthly payment over a given number of years (often 15 or 30 years).

Mortgage, Good Faith Estimate: Projection of estimated costs in securing a mortgage; i.e.:

1. Appraisal -- $275
2. Home Inspection -- $250
3. City Fees -- $50
4. PMI -- $250
5. Points (1 percent X $100,000 = $1,000) ($100,000 / Mortgage Amount)

(Etc., etc.)

Mortgage LTV (Loan to Value): A percentage ratio comparison of the mortgage amount to the sales price of the house.

Mortgage, Points: The fee/charges added to a mortgage by a bank or mortgage company. If the current rate of interest is 7 percent on a 30-year mortgage for $100,000, a lender (bank, mortgage company, credit union) may charge the borrower two points as an additional charge. Each point is 1 percent of the mortgage amount. In this case, it would be 2 percent, or $2,000.

Mortgage, Pre-approved: In the mortgage process, after being qualified an applicant is approved for a dollar mortgage amount; i.e. Joe and Mary Jones are pre-approved for a $150,000 mortgage and can home shop in that value range, plus whatever down payment their budget allows.

Mortgage, Pre-qualification/Pre-qualify: The process of determining the mortgage amount the borrower is eligible for through a process analyzing monthly income and monthly obligations. Then an affordability analysis is calculated correlated with the L.T.V. (loan to value of the house).

Naturally Durable Wood: Redwood, cedar, black locust, and black walnut. Wood in contact with the ground or embedded in concrete must be pressure treated or naturally durable wood according to the BOCA Code.

Negative Drainage: Water flowage via surface water runoff (rainfall), or sub-soil flowage to a house.

Neighborhood: A residential area/region often composed of similar styles and value ranges of homes. Boundaries can be natural (river, mountain, cliff, seashore, etc.) or manmade (railroad, interstate highway, etc.).

Oakum: An old style material used to pack pipe joints, often for soil, drain, or sewer pipes.

Occupancy Permit: A government-issued document usually for a newly built home granting the owners the right to live in the dwelling.

1. Temporary occupancy permit: Allows use/living in the dwelling for a specific time, with conditions that certain repairs/conditions are finished or repaired.
2. Permanent occupancy permit: Allows inhabiting of the dwelling without a time limit, nor is it based upon certain conditions/repairs to be met.

Octopus-type Furnace: Older gravity-style furnace, circa 1900s-1930s, with multiple tubular arms, looking like an octopus.

Orientation of the House: How it is situated on the building site; i.e. north, east, west, south, shaded, sun-rise side, sun-set side, flat, hillside, in the woods, open.

Parish: In Louisiana, a state land division similar to a county.

Percolation: The process of septic water to seep downward into the ground.

Percolation Tests: Often large holes are dug and filled with water. The downward seepage is studied and compared to local health department standards. This determines the type of septic system needed, or if one is allowed.

PMI (Private Mortgage Insurance): See PMI chapter.

Pocket Door: A rolling interior door that disappears into a wall cavity when opened, often used as bathroom doors.

Polarity: Electrical outlets:

1. Proper polarity; properly wired outlet.
2. Reverse polarity; opposite of how an outlet is to be wired.
3. Open ground; when an electrical outlet is not grounded.

Plug-in testers, with symbols, indicate the above situations.

Pole Barns: An economical construction method, installing vertical structural timbers into the ground versus conventional footings for framing. Usually covered by metal panels for siding, and occasionally roofing. Some roofs use wood decking and composition shingles. Used for storage and agricultural purposes. The vertical members are chemically pressure-treated wood to preserve them.

Positive Drainage: Water flowage via surface water runoff (rainfall) or sub-soil flowage away/out from a house.

Pressure Relief Valve: A safety device, often on a water heater, to release over-pressure buildup, to prevent an explosion.

PUD (Planned Unit Development): Real estate development of clustered lots smaller than usual, often with joint ownership of open/common areas; i.e. parks, nature trails.

Punch List: A list of completed or incomplete construction items often used with a final inspection of satisfactory completion.

Quad-level House (split-level): See drawing.

QUAD-LEVEL (split level) with 3 finished living levels and a basement.

Radon: An undetectable, potentially harmful gas (detected with monitors) emitting from the earth, often occurring in specific regions. See Home Inspection chapter.

REALTOR®: A member of The National Association of REALTORS® and the Local State Association of REALTORS®, with a Code of Ethics and regulations for the real estate industry.

Retention Pond/Swale: An area for the temporary accumulation of surface water runoff, away from buildings or site improvements.

"**Running Bare":** Builders with no workers comp insurance, no insurance, no office, no overhead.

Saddle/Cricket: See Roof chapter.

Safety Reverse: Mechanisms on overhead garage doors, often with an optical sensor to keep the door from closing onto a person or object; i.e. to prevent crushing a baby or child.

Sales Comparison Analysis: See Appraisal chapter.

Sales History: Records from the assessor card or MLS sheet, denoting the last sale date and sale price.

Salt Water Maps (Wells): Local well drillers often have maps indicating salty well water areas.

Secondary Market: Where mortgages generated locally are bought and sold by banks and mortgage companies.

Section: An area of 640 acres.

Seller's Disclosure Statement: Many states require them (in Michigan since January 8, 1994). Sellers are required to identify the working order of appliances, property conditions, and other information on a Seller's Disclosure Statement report form.

Service Door: Often a steel paneled door used for interior pedestrian access to a garage and vice versa. Allows people to access the outside from within the garage.

Service Walk: A private walkway, often to a front or rear entrance.

Setback: City/township/state zoning regulations stating distance requirements that houses, sheds, garages are to be situated from the property line; i.e. house must be 100 feet back from the edge of the street (which is used as the property line in this example).

There are usually regulations for distances from the side and rear lot lines. These can vary due to irregular side lines.

There may also be height regulations, restrictions as to how many stories or the number of feet the structure may be; i.e. homes less than 25 feet in height are allowed, older homes built prior to this regulation may be "grand-fathered" (allowed) in.

There have been many lawsuits over these issues. Get a stake survey when building or adding on, and review local building codes. (*This has been a volatile issue around lakefront properties. For example, old one-story cabins are torn down and a 2½-story mansion is built, blocking the lake view of the home built on the next street to the rear. Do your homework; be a smart buyer. The 2½-story mansion for sale may not comply with zoning regulations. A lawsuit may be in the works. I've heard of "good friends" selling their cottage at the rear over these issues. The friendship usually ended after that episode.)*

Settlement Statement: A report of costs of the real estate transaction for the buyer and seller.

Shower pans: The shower component used as the base, or floor. Leaks often begin in 30- 40-year-old houses.

Sidewalk: Usually a public-installed walkway adjacent to a public street.

Site Condominium: A method of residential development, similar to a subdivision in appearance, with possible restrictions on lot ownership. Used in this region to expedite residential development via simpler regulations at the local government level, rather than state regulation/supervision.

Site Improvements: Landscaping, sprinkler system, fences, service walk, driveway, yard lights, etc.

Site Plan: A formal engineered drawing or rough sketch, showing the outlines of a house and/or other buildings on a lot in relation to the lot lines and other significant features. See attached example.

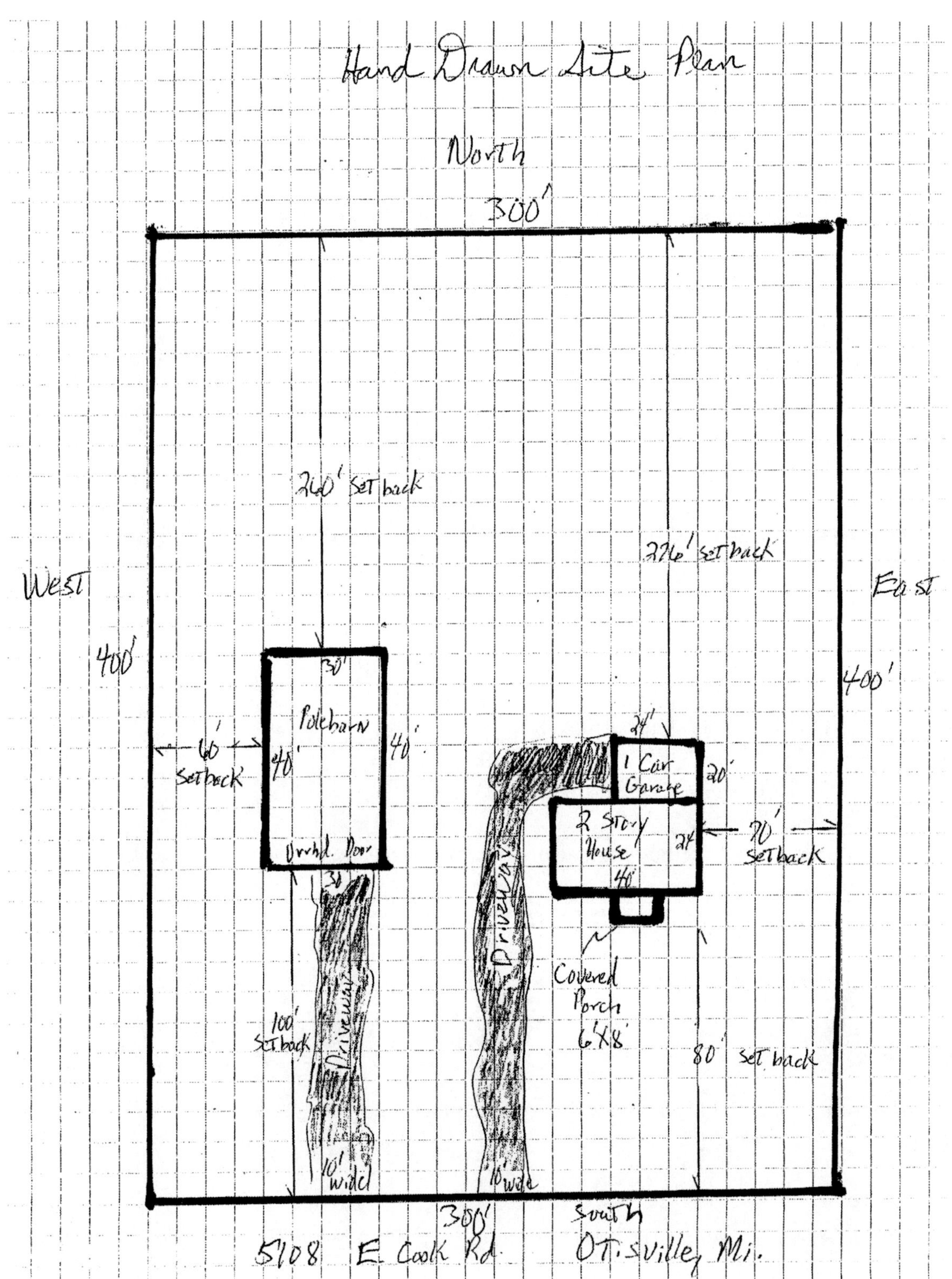
Hand Drawn Site Plan
North
300'
260' Set back
276' Set back
West
East
400'
400'
30'
Polebarn
40'
40'
60'
Setback
Ovrhd. Door
30
24'
1 Car Garage
20'
2 Story House
24
40'
70'
Setback
Covered Porch 6'X8'
100'
Setback
Driveway
Driveway
80' Set back
10' wide
10 wide
300'
South
5108 E. Cook Rd Otisville, Mi.

Solar Panel: A heating device situated to collect the sun's energy for heating purposes.

Split Package: An informational packet and documents for dividing land/lots. Often includes: application form, Land Division Act History, Allowable Number of Divisions Chart, Homeowner's Principal Residence Exemption Affidavit, Property Transfer Affidavit, Notice to Assessor of Transfer of the Right to Make a Division of Land, often available/provided by local units of government, i.e., City offices, Township offices, etc.

Square: An area measurement; i.e. 10 feet x 10 feet = 100 square feet. Used for evaluating areas of roofing or siding materials.

SRA (Senior Residential Appraiser): A professional appraisal designation granted after completion of course work, verified experience, and passing of a thesis. Similar to a CPA in the accounting field, or a Masters degree in appraising.

Stake Survey: When markers are physically imbedded to mark property boundaries.

Sump-pump: A device to remove water to the outside from an internal collection pit in a basement connected to drain tiles around the underground footings of a house.

Survey: A document specifying the property boundaries prepared by a registered land surveyor, often with land, house, shed(s) dimensions.

SWAG Method: Silly Wild _ss Guess; valuation method often used by Uncle Joe and the "guys at work," superseding a detailed comprehensive appraisal. Often used when a value disagreement arises.

Tax Identification Number/Parcel Number: It identifies the home and/or lot by its county, township or city, section, and even neighborhood/block in metropolitan areas.

Title: Evidence of ownership in real estate.

Topography: How the land lays, and its covering; i.e. flat, rolling, steep, wooded, sloping.

Townhouse: Semi-attached home with zero lot lines, without condominium rules and fees.

Township: An area usually consisting of 36 sections, subject to city boundaries or geographical features, like a Great Lakes shoreline, which could reduce the size.

Tri-level House (split-level): See drawing.

SELLER'S DISCLOSURE STATEMENT
FOR VACANT LAND

Property Address (or Tax Description): ______________________ Street ______________________ City, Village, or Township ______ Michigan

Purpose of Statement: This statement is a disclosure of the condition of the property and information concerning the property as known by the seller. Unless otherwise advised, the seller does not possess any expertise in matters pertaining to the law, taxation, engineering, land surveying or any other specific matter related to the condition of the property, and the buyer is advised to seek the advice of professionals regarding these matters. This statement is not a warranty of any kind by the seller or by any real estate agent representing the seller or buyer in this transaction, and is not a substitute for any inspections of the property that the buyer may wish to obtain.

Seller's Disclosure: The seller discloses the following information with the knowledge that, although the disclosures herein are not a warranty, the seller specifically makes the following disclosures based on the seller's knowledge at the time the seller signs this form. The seller authorizes the seller's agent(s) to provide a copy of this form to any prospective buyer in connection with any actual or anticipated sale of property. The following are representations made solely by the seller and are not the representations of the seller's agent(s) or buyer's agent(s), if any. **This information is a disclosure only and is not intended to be a part of any contract between the buyer and the seller.**

Instructions to the Seller: (1) Complete this form yourself. (2) Answer all questions. (3) Report known conditions about or affecting the property by selecting either "YES" or "NO." (4) Attach additional pages with your signature if additional space is required to adequately report known conditions. (5) If you do not have knowledge of a particular condition, check "UNKNOWN."

PART 1: GENERAL PROPERTY INFORMATION

1. **Property dimensions:** Are you aware of the property's approximate dimensions and/or size in square feet or acres? ...... Yes ☐ No ☐
   If "Yes," please state: ______
2. **Survey:** Do you have an engineering survey of the property in your possession? ...... Yes ☐ No ☐ Unknown ☐
   If "Yes," can you provide the buyer with a copy? ...... Yes ☐ No ☐
3. **Zoning:** Are you aware of the property's zoning classification as designated by the municipality? ...... Yes ☐ No ☐ Unknown ☐
   If "Yes," please state: ______
4. **Services/utilities:** Are any of the following services and/or utilities available to the property line?
   a. Municipal water ...... Yes ☐ No ☐ Unknown ☐
   b. Municipal sewer ...... Yes ☐ No ☐ Unknown ☐
   c. Electric ...... Yes ☐ No ☐ Unknown ☐
   d. Natural gas ...... Yes ☐ No ☐ Unknown ☐
   e. Cable television ...... Yes ☐ No ☐ Unknown ☐
   If either municipal water or sewer is available, are laterals extended into the property? ...... Yes ☐ No ☐ Unknown ☐
5. **Assessments, etc.:** Are there any outstanding, deferred or pending assessments or other similar charges against the property? ...... Yes ☐ No ☐ Unknown ☐
   If "Yes," please describe and state approximate amounts if known: ______
6. **Soil conditions:**
   a. Have soil borings ever been conducted on the property? ...... Yes ☐ No ☐ Unknown ☐
      If "Yes," can you provide the buyer with a copy of the report? ...... Yes ☐ No ☐
   b. Has a percolation test ever been conducted on the property? ...... Yes ☐ No ☐ Unknown ☐
      If "Yes," can you provide the buyer with a copy of the report? ...... Yes ☐ No ☐
   c. Have you ever been denied a septic or building permit because of adverse soil conditions? ...... Yes ☐ No ☐ Unknown ☐
      If "Yes," please explain: ______
7. **Drainage/flooding:** Does the property periodically or regularly experience drainage and/or flooding problems? ...... Yes ☐ No ☐ Unknown ☐
   If "Yes," please describe: ______
8. **Mineral rights:** Do you own the property's mineral rights? ...... Yes ☐ No ☐ Unknown ☐
9. **Topography:** Has there been filling or grading of the property other than by natural forces? ...... Yes ☐ No ☐ Unknown ☐
   If "Yes," please describe: ______

PART 2: PROPERTY RESTRICTIONS

Are you aware of any of the following restrictions or conditions that may limit or restrict the buyer's use, enjoyment and/or development of the property?

1. Oral or written leases for crops, hunting, logging, oil, gas, mineral rights, etc.? ...... Yes ☐ No ☐
2. Public or private use restrictions or limitations including, but not limited to, deed or subdivision restrictions, conservation, forestry or agricultural agreements, or any tax deferral programs? ...... Yes ☐ No ☐
3. Any sale, transfer or reservation of development, water or drainage rights? ...... Yes ☐ No ☐
4. Any sale, transfer or reservation of oil, gas or mineral rights? ...... Yes ☐ No ☐
5. Encroachments, easements, zoning violations, non-conforming uses, or condemnations? ...... Yes ☐ No ☐
6. Any portions or features of the property co-owned or shared in common with other persons? ...... Yes ☐ No ☐
7. Any association that has authority over the property and that may charge fees or enact restrictions? ...... Yes ☐ No ☐
8. Any pending litigation that could affect the property or the seller's ability to convey marketable title to the property? ...... Yes ☐ No ☐
9. Previous divisions or splits of the property since March 31, 1997 pursuant to the Land Division Act? ...... Yes ☐ No ☐

If the answer to any of the previous questions is "Yes," please explain. Attach additional signed pages, if necessary: ______

PART 3: ENVIRONMENTAL CONDITIONS

1. Are you aware of any of the following environmental conditions that may limit or restrict the buyer's use, enjoyment and/or development of the property?
   a. Any past or present use of the property that may have created soil or water contamination? .... Yes ☐ No ☐
   b. Any past or present drilling for oil or gas, or mining for minerals? .... Yes ☐ No ☐
   c. Any operating, capped, uncapped or abandoned wells? .... Yes ☐ No ☐
   d. Any past or present above-ground or underground storage tanks used for fuel or other chemicals? .... Yes ☐ No ☐
   e. Any past or present use of any portion of the property as a farm or household dump or as a landfill? .... Yes ☐ No ☐
   f. Any known soil or water contamination? .... Yes ☐ No ☐

   If the answer to any of the previous questions is "Yes," please explain. Attach additional signed pages, if necessary:__________

2. Have there been any environmental assessments or studies done on the property? .... Yes ☐ No ☐ Unknown ☐
   If "Yes," Phase I ☐ Phase II ☐ Phase III ☐ Other __________
   If "Yes," can you provide the buyer with a copy or copies of any reports? .... Yes ☐ No ☐
3. Has there ever been any determination that any portion of the property constitutes a wetlands, antiquities or dunes area, or other similar determination? .... Yes ☐ No ☐ Unknown ☐
   If "Yes," can you provide the buyer with a copy or copies of any reports? .... Yes ☐ No ☐

PART 4: OFF-SITE CONDITIONS

Are you aware of any of the following off-site conditions within the vicinity of the property that may limit or restrict the buyer's use, enjoyment and/or development of the property?

1. Farm or farm operation? .... Yes ☐ No ☐
2. Dump or landfill? .... Yes ☐ No ☐
3. Airport? .... Yes ☐ No ☐
4. Shooting range? .... Yes ☐ No ☐
5. Racetrack? .... Yes ☐ No ☐

If the answer to any of the previous questions is "Yes," please explain. Attach additional signed pages, if necessary:__________

PART 5: NOTICES TO THE BUYER

1. The seller has owned the property since __________ (date).
2. The seller has indicated above the condition of the property based on information known to the seller. If any changes occur in the property's condition as disclosed or if the seller becomes aware that any disclosures herein are inaccurate, from the date of this form to the date of closing, the seller will immediately disclose the changes to the buyer. In no event shall the parties hold the seller's agent(s) or buyer's agent(s) liable for any representations not directly made by the seller's agent(s) or buyer's agent(s).
3. The seller acknowledges that the information in this statement is true and correct to the best of the seller's knowledge as of the date of the seller's signature below.
4. The buyer should obtain professional advice and inspections of the property to more fully determine its condition.
5. The buyer is advised that certain information compiled pursuant to Michigan's Sex Offenders Registration Act, 1994 Public Act 295, M.C.L. 28.721 to 28.732 is available to the public. If the buyer seeks such information, the buyer should contact the appropriate local law enforcement agency or sheriff's department directly.
6. The buyer is advised that Michigan's Right to Farm Act protects farming operations from litigation if those operations meet generally accepted agricultural practices regarding noise, dust, odors and other assorted conditions.
7. The buyer is advised that the state equalized value, taxable value, tax exemption information and other real property tax information pertaining to the property is available from the appropriate local assessor's office. The buyer should not assume that the buyer's future property tax bills will be the same as the seller's present property tax bills. Pursuant to Michigan's General Property Tax Act, real property tax obligations can change significantly when the seller conveys legal or equitable title to the buyer.

Seller __________ Date: __________ Time: __________

Seller __________ Date: __________ Time: __________

Buyer has read and acknowledges receipt of this two-page disclosure statement.

Buyer __________ Date: __________ Time: __________

Buyer __________ Date: __________ Time: __________

TRI-LEVEL (split level) 3 living levels without a basement.

Tripidity: See Home Inspector Interview.

Tsunami: See cover.

Underground Storage Tanks: Storage facilities used with home heating fuel oil, often very costly to remove after conversion to LP or natural gas. Potential leaking contaminant to soils and wells can be a costly environmental hazard to clean up.

Underwriter: A reviewer at a bank or mortgage company giving the final approval of a mortgage.

Updated Appraisal Report: A report completed after the original appraisal, reworking square feet and/or certifying the original value or a new value.

Urea Formaldehyde Foam Insulation: a sprayed-in insulator used in the 1980s, thought to have created health hazards.

USPAP: The Uniform Standards of Professional Appraisal Practice - federal appraisal guidelines and procedures.

Vacant Land / Seller's Disclosure Statement for Vacant Land: – see attached sample

Valley: Where the Holly Clean Giant lives.

Valley (Roof): Junction/intersection/meeting place of two roof areas/planes.

Walkout Basement: With a home built on a sloping lot so the end or rear of the house allows for a doorway(s) to exit or enter the basement onto the sloping lot, usually without steps or stairs to the doorways.

Warranty Deed: A deed passing ownership from one party to another, but also guaranteeing that the seller is the owner.

Wood Destroying Insects: See Home Inspector Interview; i.e. termites, carpenter ants, power post beetles, wood boring bees.

Wood Stove: A main or auxiliary heating system, standing alone or connected to a fireplace, or in conjunction with a forced warm air furnace.

Woodland: Local woodland ordinances which could dictate what, if any, trees you can cut on the lot you just bought, and if you are required to plant trees. If there is a 200-year-old tree on the middle of the lot where you wish to build your house, a woodland ordinance could forbid cutting it. Ask local builders, neighbors, local government building departments.

Zero Lot Line: The situation of a home resting directly on the boundary line, without any set-back of the home.

Zoning: Government regulation of real estate into districts or areas; i.e., R1 specifying minimum requirements of only 1- and 2-story homes of 1,000-1,800 square feet on lots of at least 1/3 acre, with at least 80 feet front footage.

Zoning Map: A map of a community depicting government regulated land use.

ACKNOWLEDGEMENTS
(Living and Past) for sharing their wisdom over the years, and assisting with this manual.

Attorney Jeffrey Birrell, Flint, Michigan

Tim Cook, Pillar to Post Home Inspections

Denise Hnatiuk, REALTOR® - Century 21 Halstead

Robert Gremel, Barnhart-Gremel-Marsh Insurance

Ruby Congdon, Republic Bank

Teri Lukas, Citizens Bank

Robert Gazall, Architect

Vernon Sadler, Appraiser/Salesperson

Rex Tyson, Appraiser/Instructor

Donald Bancroft, Appraiser

Scott Newcomer, American Home Inspectors Training Institute

Arden O'Neill, Appraiser/Adjuster

Donald Bancroft, Jr. Appraiser

Joey Richvalsky, Appraiser/Broker

Richard Kinkle, General Contractor

Mike Walker, General Contractor

Harvey Castles, General Contractor

Jeff Bennett, Architect

Char Proffer, Centennial Title

Peter Banwell, Broker/Instructor

Mary Ann Bush, Broker/Instructor

James Romano, Guaranty Title

Doris Nurenberg, Flint Area Association of REALTORS

Bill Temple, Sr., Appraiser/Assessor/Building Inspector

Barb Smith, All Typing Service

Eileen Lawson, Your Secretary

Bob Noonan, Cartoonist

Randy Zimmerman, Cartoonist

Mike McMillan, Author/Instructor

Del Pratt, Builder

Brad Schultz, Delta Surveying

Reverend Elmira Vincent, Mission of Peace Home Counseling Center

Numerous Continuing Education Instructors

Numerous Author Friends

Numerous Co-Workers, Co-Students at Continuing Education Classes

Numerous REALTORS

Numerous Appraisers and Home Inspectors

General Adjustment Bureau Training Schools

Celina Mutual Insurance Company Training Schools

American Home Inspectors Training Institute

Numerous Surveyors

Numerous Attorneys

Numerous Builders

Vale Tech Training Seminars

Jack A. Miedema, Great Lakes Realty Systems, Inc.

If individual home buying experience were assigned, there easily would be thousands of years of knowledge.

Index

A

B

C

D

E

F

G

H

I

J

K

L

M

N

O

P

Q

CLOSING REMARKS

Congratulations ... you are on the way to becoming Smart Homebuyers.

Mold is a hot topic. You did not find a detailed discussion in this book. Very likely I have attended more classes and heard more discussions on mold than most people. But I am not a qualified expert. Research the sources in the reference section for their booklets and bulletins. They are the best source.

Recently in many urban areas around the country (per articles in real estate trade magazines), many homebuyers have had challenges getting homeowners insurance in urban areas. Home buying deals have fallen through as a result.

When banks/mortgage company financing is involved, the lenders demand insurance protection on the home to protect themselves against fire, windstorms, and other common hazards.

Smart homebuyers get pre-qualified by their insurance agent as part of the home buying process.

Don't let the deal fall through due to this technicality.

Perhaps I have hit a nerve with the horror stories and nasty problems. Sorry, but let your newfound wisdom make it worth thou$ands of dollar$ for your wallet and your sanity.

Let us take **action** today.

P.S. -- After buying your dream home and heading out on a well-deserved extended vacation, don't forget to turn off the water lines to your automatic washer. Water pressure can build up in those flexible rubber hoses and burst ... flooding the house. Be smart homeowners.

Best Wishes, Richard C. Smith

Answers: Broken doors, fascia, screens, shutters, soffits, steps, windows; curling/loose shingles, foundation shifting, loose siding, raccoon tenant, rattlesnake tenant, skunk tenant, tsunami wave, volcano eruption.

40 PAGE BONUS WEBSITE REPORT PASSWORD

WWW.besmarthomebuying.com/bonus